THE

ULTIMATE

Self-Help

BOOK

How to Be Happy, Confident, Stress-free, & Change Your Life With the Law of Attraction & Energy Healing

Yvette Taylor

INFIN8 FREEDOM PUBLISHING an imprint of MAKE YOUR MARK GLOBAL PUBLISHING, LTD

USA & French Riviera

The Ultimate Self-Help Book © 2018 Yvette Taylor

Published by Make Your Mark Global Publishing, LTD

Book cover design: Andrea Danon & Stefan Komljenović

Illustrations: Tamara Višković

Editor: Carol Taylor

Paperback ISBN 978-0-9992579-5-1

Library of Congress Control Number: 2018960992

Dedication

I dedicate this book to all women, men, and children who are ready to change their lives and live in a state of flow.

May your world be filled with love, passion, happiness, and inspiration at every step.

Together, we can change the world.

Just Giving

Have you felt the magic of giving a gift? Whether you call it paying it forward, giving back or making a difference, I believe it is an inherent part of who we are as human beings. We love to give and make others happy. Well, this book is no different. There are two ways you can do that with The Ultimate Self-Help Book too.

YOU'VE ALREADY GIVEN.

Simply by buying this book you have made an impact somewhere in the world. A percentage of profits from every book sale goes to support one of 500+ Just Giving projects as part of B1G1 Community. These projects provide health, education, food, water and other essential resources to meet sustainable development goals around the world.

GIVE IT AS A GIFT

How many people do you know who would love to know how to change their lives? Maybe it is a friend, a loved one or someone at work. Whether it is a birthday present or just a gift of love. Maybe you'll choose to help a stranger. You could leave a copy of this book on a train or at the coffee shop. How can you pass on a message of hope and inspiration to help someone change their life?

YOU CAN CHANGE YOUR LIFE

Once you've read the pages of this book and implemented it in your life, pass it on. Whether you gift the book or leave it for someone else to find, write your message here and watch the magic unfold.

Leave your message & share the love

Contents

Foreword

With this book in hand you are standing at the gateway to a totally transformed life. Yvette Taylor has effectively written one of the most comprehensive books ever to truly empower you on your journey to deep healing and elevated well-being. By absorbing and applying the information within these pages you can and will create an entirely new life for yourself, including your relationships and personal health as well as your work, finances, and overall life purpose.

This sounds like a lofty promise that I, a Western trained physician, would typically avoid. And yet, with my background and training in Traditional Chinese Medicine, acupuncture, and positive psychology I agree wholeheartedly with Yvette's knowledge and her work with the Energy Alignment Method (EAM), particularly since over the last two years I have personally seen her work transform lives.

Having trained in the United States as a medical doctor and surgeon 20 years ago I am well aware that making a claim that by harnessing the power of our mind and energy field we could heal ourselves of allergies, injuries, or illnesses seems far-fetched at best, and New Age 'woo woo' at worst. Today, however, medical science has acknowledged that so many illnesses, both mental and physical, are linked to our beliefs, emotions, and lifestyle. Modern geneticists and emerging authorities in the science of epigenetics, the field that studies the effect our environments play in our gene expression, agree that even at the level of our precious DNA we have more control over our well-being than the world's greatest doctors, surgeons, and medical treatments.

While advances in medical science are great, and despite the widespread complex diagnoses that too many of us carry, the time of relying on doctors, therapists, and prescription medications as the sole source of healing, has come to an end. We are each being called to heal ourselves. Within this book, which Yvette has carefully laid out for you, is the very information you need to do just that. *The Ultimate Self-Help Book* will help you identify the source of your dis-ease, pain, and blockages. You will understand how to use a simple method to identify your own resistance or blocks to healing, relationship harmony, and success. Then you'll unlock your potential to thrive.

I am a longstanding advocate for self-help. As a former news anchor and host of documentaries in my role as Medical Director for the Discovery Health Channel, I've used the media to teach how our thoughts, beliefs, and our speech — including our internal, unspoken conversation — impact our mood and health. For over 2 decades, in my own integrative practice of medicine, and in my own books, I have spent countless hours teaching my clients about the esoteric subjects of qi, the Chinese term for life force energy. I know that we each have the potential to become masters of our qi and that we can use our life force to heal, grow, and transform. Now I can finally hand my clients a book that will provide a clear understanding of the principles of manifesting good health, personal confidence, and harmony in life.

I met Yvette in London after having given a keynote speech about creating a global business with authenticity, integrity, heart, and soul by becoming a Global Luminary. From our first interaction I understood that Yvette fully embodies the characteristics of Luminary. By *living* the principles behind the Energy Alignment Method herself, she has evolved into a powerful transformational teacher who radiates compassion, warmth, and light to guide others to true healing.

Having seen Yvette in action at her events and workshops I've watched hundreds of people take responsibility for their lives and transform traumatic past experiences into fuel for growth. I have personally witnessed and interviewed people who've applied her self-help technique to heal from conditions and diseases that defy logic. Now Yvette has painstakingly brought the wisdom transmitted in her live events into the written word.

The Ultimate Self-Help Book will give you a thorough understanding of the concepts of overall life energy management, the elusive Law of Attraction, neuroscience, Neurolinguistic Programming (NLP), and Chinese medical philosophy. The depth and breadth of the content in this book are what merit the ambitious title, and what will deliver the results you're looking for in life.

As you consume and digest the information in this book you will find yourself brimming with newfound optimism and excitement about the life you can confidently bring into reality. As a witness to the power of applied self-help techniques I was inspired to write this Foreword to add my endorsement to Yvette and the Energy Alignment Method as well as to give you, dear reader, my vote of confidence *in you*.

You have the potential to tap into your innate potential for vitality, joy, and real self-love. This book will help you to unlock that potential and use it to transform the area of life most important to you now, and in the future.

With sincere blessings to you,

Andrea Pennington, MD, C.Ac.

Founder & Managing Director, In8Vitality, LTD.

Cannes, France

September 2018

Introduction

Finally! You found it. After all this time and searching you have in your hands the answers you've been looking for. I know it's a BIG claim, "The ULTIMATE Self-Help Book". Yet I know that once you truly understand and master what I share on these pages you'll never need another self-help book again.

You see, self-help books usually focus on one thing like relationships, wealth, or mindset. To truly change your life, you have to work on EVERYTHING. You need a whole-istic approach. That may seem huge but the good news is that it's achievable. Most people try to change their life the wrong way around. Here, I'll share with you the exact steps to changing your life, in the exact order you need to do them.

Everyone is looking for a way to feel happier, healthier, and more in control of their life in our fast moving and hectic world. The Energy Alignment Method ® ("EAM"), is a transformational self-help technique that can enable you to change your life. I've spent over 20+ years searching for answers to changing my mindset, to feel in control of my life, my emotions, my health, and well-being. Yet even after every self-help book, every wellness course, every workshop, every therapy, every guru... I still felt like I was missing the one thing that connected them all.

When I found that missing piece, everything fell into place.

It's ALL about energy.

EAM is founded in years of working in energy medicine, the Law of Attraction and traditional Chinese medicine. Its methods include elements of Kinesiology, neuroscience research, NLP, Positive Psychology, and Eastern spiritual principles. The magic of EAM is that it enables you to shift energy, let go of repetitive thoughts, and overwhelming emotions. It helps you to release physical or emotional pain, negative feelings, painful memories and traumatic experiences to be free from stress, anxiety, and feeling overwhelmed. As you let go of what holds you back, it is no longer held in your energy and your subconscious. You can then choose to create and embody a new energy, thought, belief, pattern, emotion or experience that serves *you*. Imagine how wonderful it would be to identify the underlying cause of what is really stopping you from achieving your dreams, or finding happiness, and wellness, and *finally* get clarity on what you want in life.

EAM is a proven process of connecting with and directing the energy in the universe, and within ourselves to be in alignment. For those who are rolling your eyes thinking this is some New Age hippy **** and wanting to see the scientific data behind EAM, just bear with me. We discuss both the science and the spirituality of EAM because ultimately it is all the same thing. It's ALL energy.

EAM shows you how to align your energy, thoughts, beliefs and emotions so you can be in FLOW. The techniques, exercises, and practices in EAM teach you how to transform your energy to create more positive thinking and shift how you feel, changing your outlook and your life. Once you learn the 5 powerful steps in EAM: Step 1. ASK, Step 2. MOVE, Step 3. EXPERIENCE, Step 4. TRANSFORM, Step 5. MANIFEST, you can apply them to anything you want to change in your life.

Working with EAM will give you clarity about the underlying cause of what is holding you back. As you tune in and begin to master creating your own positive energy, you'll feel free from stress and more in control of your life. You'll also create more harmony in your relationships and get relief from physical or emotional pain, negative feelings, and traumatic memories and experiences that have trapped you and kept you from moving forward.

One of the guiding principles of EAM is that you already have everything you need inside you to change your life. EAM enables you to access your power and to direct it to correct and realign the areas that are out of FLOW. Everything in the world, everything that is all around us and inside of us, is energy. You have the power to not only tap into this state of energy FLOW, *but also to direct and change it.*

It can be so easy to get wrapped up in our own lives, thinking that we are individual, separate. When the truth is, you are part of something far bigger, far greater. We are all connected. Because everything is energy, what you think and feel affects others. By creating energetic changes in yourself through EAM, you'll change your life and the lives of those around you. As we reclaim our power and take control of ourselves and our lives, we can create a positive change. We are here, each of us, at this point in time, and we can create a positive energetic change in ourselves that can ripple out into the world and change humanity.

Your life IS the single most precious thing you have. We only have a tiny amount of time on this planet to truly find ourselves, create our greatest expression, and make a difference. My greatest wish is that we can all live in a state of FLOW, love, and peace, enjoying the people and experiences in it to the fullest. You can do that by being in FLOW with life and making your alignment a top priority.

Your energy, thoughts, beliefs and emotions have already attracted this book. You manifested this! You chose this book for a reason, and whatever that reason, the universe has provided! Now it's up to YOU to take the next steps. If you've been asking for help, if you've been looking for the answer you've found it. The book you're holding in your hand is the universe pointing you in the right direction — EAM is the missing piece of the puzzle.

WHAT IS FLOW?

The state of FLOW is that moment when you feel in tune with life around you. It is that moment when anything and everything seems effortless and easy. FLOW can be described in many ways, and we'll explore them all inside the pages of this book. FLOW is not an esoteric New Age principle. It is an energy state in your body, which can be scientifically measured.

On a physical level, FLOW creates changes in your brain and heart waves. It changes your hormone levels and releases endorphins, which makes you feel happy. Being IN FLOW resolves stress and promotes a feeling of calm. It reduces the need to overthink and feelings of being overwhelmed. The FLOW state helps your body to heal on a physical level as well as a metaphysical level. It alters your brain structure, which enables you to change your perception and change your life. FLOW helps to improve your mental and emotional stability. It also changes so many things on an energetic level for you too.

So why would you choose anything else but FLOW, when it can literally change your entire experience of life?

WHY FLOW MATTERS TO YOU

Everything we experience in our lives is because of our state of FLOW and that of the people around us. So, what does being OUT of FLOW look like in your life?

Being out of FLOW can feel like being stuck in the past, or in painful emotionally or mentally unstable relationships. Physical pain, tiredness, and fatigue can also mean we are out of FLOW. When we fear change, failure, success, happiness, loneliness _____ (you fill in the blank) we are out of FLOW. Harsh self-judgement, self-sabotage, self-doubt, low self-esteem, lack of confidence, feeling unworthy, or not 'good enough' come about when we are out of FLOW. When we carry guilt, place blame, feel shame and jealousy, are overwhelmed, stressed, or anxious, it is because we are out of FLOW. Procrastination, obsession, chronic debt, poor boundaries, confusion, indecision, and frustration are all indications that we are out of FLOW.

These are energy states that we have all been in at one time or another. I want to show you how to release and let go of those feelings, so they are no longer a habit or default. Using the 5 Steps of EAM will help you to create a pattern of FLOW and ease so that you CAN change your life.

FROM THE OLD PARADIGM TO THE NEW

So many people are searching for the answers to feeling happier and to changing their lives.

Like many, I started the journey toward change to find out more about myself but it quickly evolved into a passion. I read as many self-help books as I could get my hands on and took workshops and courses. I studied and qualified in every field that seem relevant.

But I was frustrated because the answers all seemed so complicated. There always seemed something missing, some 'secret' that no one would share. I was searching for the ONE core principle, the one fundamental element that brings everything we've learned or want to achieve — optimum health, abundant wealth, fulfilling relationships and work — together. Whilst no one was saying it I eventually learned that all those courses, workshops, books, blogs, and videos were really talking about ONE thing. ENERGY. Energy is all around us, everything is comprised of energy, our thoughts and emotions are expressions of energy. It is the framework, the conduit, that connects us to each other and to the universe. It is ALL about ENERGY. All of it. Everything you've been taught and everything you are trying to do is about manifesting and managing your energy AND you have the ability to create it, direct it, and change it.

6 SELF HELP MYTHS WHICH STAND IN OUR WAY

The answer to changing your life and manifesting what you want IS NOT OUTSIDE OF YOU. It is IN YOU. It IS YOU. When you learn to direct your personal energy, that is when the magic begins. All my years of searching had only shown me HALF of the story and led me to believe in some misguided 'truths' or myths, which many courses in the self-help industry are based upon.

Myth 1 - To change your life JUST think positively and say affirmations.

Myth 2 - The Law of Attraction is quick; you always get instant results. It's a secret.

Myth 3 - It is just about an abundant mindset.

Myth 4 - Just ask and you will receive.

Myth 5 - That you have to 'dig' for the root cause or your unhappiness or talk it out.

Myth 6 - That you must set SMART goals.

I address each of these myths in the chapters that follow and I offer realistic solutions using EAM for each of them.

How much of your life have you spent searching for the answer? It took forever to find what worked for me. It was only when as the pieces of the puzzle came together that I created the Energy Alignment Method, saw the whole picture, and knew the full story.

All this time you've been searching for something outside of yourself. What these myths forget to tell us is that we already have all the answers inside us.

Whatever you believe, you are reading this for a reason. This is the universe pointing you in the right direction. The question is, are YOU ready to take ACTION?

The world you see outside of you is not broken. We are in the process of change and you know that change looks messy. The change we are in the process of is about moving everything in our life from the old paradigm to the new. The old paradigm is one based on fear and control. It is about domination and who will 'win' and who will 'lose'. It is about 'having more', and what is bigger, better, faster. It is based on competition. It is a world where we place blame, point the finger, and say who is right and who is wrong. Now, that's all changing. People like you and I are waking up. We want to live in a world of love, where we all win and everyone is better off for it. As a society, we want to be empowered to create peace, compassion, and connection. We want to take responsibility for ourselves and our lives. It is a world that we shape, that we change and create for ourselves.

WE ARE PART OF IT ALL

Think for a moment of the vastness of the universe with all of its galaxies, solar systems, and planets. Think of our earth. Earth has been sustaining itself for 150 million years. The ecosystem, the wildlife, the sea life, the vast mountains, and seemingly endless plains, the flora and fauna, and many different species. Think of all the trillions and trillions of cells making up life on this planet right now. Think of the DNA and the trillions of years of life existed on this planet before us. It is so vast as to be almost incomprehensible.

Right now, there are 7.6 billion humans on Earth. Every day there is around 360,000 births and 150,000 deaths. In amongst it all there is you. You and I are made of the exact same things that make up the stars and planets in our known universe. What is the ONE thing that holds it all together? Throughout the billions of years and trillions of lifetimes and cells, the one constant in it all, is energy. It is the one defining connection that has been consistent throughout all measurable time. Energy is the only thing that never dies, it simply transforms. As human beings, it is important to learn how to FLOW with the change of time and space and energy to transform again and again. We are not separate from the energy that created the cosmos, we are a part of it. We are powerful. We are made of the same energy as the universe and we are able to manifest, direct, and transform using that energy.

PREPARING FOR THE JOURNEY

So here we are. The beginning of a journey we're going on together. I'm here with you. Whilst we may not have met in person yet I'm with you all the way. In this book, we'll be going on a journey together. There is a reason we've created the book the way we have. It will take you on a journey that will help you understand how to change your life.

In Chapter 1 we'll take a look at the mainstream science, physics and psychological basis of transformation and how we shape our reality. In Chapter 2 we'll discover how your energy is structured and how it influences your life experience. In Chapter 3 you'll discover how to use this life changing tool, EAM, to shift your energy and create more flow. In Chapter 4 we'll use EAM to overcome the biggest hurdles that stand in the way of changing your life. Chapter 5, 6 & 7 is where we get to work using EAM to change the key areas of your life, like health, wealth, passion, purpose and relationships and so much more. In Chapter 8 we'll explore our potential to impact change on the whole planet.

This is going to be a co-creative experience. You are not alone. You can always connect to our bigger community and meet the other people on this journey. Come over here to join us
www.energyalignmentmethod.com/join-the-community

Myself and our team of awesome EAM mentors are there with you too. You are already changing your life just by taking the lead and reading this book. You don't *need* me ... but we will be here to empower you. Ultimately, this journey is about YOU becoming more self-responsible because only you can change your life. Just reading this book will not do it. You must put it into practice. When we invite you to do the work and explore the subject with EAM, please do so. *That* is what will create the change in your life.

WHAT THIS BOOK IS

With this book and the wider work, we're doing with EAM, we are bridging some of the 'gap' between Science and Spirit. In *The Ultimate Self-Help Book* I share with you what is missing from most personal development and self-help books and bust some of the myths that are so prevalent in our industry. I want to serve as your private coach or guide who you can turn to at any time. My wish is that you'll understand all of the concepts and ideas that you've read and needed to make sense of. We will get to the point AND give you the explanations, as well as the theory we'll be putting things into action. I'll share with you real life stories of people who have changed their life with EAM so you can see by their example, that it can be possible for you too.

My wish is that you'll finish this book more empowered than you were at the beginning. I hope that you'll use the 5 Steps as well as the exercises that go with them and implement positive, far-reaching changes in your life. I'll show you how to stop other people from affecting and influencing your energy, and how to change your relationships and connection to others. You'll learn what to do when everything around you appears to be going wrong, and how you can transform your life to achieve your dreams, find your calling, help others, and become the person you know you are meant to be.

WHAT THIS BOOK IS NOT

In these pages, we won't be about dredging up the past, taking deeply emotional trips into our childhood, or placing blame on others. We won't be painfully reliving situations or 'talking it through'. If you're already a therapist, coach, healer, or mentor I know when you see the power of this work you're going to want to use EAM with your clients. However, this book is only the tip of the iceberg of what you need to know to apply it others. To safely facilitate a lasting transformation in others you must first go on the journey yourself. This is one of the reasons why our EAM mentors have 18 months of training before they are qualified. If you really want to use EAM to change lives, then get in touch and speak to us and find out how you can. Just pop here find out more www.energyalignmentmethod.com/book-a-call

Go through the training and become an EAM mentor and a true master of energy alignment. We welcome you.

WHO THIS BOOK IS FOR

This is the self-help book for people who think they don't need one and maybe even think that self-help isn't for them. You just want life to feel better than it does right now. This book is for you if you are already on the path and are looking for answers to questions you may not yet know even exist. You do not need to be a spiritual superhero already. If you're already somewhere along your path, then this guide book will help you find your way.

It's also for those metaphysical 'lost souls' who once they read, or see this information, will just get it. For some of us, we feel an instant connection because EAM is simply reminding us of the true foundation of our life, which we know on a deep level already. So many of us are searching for something new, empowering, and enlightening to take us to the next level. If you feel like you're stuck in a rut, or you're on a quest to your true self, and your soul purpose, you can discover the answers inside the pages of this book, like so many who have been on this journey.

MORE THAN YOUR AVERAGE BOOK

This is not your typical self-help book. On this journey, I'm not going to tell you that "It's all your parents' fault" or "Let's just talk about it", or that "you can manifest anything you want just by thinking." If that's what you are looking for, you won't find it here. I'm not a professor, scientist, psychologist or neuroscientist. I began my journey just like you. My life put me on a path to wanting to discover HOW I could create a life I LOVED, one that empowered me to know how to change my life. Along the way I have spent more than 20 years understanding energy and learning about FLOW. I became qualified in and taught almost every holistic therapy you can think of and studied a 3-year degree in energy, human beings, and our interactions with the world. I spent 10 years coaching, guiding, mentoring, and studying thousands of people and what I am sharing here is the outcome of that work. AND you know what? I'm still learning. We all are. Because every client is different. Every lifetime is different and as you'll see in this book, working with energy is always different too.

I've been doing this work for a while and when I'm looking for my own coach, guide, or mentor I never settle for anyone who thinks they have it all down. Why? Because it means they have given up. They have stopped learning. They have closed off to new ways of being or becoming and I believe that no one has all the answers.

HOW TO READ THIS BOOK

I know this book is epic in size. It's because there is so much to share with you (and believe me this is just the beginning).

You may be thinking, how can you fit this into your schedule along with your everyday life? Here are a few simple ideas. Limit your TV watching. Get up 30 minutes earlier and have a cheeky read in bed. Instead of scrolling through Facebook or other social media sites pick this book up instead. Do some of the EAM exercises in the shower, whilst cooking dinner or on your commute. Make it a part of your ever day life. The concepts, tools, and exercises will only change your life when you IMPLEMENT them. That is where the magic begins.

I have created a set of free resources to accompany this book. You can download them here www.energyalignmentmethod.com/tush-freebies

Get yourself a journal because we're going to do something productive with what you write in it. Throughout the book from Chapter 4 onwards you'll see tips, hints and ideas on ways you can ◊:◊ **EXPAND YOUR ENERGY WITH EAM**. These will be little exercises for you to implement. We're going to use it to work through all of the things that will come up when you recognise the beliefs and the stories that have been holding you back. Use your journal to write your notes for each of the exercises given throughout this book and then you can EAM all the things that come up. Be mindful whom you share this with. Some people will think it is weird and crazy, which can draw your energy away from the work you need to do. WHEN you have changed your life, and they see your energy shift, change, and transform they will ask you what you've been doing. THEN you can explain it to them.

You Can Change Your Life

There are so many ways that the impact of our life experience can influence and affect our energy. You'll see many examples of them throughout this book. Everything that happens to us affects our energy somehow. It is the energetic, emotional and mental impact of these situations which often sends us on the search to change our life. We want to feel better than we do, or to make us reach for something more.

Often when we meet others we only see them for who they are now. We do not know their life experiences, the journey they have been on or what they have overcome. Like you I wasn't always the person you see today.

Throughout my life I had been battered and bruised by many of my life experiences. During my younger years I lived in fear, constantly feeling on edge, wondering if Dad would come home again drunk and belligerent. Often I would be cowered behind the bedroom door holding hands with my sister, as we listened to our dad beat our mum. Feeling hopeless to do anything to protect her, at the same time believing this was how 'normal' family life was meant to be.

Dad was tight with money and would only provide the bare minimum, which meant mum worked had to work as a dinner lady and cleaner at school to make ends meet. Whilst my friends where playing, I would be wandering the empty corridors of the school or helping my mum scrub floors before I went home.

At the age of 7 my dad had a serious accident. He fell more than 40 ft from a warehouse roof straight onto a concrete floor. He broke his neck and back, had severe head injuries and spent months in intensive care and recovery in hospital. His head injuries seemed to escalate his violence and his drinking became worse.

At the age of 8 I seemed to be rapidly gaining weight... within a few days my whole body had swollen, my face was so puffy I could barely open my eyes. The doctors had ignored my mum's repeated pleas for help every time saying "I will be alright; it is just puppy fat". On my seventh visit we got to see the family doctor, who immediately called an ambulance. I had developed a rare condition known as nephrotic syndrome, which meant my kidneys were failing. By the time I got to hospital I was less than 24 hours from death. Over the next 3 years I missed school, bouncing from hospital to home. I had spent so much time in hospital without my family, left feeling lost and alone, I believed that I had to do life on my own. Every time I went home I would relapse and end up back in hospital for a few months. In a last-ditch attempt, doctors decided to try a cancer treatment before putting me on dialysis for life. Whilst the medication worked the doctors had said I would forever be infertile and unable to have children of my own.

KEEPING SECRETS

For years, I held onto secrets. I became fiercely independent and didn't want help from anyone. I thought I was 'grown up' and could do whatever I wanted. At the age of 11 I had unknowingly lost my innocence whilst drunk at a friend's party. Having told my friends and their older sister, no one believed me. I kept it quiet, feeling petrified I would get in trouble. A few weeks later when on holiday I was raped at knifepoint in a bathtub by a 'friend' of the family. So, I once again kept quiet for fear of bringing shame on the family. Sadly, it wasn't the last time it happened to me. I began to believe that this is just how men were.

I bottled it up inside, keeping my secrets and becoming angry at life. Turning to alcohol, drugs and partying to temporarily numb the pain. I felt unloved, unwanted and unworthy. To find relief from the pressure, sadness and pain I began to self-harm. Setting fire to myself, stubbing out matches or cigarettes on my arms and legs. Cutting or punching myself in the face. Whilst none of them worked it was the only way I knew to control how I felt inside.

At the age of 14 I fell in 'love' with a man who was far too old for me. I would disappear for days or weeks on end. When I would return home, I was angry, frustrated and violent. My mum was desperate at home never knowing where I was or what I was doing.

TIME FOR CHANGE

When I was 17 years old I discovered energy, eastern philosophies and therapies, which empowered me and spoke to my heart. I trained and studied in every modality and technique I could. It helped me to make sense of the anger, hurt, and betrayal I felt inside. As I learned that what was happening outside was always a reflection of what was within, it gave me a new outlook on life. I was able to release the pain from the past. I finally understood that I had to go within to change what was happening in my life. I was finally able to feel a sense of peace and freedom inside. As I began to share this work with others, by the age of 24 I was running my own well-being centre and helping people heal as well.

I got married young. We had met at the age of 17 and both loved the party life. In fact, that was all we knew. Whilst he was a nice man, I knew in hindsight I knew I had married for the wrong reasons. Everyone, including me, believed I had the best relationship, yet inside I felt trapped. Whilst I ignored it at the time, I was desperate to create some safety and stability in my life, so it seemed like the right step. At 26 I took the bravest step to change my life. Whilst it was so hard to leave I choose to split from my husband. I moved hundreds of miles away from my friends, family and everything I had built with my business. All I had was a pull in my heart to take the leap. It felt as if life was controlling me, yet I knew it was right and time to begin a new chapter.

NEW BEGINNINGS

I soon bounced into a new relationship, this was one my heart had wanted. He was exciting, handsome, loving and supportive. At that point in my life I felt I'd dealt with my past and was able to start looking more to my future, where I wanted to go and what I wanted to do.

I began to push all my energy into my career. Juggling three businesses, studying a full-time Acupuncture degree and working all hours to earn the money. I still believed that 'happiness' and 'success' were wrapped up in the ideal lifestyle. I was driven by a need to prove to everyone from my past that I could be successful. I would have the car, the home, the holidays, the marriage and finally live the 'happy ever after'.

Yet in my heart I knew this was not the way. Somehow believing I could be the one exception, I ignored the clear signs from the universe that this was all out of flow. I ignored the pain, sadness, and frustration, quieting the voices in my head with wine and chocolate and more work. I pushed and pushed, sacrificing my happiness, health and well-being along the way. It was not long before it all collapsed.

In just three weeks two businesses disappeared. Leaving me with £40k debts, which was money borrowed from family and business loans. With no way to pay it back. Despite everything I had been through this felt like my rock bottom – not for me, but because I felt I had let everyone down. I felt as though I had failed and could not see a way out.

FINDING OUR FLOW

From this place, there was no choice. I had to go back to what I knew: my energy work. Instead of focusing on building my life from the outside, once again I had to go within to change the way I felt. I had to find a way to release the energy of debt, small thinking, and stop focusing on what I lost to create my future. I aligned my energy, thoughts, and emotions in my life. Then I did only the things in alignment with my vision and what I was called in my heart to do. As I started to put EAM into practice and follow the steps to rebuild my life, I became more congruent, and my ability to attract money grew. But I still ignored the call in my heart to share this energy work, and instead rebuilt my work life as an 'online marketer'. Too ashamed to come out of the spiritual closet I would secretly work with my clients on their energy.

In 2014 I became happily pregnant with the little baby I was told I would never conceive. Having used EAM and energy healing to do so much work on myself, my hara, my health, and allowing myself to be in flow. Life just felt so exciting thinking about the amazing future that was to come. Just six weeks before he was born my third business failed and I lost another £70k! Now for many this would have been devastating but I was thrilled. It felt like the biggest gift. Now I was free to spend time with the little one, to listen to my heart and to pursue my passion. Whilst I sat at home with no money left and no source of income, I had no stress, no worries, no business or commitments, and no idea what to do next. I was just able to be present. As I stared into the eyes of our gorgeous little boy, I remember saying out loud to the universe, 'Right, if I am taking away any time from this beautiful little man it absolutely has to be the thing that I am here for. I am not f****** around anymore!'

I had allowed myself to stop the 'PUSH' of life. To be honest, I had no choice but to sit and receive. During that time, I just received download after download. I would wake in the night to scribble down notes, as pieces of the puzzle came together. As I allowed truly connected to this voice inside I realised I had been living my purpose and following my passion to help others change their lives all along. That is what I knew I was here for. Having my little boy Kye had inspired my heart. I wanted to make a difference in the world for him.

Just four months after he was born I began sharing my passion for energy. The inner voices crept in nagging, "Who are you to be doing this?". "You don't have the flashy house / car / lifestyle?". "You're not 'qualified' enough" and "What if people say that you're wrong?". Yet the feedback from others was incredible, every day I received emails and messages from people saying how much it had transformed and changed their lives. I finally felt that I was in flow.

LETTING GO WITH EAM

My journey to self-love, alignment and to changing my life began way before EAM was born. Despite all the work I had done on myself with other methods once I began working with EAM I was able to create much bigger shifts, transform and let go of the stuckness I still felt. The lessons I learned along the way inspired so much of this book and became the basis for EAM. I wish I knew then, what I know now. I can see how much quicker life would have changed. Looking back at the journey I was on it makes sense now. Seeing the impact of the upbringing I had, the experiences and life choices I made. The good news is that it is all just energy. Whilst it used to be my story it is no longer the basis of who I am. I no longer operate from this place; I am still on the journey to becoming. We all are and always will be.

A NEW JOURNEY

I know now that I had to experience the suffering and setbacks of my childhood, it made me the woman I've become. Without that pain I would never have started on the journey of self-discovery. Without that EAM would never have been born. I know we have all been on our own journey. Everything we have experienced is because we are strong enough to take it. There are lessons in your past who have made you who you are. In this book, we will find the gift in your journey to who you are. If I could speak to my younger self here is what I would want to say;

"I know how much you have been through. You were brave, courageous and strong. I admire the determination you showed even in the face of your greatest fears. I thank you for never giving up. You taught me to stay strong and to find friendship, be kind, and to love others. You taught me to forgive and to let go. You taught me to be keep on going until I found happiness. I thank you to the fullest expansion of my heart. These are the lessons you taught me so I could become the woman I am today."

At the beginning, I never dreamt I would end up creating a transformational self-help method or sharing what I learned about energy. Yet here I am teaching it to thousands of people. Along the way all I had inside was a calling in my heart that said "life has to be better than this". I had to find a way to align to the life I wanted to find happiness, contentment, and discover my true calling. EAM has changed my life. No matter where you have been or what you have been through I know you can too. I hope this book and what you will learn inside these pages will inspire and enable you to change your life too.

PART ONE

The Explosion of Energy

IN ALL ITS FORMS

CHAPTER 1

The Science & Theory

"The day science begins to study non-physical phenomena; it will make more progress in one decade than in all the previous centuries of its existence."

~Nikola Tesla

It all began with the Big Bang. The explosion of energy that created life itself. In this chapter, we're going to take a walk with the sciences and talk about energy from the scientific paradigm. It will allow you to understand some of the key energy principles which will apply to your journey to change your life.

The Newtonian Laws we were all taught in school only apply to things that happen on a macroscopic scale. The 'real world' life you see does not apply to life in the microcosm, things that happen at a tiny level. For that we need to know about quantum mechanics, the New Age science that has actually been around for many years. Yet I was never taught it at school (and I'm pretty sure you weren't either).

SCIENTIFIC ENERGY THEORY

Our current scientific, western medicine, and physiological perspective of life are evolving at a significant pace as deeper and better understandings emerge from various aspects of science and extensive research. Despite the numerous claims NO ONE yet has the full picture. There are so many streams of science each designed to speak to a certain aspect of our current known universe. From geology to astronomy, from physics to chemistry, from maths to psychology. They analyse everything from string theory to parallel universes and everything in between. Our known universe is made up of elements that are so huge they are almost beyond comprehension, to particles so tiny they're impossible to imagine.

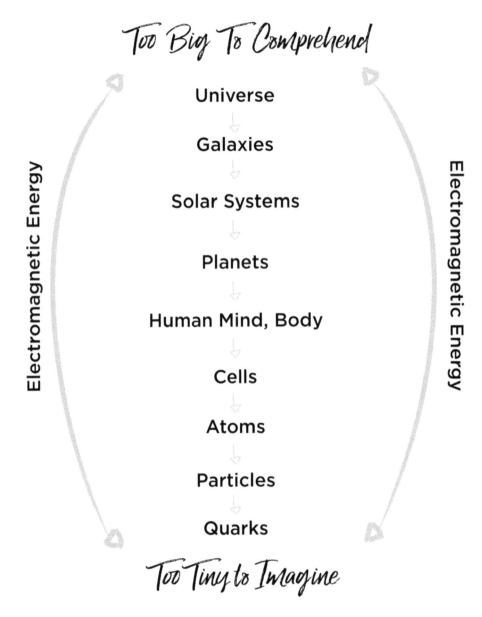

Too Big To Comprehend

Universe
↓
Galaxies
↓
Solar Systems
↓
Planets
↓
Human Mind, Body
↓
Cells
↓
Atoms
↓
Particles
↓
Quarks

Electromagnetic Energy

Electromagnetic Energy

Too Tiny to Imagine

The Range of Electromagnetic Energy

What brings them all together is that they are all energy in its many different manifestations. Energy is the one constant throughout all the main sciences. You may be thinking, but this isn't scientific. Well what is SCIENCE? There are many different streams of science exploring different possibilities into so many different theories. Some 'scientists' are coming to the same conclusions while others are coming to completely opposite findings. They are all 'scientific' yet even they cannot agree on the same answers. Not ONE school of science or research currently has the one answer that explains *everything*, the meaning of life, consciousness, and how matter or energy work on a microscopic, macroscopic, or quantum level. NOT ONE.

I want to share with you some ideas, some possibilities and concepts, which are based on science and research within their chosen fields. Whilst some of the concepts may differ theoretically or come to different conclusions, they give you a broader perspective and hopefully a better understanding of where and how their research connects. I'm not trying to turn you into a neuroscientist or quantum physicist. I use these theories to better help you to understand how you can change YOUR life using the energy all around us and inside of us of which everything is made.

There are unknown scientific gaps, which we can more easily discuss in terms of Eastern energy and philosophy. We have corresponding processing of information within our energy bodies, through our *meridians*, which are channels of energy, your *aura,* which is your electromagnetic energy field, and *chakras*, which are energy centres in the body. We will explore these in chapter 2.

There are a few principles that I believe all sciences can agree upon:

- The one constant in it all is energy

- There is more to life than what we know.

- There is more to life than what we can see with the naked eye.

- There are answers to questions about the universe that need to be answered.

- There are questions about life and why we are here that still need to be asked.

- There is (as yet) no ONE explanation for all matter and consciousness in the known universe.

Let's do our best to piece this together with what we know. Let's start with the SCIENCE.

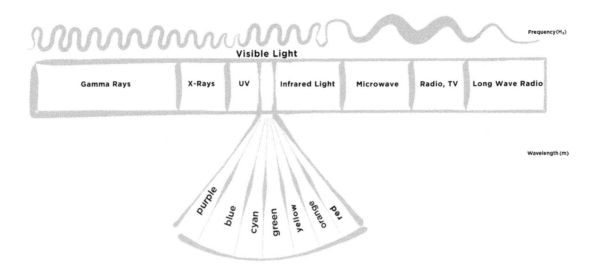

Electromagnetic Frequency Range

Everything is energy vibrating at different levels. This graphic represents the different vibrations of electromagnetic energy all around us. Science has proven that everything in the world is connected by one field of energy called the electron mat. Imagine it's one big flat mat of electrons in different shapes depending on the vibration of the energy. Picture energy like the blades of a fan. When a fan is spinning SLOWLY you can see the blades rotating. When it is spinning quickly it is undetectable to the human eye.

On the left, you can see energy vibrating at a very fast high vibrational space, these are known as gamma rays. This is shown by the short sharp movement of the energy. These rays affect our energy. They are used in nuclear bombs, to kill cancer cells, and to sterilise hospital equipment. We know the devastation a nuclear bomb can create. In this same family are X-rays and UV (ultraviolet) rays. We know the impact X-rays can have; they can make us sick if we have too many. UV rays radiate from the sun. Imagine you're sitting outside enjoying an ice-cold drink in the sunshine, or having a BBQ and soaking up the rays. Later when you go inside you may notice your skin is burnt to a crisp from those invisible but powerful UV rays.

In the middle of the image you can see the visible light spectrum; the rainbow colour patch is the only piece of the energy spectrum that we are visually aware of. Light is also electromagnetic energy and everything that vibrates on that similar frequently is what we see. On the other side of that are infrared rays, microwaves, radio waves, TV, and long wave radio. We use them every day in our phones, watching TV, listening to the radio, or to cook our food. We know that these other forms of energy exist. Although we do not 'see them', we use them in our daily lives. We behave as if the only things that 'exist' are those things we can see or feel. We forget that we are surrounded by, affected by, implement, and interact with and within this energy, like a fish in water. It's all around us.

FAST AND SLOW, HEAVY AND LIGHT

We call the faster shorter wave energies, higher vibrations because they are short and fast and light. The longer vibrations are slower, heavier, and often denser in energy. This is an important principle to understand because you experience the difference in the vibration of different energies and therefore the differences in their impact on you each and every day. This 'faster' and 'slower' vibration of energy is also responsible for the speed at which you can manifest something or influence the rate of change. For example, a belief, a thought, a memory, or emotion can change very quickly because they are faster vibrating energies.

Let's consider this in terms of changing your life. If you want to change something that is manifested in a physical world, like a house, car, or money, because they are a slower vibration, it takes more consistent, focused, ALIGNED attention on the change you want to see in order for it to transform. Yet most of us don't give ourselves the time or space to do that. When we use EAM we are working with energy. Whether you want to look at it as the science energy or more spiritual energy as QI (pronounced chee) or PRANA, they are all the same. It is these unseen forces of energy that influence our daily lives. Although we don't see them with our eyes, we feel their effects.

ELECTROMAGNETIC ENERGY IN SPACE

What about the influence of energy from space? One cosmic solar flare is equivalent to 100 million atom bombs exploding at once. The energy and debris emitted from these can seriously damage spacecraft and people if they are out in space. Solar flares release all kinds of energy along the electromagnetic spectrum. Everything from radio waves to gamma rays. This means that solar flares can and do impact many things we see and use in our everyday lives. They are known to disrupt equipment, satellites, and power lines, overload cameras, and expose us to toxic levels of energy.

Think of all the planets and galaxies in our universe sending out these massive waves of energy. Even the planets within our solar systems have their own electromagnetic frequencies influencing us every day. In the same way, our beautiful moon has a small magnetic charge—though weaker than that of the earth—its lunar gravitational pull influences the ocean's tide. Considering that we are 80% water, if the moon can affect our massive oceans, imagine its pull on the water energy inside us. These cosmic giants are sending measurable electromagnetic frequencies, which affect our planet on a global level. Could it also be possible that these planetary and intergalactic energy waves have an effect on our energy too? The effects may be undetectable to the naked eye but they are still exerting their energies which impact us in many ways. These massive waves of energy could also be influencing our physical and energetic bodies.

WE ARE ALL CONNECTED BY ONE FIELD

We learned in school how the universe is the beginning of everything. And you may have heard the phrase, we are all one. What this means is we are ALL part of one unified field of energy. At the smallest, most infinitesimal level we are all connected by one large mat of energy called the electron field. EVERYTHING.

This is more than just a human to human connection. The electron field connects everything:

The chair you're sitting on...

This book or the tablet you're reading this on...

Your next-door neighbour...

The animals in the wild...

The planets in our galaxy...

The far-flung galaxies themselves...

In fact, anything you know, believe or perceive within our universe is connected to this field.

This unified field is made of electromagnetic energy. At its simplest foundation, this helps us to understand that everything around us is made of *one* thing. Something smaller than electrons. Our body is made of bone, tissue, and blood. Those elements are made of cells, which are made of organelles, which are made of proteins, which are made of amino acids, which are made of atoms. Atoms are made of protons, neutrons, and electrons. Electrons are made from the electron field. So what on earth is that field made of? Potential energy. This brings us to the world of quantum mechanics.

A LITTLE QUANTUM PHYSICS AND MECHANICS

Despite the differing and often opposing theories and models, quantum mechanics is far from a New Age fad. Quantum mechanics have been busily powering our phones and computers, and innovating technology, for decades. It is working in other areas of our everyday lives, too. Quantum physics is a set of theories that underlay our life experience. It is through many new scientific quantum mechanical understandings we live our life today. Quantum is about the world of explaining things that happen at atomic and subatomic levels of our life experience. Way smaller than we can see with a normal microscope, they do not always apply to the way we experience life at a macroscopic or everyday level. Quantum mechanics is often described as the science of possibility, which is such a profound and exciting concept. Science has shown that at the quantum level everything is energy. In that nothingness comes *everything*. Everything you believe to be possible.

There are many different schools of thought on quantum physics. Some believe that we are part of multiple realities. In the many worlds theory, the belief is that many universes are working all at the same time, where every possible event is occurring. For whatever reason, our awareness only sees one. The school of thought known as the Copenhagen interpretation theorises that it is more about the waves of energy. They believe that we create our experience from an infinite number of possibilities. When we give our attention to something it becomes the physical form. As intriguing as this is, theories are not facts. So how on earth do we know what is real? The world of quantum is fun, to say the least, though it may not make sense. Even quantum physicists are trying to understand it all. So many theories, models, and explanations that not many of them agree on.

THE DOUBLE SLIT TEST: THE OBSERVER IS THE CREATOR

Science and maths are not my strongest subjects and I'm not a quantum physicist, yet I wonder at the magical effect it has on us. One of the most exciting experiments that has been undertaken in the world of quantum physics is known as the double slit test. This incredible experiment proves that everything around us exists by being experienced by YOU or ME, the observer!

Let's start by getting into the world of quantum. Imagine you are playing ping-pong with tiny electrons. There is no one around to play with so you give yourself a target on the wall. In front of that is a screen which has a slit in it. Your job is to get your balls through the slits. When you smack those tiny electrons some of them travel through the slit and hit the wall behind it leaving a mark the shape of the slit. We now have two slits on the screen in front of the wall. You carry on hitting the electrons. Our logical mind would expect to see two sets of marks on the wall behind; instead, you end up with marks that look like we created several slits in the screen but we only had two! Weird? Definitely. So, what made that happen?

The easiest way to think about it is that our electron is behaving like a WAVE of water rather than a ball. Every time you hit the electron it creates a WAVE that FLOWs towards the two slits. The electron separates to go through the two slits to the other side it. This creates a series of waves, which create the multiple impact marks on the wall. But why would our electron ball behave like a wave when it passes through double slits? It is believed that as the electron splits in two when it reaches the slits in the screen and travels through both *simultaneously*. It then creates a wave effect as it comes through the screen, this is explained by the 'Quantum Theory of Non-Locality' where something can be in existence in two places at once. Mind-bending, right?

ELECTRONS MAKE CHOICES

Of course, being scientists, they wanted to prove this was true so they placed a small device to observe what our electron ping pong ball did when it went through the two slits in the screen. This is when it all went a bit SCI-FI. Instead, what they saw on the wall were two neat little columns instead of the smaller wave-like impacts. You're probably thinking *huh*? Yep, tiny electrons 'decide' what to do in response to being observed. When watched, it behaves like a ball and when it's not being watched, it behaves like a wave. An electromagnetic wave is an energy; it is a vibration. What does this mean to us? We already know everything in our world is made of energy, and that we are all part of this one field of electrons. *Those electrons are actually affected and therefore behave differently, depending on our observation, when a MIND is present.* It ONLY appears as matter WHEN it is being observed. Deep, right? Yes! Empowering? ABSOLUTELY! Because this means that ALL of our reality is actually one big field of energy with potential for *anything* because how we observe it changes its (and our) reality.

Why is this important to you? Because this experiment shows that it is US who shapes the reality we see. It is our energy, our thought, and our conscious awareness of what we see that enables the electrons to behave like balls instead of waves. It is US who experiences this sea of energy around us as matter; therefore, we have the ability to change what we see outside of us by changing our perception, which then alters our reality.

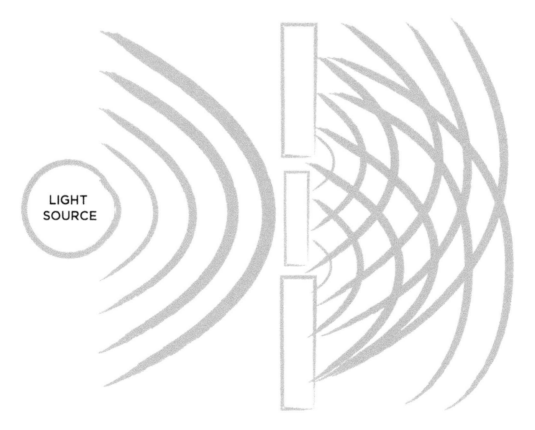

Double Slit Wave Experiment

This energy field which we can influence is what many ancient Eastern philosophies talk about as the Tao or beginning of time; in science, it is known as the Big Bang. In whichever context, it is the point at which all life and energy was created. In fact, it does more than connect us... we ARE it and it IS us. We ARE energy — Energy IS us. You are NOT a separate human being from me. I am you and you are me. We just believe that we are separate because that is what we see on a day-to day-basis.

If we could see this energy field around us we would know that we're all connected. Whilst many branches of science are yet to agree on the ONE thing, it is currently the holy grail of understanding the way the universe works. *This experiment shows us that we play OUR part in the reality we see.* Everything is energy and OUR energy influences reality on so many levels. Our thoughts and feelings have the power to shape our reality. Things do not 'exist' without us seeing them. Nothing is REAL without observation. If that is the case, it stands to reason that what we see in our world is made up. But how? We'll explore this in a minute.

We play

our part in the

reality we see.

THE THREE FLOWS OF ENERGY

All electromagnetic energy can be in one of 3 states. It is either moving in one direction from one place to another, not moving, or moving in the opposite direction. In this context, FLOW means moving steadily and continuously without stopping. RESISTANCE is a force that stops the progress of something or makes it slower. Or, it is the degree to which something prevents the FLOW of an electrical current. The scientific definition of RESISTANCE is *a measurement of the difficulty encountered by a power source in forcing electric current through an electrical circuit, and hence the amount of power dissipated in the circuit*. REVERSAL is the act of changing or making something change to its opposite. You will find these terms used in physics in relation to the FLOWs of energy. We also use them in terms of energy psychology, which we'll discuss in Chapter 2. ELECTRICITY is a form of energy resulting from the existence of charged particles (such as electrons or protons), either *statically* as an accumulation of charge, or *dynamically* as a current.

MAGNETISM

Magnetics is when something of a like match, or vibration, is drawn to it. Magnetism is what creates mass. This is how planets are formed. As things of a like matter with the same electrical charge are drawn to one another, they collect, gather, and they grow as more things of a like nature come to them. This is caused by magnetism. Energy moves in circles and cycles. These cycles are the results of the FLOW of electromagnetic energy. An electromagnetic field (also EMF or EM field) is a physical field produced by electrically charged objects. These objects are electrically charged by ELECTRONS.

As the name suggests this field is both *electric*, meaning it holds a charge, and *magnetic* meaning it attracts things of the same vibration back to it. By its very nature of being electric and magnetic these electrons affect other electrons in its vicinity. When you look at energy at transmission systems, such as radio waves, there is something in the signal itself known as the carrier wave. It is a waveform with the purpose of transmitting information as an electromagnetic wave.

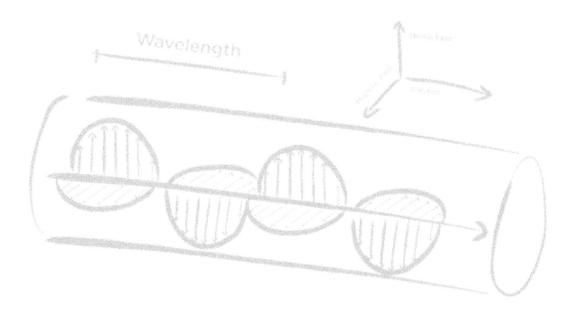

Electricity, Magnetism & Carrier Wave

When you think about the structure of energy, imagine it in three components, the electricity, the magnetism and the message. The FLOW of electricity travels UP and DOWN. This is the two extremes of the energy, the yin and the yang, the positive and the negative. The magnetic element is flowing left and right creating our horizontal experience in life and drawing things in or pushing them away from us. The third is the 'message' or communication of information which is sent via a carrier wave. This FLOW of electromagnetic energy affects everything. Whether we are talking about a tiny cell in our body or the environment around us. They are all connected. Everything within and around us is energy in motion and we are influenced by it all.

OUR SENSES INTERPRET VIBRATION

We have five physical senses—sight, sound, touch, smell, and taste. Each of these senses have a specific role and is a translator of a particular type of energy vibration. For example, our eyes receive and interpret a particular range of electromagnetic energy known as light waves. Our ears interpret mechanical energy in the form of sound waves. Our skin interprets a particular range of pressure, temperature and pain. Our sense of taste and smell are more interpretations of molecules which lock into receptors and send signals via the nervous system. In its own way, each is an indicator of vibration. Animals also experience different ranges of energy. For example, a dog has a greater perception of the range of smell and sound. Some animals can see in the dark using infrared waves. It's possible for biology to perceive a large wave of electromagnetic frequencies, but our human bodies are not yet adapted to do so.

In order to process all of that information coming at us, our brain and body have to filter through all of that data. It does this in a part of the brain known as the thalamus. If it didn't filter out all that extra information and noise, we'd go mad! Our senses are picking up far more information from this sea of energy than we consciously perceive in our reality. What you see in your world is not truly an accurate or complete picture. It is just your interpretation of the energetic information around you. Those interpretations are made from the filters we have from our own experiences. We are built to interpret vibration of energy in all its different forms.

THE SCIENCE OF THE FLOW STATE

The FLOW state is a way of operating and performing that is often used in top performance coaching. High level athletes are trained to get into and stay in their FLOW state for peak performance. There are many different institutes studying the flow state one of them is the Flow Genome project. Your FLOW state is probably best known to you as 'being in the zone'. It's those moments when everything just works. When you feel like you're on top of the world. Many of the biggest and most innovative companies understand the power of FLOW. They see how the state of FLOW can drive change and create new ideas and ways of working throughout their businesses, too. Now this is a very exciting concept for you on a personal level, whether you work for yourself, in a small business, or as part of a large corporation. Imagine what you or your team working in the state of FLOW could accomplish.

Studies have shown that when working, team members or top executives who were in their FLOW state were five times more productive than those who were out of FLOW. I can vouch for this myself; I get so much more done when in FLOW than out of FLOW. We can all become more productive if we increase our FLOW state by just 20%. I will show you how using EAM you can increase it a whole lot more.

WHY BE IN FLOW?

There are so many proven benefits on different levels to the state of FLOW. Physically, being in FLOW has been shown to increase the fluid exchange into and out of cells, create better filtration of blood and fluids, and better absorption between the capillaries and tissues. These have long-term effects on your health too. Being in FLOW also creates measurable changes in hormonal activity and balance in the adrenal and cortisol levels. This is ALL because you feel good! Ultimately, it creates a better efficiency of energy across the whole system.

There are an increasing number of studies and documented evidence that shows the improvement in health and well-being by changing how we think and feel. On a psychological level, there are marked changes in our ability to think clearly, recall and access information, as well as an increased emotional stability and sense of well-being. Studies across various groups have shown that being in the FLOW state creates a measured drop in the effects of stress, increased positive mood, and a change in the quality of life and attitudes of people using coherence or FLOW building techniques like EAM. ALL from being able to manage our state of FLOW!

BRIDGING THE GAP BETWEEN SCIENCE & ENERGY PSYCHOLOGY

To fully understand how FLOW works in the body, let's take a look at some of the research from The Heartmath Institute and Resonance Science Foundation. For more than 40 years the researchers at The Heartmath Institute have studied the effects of energy, the science behind our electromagnetic energy, and the physiology of the body and the way we experience our world. Much of their work is based on monitoring the effects of the electromagnetic influence of our heart and our brain on the rest of our body and environment. They focus on a specific physiological and energetic state of energy called COHERENCE (in EAM we call this FLOW). This is a measurable state, which they believe reflects our current emotional state. This model is grounded in and consistent with research in the fields of neurocardiology (the study of communication between heart and brain) psychophysiology, (the study of physiological bases of psychological processes), and neuroscience (the study or neurons).

In Heartmath, coherence is a specific measure of the heart's rhythms that appears as smooth and orderly wavelike patterns. In this state, all of our energy is Flowing and there is a natural synchronicity in our body systems. During this time, many people experience more energy, feel more alive, are grounded or composed, and are able to think clearly. Physiologically, their body shows a more synchronised rate of breathing, better blood FLOW, improved nervous system function, boosted immune function, and a better hormonal balance.

The Heartmath Institute has shown that EVERYONE is capable of being in this state of coherence. They have developed several techniques and methods designed to help people maintain a higher level of coherence in the heart. Their tried and tested techniques such as their Quick Coherence Technique involve noticing your current emotion and choosing to move your emotion to something more coherent. There are many ways to achieve it, yet one of the quickest ways to do so is to feel positive emotions such as love, compassion, happiness. This is exactly what we will do with Step 5 of EAM — MANIFEST.

Within EAM we use this same principle of choosing to shift our emotions from an incoherent or RESISTANT state to a coherent or in FLOW one. This is the main foundation of the EAM. In fact, it's why we do everything else. This process of recognising our state and choosing to shift it has been shown in numerous scientific studies to have considerable physiological and psychological impacts.

THE INFLOW AND THE OUTFLOW STATE

The image below is an example of a heart that is out of FLOW. You can see the erratic and irregular pattern. This is often what it feels like as we experience negative emotions like, stress, frustration, or feeling overwhelmed.

Heartwave out of flow state

Below is an example of our heart rhythm energy when in FLOW. You can see how it creates an even wave coming in and out, flowing evenly up and down. This is what happens when we experience positive emotions such as love, peace, connection, freedom, happiness and joy.

Heartwave in flow state

ENERGY PSYCHOLOGY & THE PHYSICAL BODY

With EAM and energy healing, our goal is to enhance your ability to successfully handle the energetic, mental, and emotional response to things that happen or have happened in life. We want to create a greater overall feeling of well-being, so you feel more connected and are able to transform your internal baseline energy to a higher, more positive vibration.

Everything we do in life is usually because we want to feel better, yet the very thing that tends to stop us is our own perceptions, thoughts, and beliefs of our experience. Most people would agree that it is our perception of experiences that creates stress, anxiety, or make us feel overwhelmed, which we call a state of RESISTANCE. What if we were better able to manage those experiences and transform our energy and physiology from the effects that these situations have on us? The good news is that we can with EAM. This is the state of being in FLOW. If we can create our own resistant experiences, we can also choose to create more positive ones by changing our experiences, energy, emotions, and thoughts. To begin, we need a better understanding of what is happening to our physiology: and the integral part that our HEAD (our brain) and our HEART (our heart) play in our cognitive, emotional, and energetic experience of the world.

A number of studies in the field of neurocardiology have shown that the neural communication between the heart and brain is far more complicated than we ever thought before; it really is fascinating. These studies have shown that information is consistently sent *from the heart to the brain* via our nervous system. Yes, you read that correctly. Our heart is sending information to our brain and not only the other way around.

THE ROLE OF THE HEART

Our heart is one of the most powerful electromagnetic communicators in the body. It can be measured up to 20 feet away from the body on a machine on a Superconducting Quantum Interference Device (SQUID). Energetically, what they are measuring is what we know as our aura. The electrical measurement of our heart is up to 60 times greater in amplitude than that of our brain. *The magnetic component of our heart's electromagnetic energy is 5000 times stronger than our brain.*

Research has confirmed that our heart does much more than just pump blood; it is, in fact, a sensory organ and acts as a super sophisticated information encoding and processing centre. That means that your heart is able to learn, remember, and make *independent* functional decisions that *do not* involve the brain. (Insert dramatic music.) Our heart is not only mechanical (pumping blood), it is also intelligent (processing and sending information). The heart is also able to detect changes in our hormones and changes in responses to the nervous system. It also creates and transforms its own hormones and neurotransmitters, a function previously believed to only happen in the brain. Our heart also influences our nervous system and the higher centres of the brain, which are involved in perception and emotional processing. Our heart is what keeps the rhythm and pace of the body. It is the primary source of what are known as dynamic rhythm patterns and it is the most consistent too. (Thank god it keeps doing its work!)

When we look at the maze of neural networks that connect the heart and cardiovascular system to the brain via the afferent or incoming nervous systems. These connections are far more extensive than those for communicating with any other major organ. This means more information is travelling from the heart to the brain than anywhere else in the body. WOW WOW WOW! It is not a new idea that information is communicated through many biological systems. We see this in animals, tress, marine life. Now we can see that it also happens with human beings.

Earlier we briefly discussed the 3 different aspects of electromagnetic energy, the electro (up and down) magnetic (left and right) and the carrier wave, which is the message component. Through years of research The Heartmath Institute has been able to show that our HEART energy also has this carrier wave component. This carrier wave is the messenger sending information to your whole body and energy systems all the time. Here are some of the amazing things our powerful heart can do. They have shown that when in a coherent heart and with a set intention to create that change, a person is able to cause physical structural changes in water, and the rate of growth in cells and the state of DNA. Cell growth was also enhanced by 20% with the energy of coherent intention and that the growth of tumour cells was inhibited by 20% too. Meaning the cells in your body respond to your FLOW state and setting an intention.

This means *your energy state and your thoughts are measurably affecting your physical body and by changing your energy to the FLOW state and setting intention you can change the structure of physical things in your environment!* (Insert more dramatic music.) Monitoring the alterations in the rates, rhythms, and patterns of afferent traffic is a key function of the cortical and emotional systems in the brain.

By being in flow &
setting intention
you have the power to
change the structure of
physical things.

WHAT IS HEART RATE VARIABILITY?

Heart rate variability (HRV), is a measure of the natural changes in our heart rate and rhythms. This is a well-regarded, tried and tested model used to explain and measure the variety of interactions within our physical, mental, and emotional health. The measurement is taken using an electrocardiogram (ECG) the same instrument used to monitor your heart rate in hospital. This is used to assess what is happening with the autonomic nervous system (ANS). The Heartmath Institute has used this measurement of HRV to demonstrate the influence positive and negative emotions have on us, in addition to the mental, emotional, and physical states of FLOW, which reflect the mental and emotional experience of the person.

THE BIOLOGY OF THE FLOW STATE

With all of this in mind we can see that our state of FLOW is something that impacts so many areas of our life experience. In the rest of the book we'll explore more of the energetic, emotional, and mental aspects of FLOW and how you can use EAM to create your own FLOW states as and when you choose. It's important to know that this state of FLOW also has massive physiological impacts too, which will in turn affect physical health and well-being of all organs, systems, and functions within the body. Getting into and staying in the FLOW state is about bringing your life together whole-istically, looking at your environment, your food, diet, relationships ... well everything! We will explore much more of this in Chapter 4 and beyond as we look at the main areas of your life.

THE EFFECTS OF FLOW

PHYSIOLOGICAL

On a physiological level, research has been able to show that the FLOW state creates a neurological synchronisation between the heart and brain. It changes the structures and associations in our brains and changes brainwave patterns, which influence our body. It reduces adrenal and cortisol levels in the body, which resolves the physiological effects of stress that can create disease. It resolves the stress responses and therefore the stress phase of the healing cycle. It promotes physical healing as the body is able to return to normal function faster. It releases tension in the body and muscles, relieves physical pain, and reduces symptoms of illness. It is able to help create changes on a cellular level, too.

PSYCHOLOGICAL

On a psychological level the research shows that when we get into FLOW and make a habit of it we can maintain our positive emotions longer. That means we can naturally and easily create more positive emotions. We also have better mental and emotional stability and our ability to adapt to changes in our environment increases. By allowing yourself to be more in FLOW *you actively seek more new experiences as your brain seeks to maintain the status quo of positivity in your environment.* You are able to rewire the brain and create new emotional and mentally positive experiences.

In Chapter 2 and beyond we'll explore more of these benefits of being in FLOW on an energetic level and the impact that these can have on your entire life experience.

THE EFFECTS OF NOT BEING IN FLOW

So obviously, the effects of not being in FLOW can affect us on a physiological level, too. We create negative associations in the brain. The body is in stress phase and pumping high levels of adrenaline and cortisol into the body. This affects normal physiological functions in digestion, heart rate, cell filtration rates, the growth and death phases of the cells. The body is usually unable to heal itself and we will find ongoing or chronic physical health conditions, and pain inflammation illnesses. When you are out of FLOW on a psychological level there is decreased brain function. This means you are unable to think clearly, make logical decisions, or function at your highest levels for any tasks you may be undertaking. When you are stressed, angry, or irritable you'll be stuck in negative emotions. You'll find that you stay in a low mood, with little or no energy. Things will seem bleak with little hope for the future.

WE ABSORB OTHER ENERGY

Research into bioenergetics (the study of energy relationships and transformations of living organisms) show that energy sources like algae can take and absorb energy from one another. We do the same thing. Have you ever noticed that when you change your environment to something more peaceful you feel better? Or when you're with certain people you feel uneasy or uncomfortable. That's because we can absorb energy from other people, too. In fact, we absorb energy from things all the time. So, who you have around you, and who you spend time with, is very important because you literally 'soak up' their energy.

Absorbing energy used to be such an important part of our energetic makeup, it's how we replenished ourselves in nature. Over the last few hundred years much of that has changed with industrialisation; we have lost our connection to nature and the many sources of energy all around us. We'll explore in Chapter 2 how your energy is affected by others, why this happens, and how with EAM you can stop it affecting you.

GROUNDING OUR ENERGY

We live on an electromagnetic planet and we are amazing electrical biological beings. We've already seen how much of our life is simply interpretations of energy on different levels. We are part of the planet and a fractal of this living organism. The term grounding means the ability to connect something electrical into the earth.

Think of your TV plugs or anything electrical in your house. All electrical devices are earthed to discharge its resistant frequencies. This prevents us from getting an electric shock. We know the potentially lethal effect of an electrical shock, which occurs when our energy is unable to discharge resistant electrical frequencies. We are the same. Our entire body, head and heart also give off electrical signals. Whilst the consequences may not be as obvious as an electric shock, if we are unable to ground ourselves this resistant energy builds up creating disturbances on an energetic, mental, and emotional level.

With EAM Step 4 TRANSFORM, we are able to transform resistant energy so it no longer affects your energy.

You can also get grounded by going outside barefoot. Yet many of us forget to reconnect to earth as frequently as we need to. We live in buildings away from the ground and we wear plastic shoes, which prevent this earthing connection. Numerous research studies have shown that this one simple act of taking off your shoes and getting grounded can positively impact our health. Releasing resistant energy and grounding can decrease inflammation in the body, reduces stress levels, and improve physical circulation. Energetically, it enables you to discharge resistant energy held in your aura almost instantly. It is useful to do EAM outside barefoot when you can.

Every day try to get outside and stick your toes in the grass. There are also many awesome grounding products available. You'll find a few in the resources section in the back of the book.

NATURE, NURTURE & THE POWER OF LOVE

Bruce Lipton, PhD is an internationally recognised leader in bridging science and spirit. He is a stem cell biologist, the bestselling author of, *The Biology of Belief* and recipient of the 2009 Goi Peace Award. Doctor Lipton's unusual scientific approach transformed his personal life too. With such a deep background into understanding cell biology, his work highlighted the simple yet powerful systems as to how our mind controls bodily functions, and how it showed the implied existence of an immortal spirit (aka energy). He began to apply this science to his personal life and physical health and he discovered that his health and mental well-being improved on every level of his daily experience. His work explored the effect of signals coming into our body from the outside world. This includes the effects of our own perception and observation of our life. The studies were able to show the impact that our thoughts, feelings, and emotions have on our body, particularly in the way the cells react and behave in different chemical or energetic environments. Doctor Lipton's work is ground-breaking. He has taught me so much about understanding this mind-body connection over the last decade or so.

Doctor Lipton studied the influence of the energy on cells. As a cellular biologist, he spent many years exploring the cells in our bodies and testing the influences and impact of them. When testing cells in a petri dish, he would add cell food to the dish and the cells would be attracted to it — they would move towards the food and nourishment, which is growth. He also tested the influence of poison, which showed that the cells moved away from the poison in the dish, which is protection. At the level of cells, which we are made up of, there are three behaviours, cells can move towards, away from, or stay stationary depending on signals presented in the environment. Our cells are also influenced by our energy, thoughts, emotions. They behave in the same way in our bodies depending on the positive or negative signal being sent. These signals are based on what is perceived in our environment. A cell can either be in growth or protection. It cannot be in both at the same time. You'll see that this directional movement reflects the same as the FLOWs of energy we spoke of earlier. I believe that our aura behaves in the same way as the cells within the body. We are forever reading and perceiving signals from our environment, which is how we adjust our state of flow. We either allow ourselves to be in a state of growth (FLOW) or protection (RESISTANCE or

REVERSAL), we cannot be in both at the same time. We will talk more about this in Chapter 2.

We grow new cells every day. If we are living in a stressful environment, are constantly in fear, or are creating resistant thoughts and negative emotions, we aren't allowing our physical body to heal and repair itself. This is where sickness, illness, and disease come in. The energy and direction of life is GROWTH, which is essential for every cell in our body and everything about us is designed for this purpose. On a biological level, our cells use a source of energy in the body known as Adenosine Triphosphate (ATP), a protein. We need ATP for our growth, for rebuilding cells and tissues, and for protection against bacteria, disease, and the effects from stress or fear for instance. When our body is in a state of growth it has a new abundant surplus of ATP and therefore energy is being created all the time through normal bodily functions. When our energy is in protection, these natural cycles and processes that create ATP are shut down or reduced. This means that if the body is in protection or RESISTANCE over a prolonged period of time, it depletes our body's physiological energy reserves and affects the growth processes in the body. So the rate at which new cells are being created in our body begins to slow down, or stops, which means our body is unable to repair itself. This is how dis-ease begins. Research into the field of Epigenetics also shows that our perception of our life and environment, is the trigger for certain DNA within the body to be expressed. It has been shown that energy healing is more effective at repairing the physical body; whilst it works in the same way as molecules, the shifts are often quicker and it works at a deeper level because it is rebalancing the energy.

HOW OUR BODY CREATES EMOTIONS

Despite the common perception that a THOUGHT triggers an EMOTION, it's actually a more complex interplay of our energy, hormones, brain, nervous system, heart, and body. Studies have shown that what helps create our emotional experience is the repeating and rhythmic patterns generated by our heart; whether they are in FLOW or out of FLOW, these patterns are like old friends to our brain. These heart wave patterns are compared to our ENERGETIC, EMOTIONAL, and MENTAL set points, which are all tracked and managed via the brain stem. Signals are sent UPWARDS towards the thalamus, hypothalamus, and amygdala, the parts of the brain centre that are involved in the processing of emotion. With this understanding we can see how our emotional system operates by recognising the patterns in our heart rhythm. As we learned the HEART is in fact guiding the brain *before* the brain knows it, many of these changes are also shown in the currents electromagnetic rhythms. As well as sending information to the brain, our HEART is also creating neurotransmitters (hormone production) and sending information to the rest of the body. These hormones also affect the brain and provide an important influence over our experience of emotion.

For example, when we are happy we release endorphins, which reduce stress and physical pain. They also work as a sedative to help you relax. These endorphins are manufactured in all different areas of our body, in our brain, and in the spinal cord. They are released throughout our body and connect to and create many of our emotions.

This data turns much of our previous understanding on its head (excuse the pun) and is important to know as our emotions are not a cognitive or linear experience; meaning we are yet to understand the evolutionary reason why we have them and why the experience of them varies between individuals. Neuroscience has yet to determine the sequential process through which emotions happen. It is almost a simultaneous process. The actual experience of emotion is therefore made up of the heart, the brain, our limbic and processing systems, hormones, changes in our electromagnetic energy sent from the heart, and a change from our set points. So our emotional experience is something which involves our whole body, NOT only the brain.

MOLECULES OF EMOTION

I have great respect for Candace Pert, an American neuroscientist. She sadly passed in 2013 and left an amazing body of work. Most notably she discovered the opiate receptor, the cellular binding site for endorphins in the brain. Her work created a tidal wave of change in many streams of modern science like immunology (the study of the immune system), endocrinology (the study of our hormones), neurophysiology (the study of brain structure), psychology (the study of mind function) and biology (the study of physical anatomy). They can no longer be seen as separate as her work has shown undisputedly that we *have a mind-body connection and each impacts the other*.

Through her decades of research Pert was able to show that our emotions are not a figment of our imagination but real on a *physiological* level. They are made of molecules; they exist and are located in our mind, body, and energetically in our aura. Her work has explained scientifically what many eastern and ancient philosophies have known throughout the ages — consciousness comes before manifesting reality! Yet, many western modalities would state that your emotions are products of your PHYSICAL brain and has nothing to do with your body or health. This is not true. We now know that in the physical body our emotions are little pieces of biochemical information created and sent as peptides to their receptors. These receptors are present through the cells of our entire body. They play a part in our subconscious (or unconscious), because they are present.

In her book *Molecules of Emotion* Pert explains, "As investigations continue, it is becoming increasingly apparent that the role of peptides is not limited to eliciting simple and singular actions from individual cells and organ systems. Rather, peptides serve to weave the body's organs and systems into a single web that reacts to both internal and external environmental changes with complex, subtly orchestrated responses. Peptides are the sheet music containing the notes, phrases and rhythms that allow the orchestra — your body — to play as an integrated entity. And the music that results is the tone or feeling that you experience subjectively as your emotions."

THE SCALE OF CONSCIOUSNESS

Dr. David R. Hawkins developed the scale below as a 'map' of the levels of human consciousness. He used Applied Kinesiology to document the nonlinear or more energetic world of emotions. In his work, each level of consciousness or emotion coincides with specific human behaviours and perceptions about life. Each level of the energy on the scale vibrates at a different energetic frequency, and this connects to and relates to our ability to attract. The numbers on the scale represent measurable electromagnetic frequencies of the emotion. The numbers themselves aren't as important as their relationship to one another.

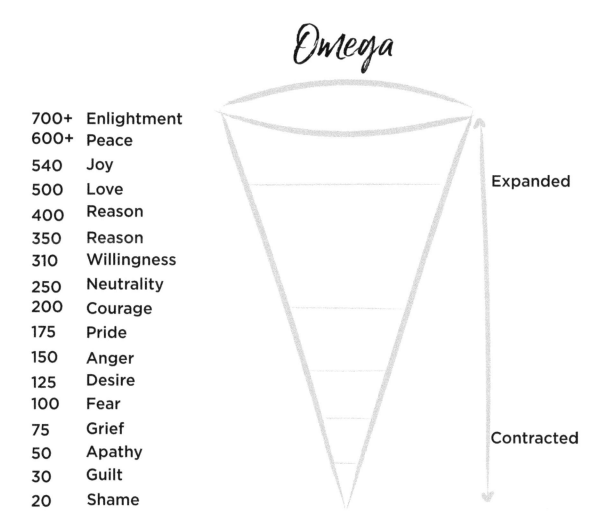

Dr David Hawkins Scale of Consciousness

I love the idea of the emotional scale. You've possibly seen many variations on this concept. It is really helpful to enable us to understand our emotions. Because we experience our emotions as individuals, they are often very subjective and therefore hard to measure. Later in this book I will show you how we use a similar vibrational scale in EAM to allow you to transform and let go of stuck emotions and raise your energetic and emotional vibration.

YOUR INTERNAL REFERENCE

Our brain is adapting and learning information all the time and rewiring neural networks. We call them set points. Within EAM we talk about these energetic, emotional, and mental set points or reference points. Our body is always trying to maintain a balance to what we know, that is exactly what these set points are for. Our emotions are governed by our reference to these internal set points. What we are unconsciously searching for is how well something matches our set points or previous experiences. When these baseline systems and our perception of the environment are a match, we feel happy because we are safe. Our thoughts, emotions, external inputs, and energetic messages are a match to that feeling of safety, love, or happiness. They are congruent so we feel great and we release happy hormones like oxytocin and endorphins into our body because our heart waves are COHERENT so we feel awesome! When we are in a state of stress or anxiety it is because the messages, our system is receiving creates a RESISTANCE or a mismatch to our internal baseline, putting us in a state of instability. This can be triggered by a thought, emotion, or any other internal, external, or energetic input, conscious or unconscious.

In these situations, our normal experiences are unable to be easily processed. Our neural system sees this as a mismatch to our past, present, or future projections of experiences. It then sounds the alarm, which is what we experience as this negative feeling or emotion. This sends our body into that adrenalineOfueled process because it perceives we are or may be in danger. This is also why our bad days seem to spiral. If we don't choose to catch ourselves and pay attention to when we are out of FLOW, that instability is still there in our electromagnetic energy. This is why that person treading on your foot on the train riles you so much. Instead of you saying, 'it's okay', you're ready to start a fight. You may not be consciously aware that energy is already on a high alert and watching out for the next thing to match its previous bad experience, which then creates more of the negative experiences.

The same is also true of our good days getting better. Have you noticed that on those mornings when you jump out of bed feeling happy, something great happens? You tell your friends. Then you find money on the floor. This occurs because we spend our time looking for positive happy situations or experiences that validate the patterns we are having, good or bad, positive or negative. And *you* can change your pattern!

The brain recalls information and uses our past experiences as a reference point for what we are doing now or projecting into our future. The brain is constantly searching for the level of congruence between the two. When it finds a mismatch between now and then, it will sound the alarm. This is often why when venturing into something new, stepping into changing your life, or doing something for the first time, we usually have a sense of fear. Our brain has no reference point for it, so it sounds a silent alarm. It will then create a whole series of 'rational' thoughts, beliefs, and ideas as to why staying where we know how to handle things and 'stay safe' is the best thing to do.

This response applies to the journey we are on now. As you go on this journey it will feel challenging. It will feel like 'hard work' as you try to do something new. You may want to give up and your mind will create a number of rational thoughts as to why that's a good idea. Knowing this, you can recognise the pattern, and once you know the 5 Steps of EAM you'll be able to use them and move forward.

UNDERSTANDING NEUROSCIENCE

Let's take a look at some more of the science. Neuroscience for me is one of THE most fascinating and exciting places to see new developments. Neuroscientists are now able to map scientifically many of the concepts that have been known to eastern philosophies for thousands of years or were previously only seen as New Age ideas. It is exciting that two seemingly opposing ends of the spectrum are able to talk about these ideas with a common language. It's all just energy.

WHAT IS NEUROSCIENCE?

Simply put, neuroscience is the scientific study of our nervous system. It combines many different elements of mainstream sciences like psychology, anatomy, biology and physiology. What neuroscientists want to understand is the basis of our memory, behaviour, perception, and consciousness (that is my favourite part). This is a rapidly developing branch of science because as new discoveries are made, more and more people are dedicating themselves to this mind-boggling and expansive field of study. So much of EAM is founded in neuroscientific understanding and research. To fully understand EAM you should understand a few key neuroscientific concepts and what our brain is doing on a structural level.

From a western medical perspective, it is our brain (HEAD) that is the root of our thoughts and emotions. It is busy managing things like our sleep, our heart rate, and movement of our physical body, plus the 101 other things it gets up to! Neuroscience offers us a glimpse into one of the most exciting parts of the human experience.

MINDSET & COGNITIVE THEORY

Let's take a look at how our mind creates our perception and interpretation of the world and why. When we say 'mind' it is more than just the physical brain: we are talking about a variety of elements that make up our experience of life. The positive side is that your life is probably different from how you think it is. The flip side is that we are living the life that our 'mind' has constructed. That construction is made of our thoughts, beliefs, memories, fears, hopes, and experiences. These all cloud our ability to see life objectively. When two people are in conversation they are hearing the same words yet each will perceive it through their own subjective understanding. We are not objective; it is impossible to be so because we view the world through our own eyes, thoughts, beliefs, and emotions and we can never experience anything outside of that. So, what creates these different realities and experiences for us individually? It's all in the way that WE interpret the information coming in through our different senses.

THE ROLE OF THE BRAIN

Through this new understanding of energy, neurocardiology, and breakthroughs in science, we are beginning to understand that the 'brain' as we know it is not the only player in our cognitive experience of life. Formerly, it was believed that our emotions originated in the brain; it is now known that they are more an experience of the heart, the brain, *and* the body working together. Our brain works like an old-fashioned analogue processor that is constantly looking for patterns, similarities, differences, and relationships between them. It is constantly trying to create a picture from the information it has. The human brain weighs about 3 pounds and energetically runs on around 12 watts of power, which is a fifth of the power required by a standard 60-watt light bulb! What a clever light bulb. Our amazing brain has 400 miles of capillaries and 86 billion microscopic neurons which are in constant communication. To put that into context, they are making around 10 quadrillion calculations every second. And yes, that is a real number!

Each neuron in the brain is like a tiny tree. They connect to other neurons, and where they touch one another they make between 4000 to 9000 connections. That is a lot of communication. It is almost too much to comprehend. These neural connections help us to generate our experiences and perceptions in each moment. They help us to think, create understand, use reasoning, manage our emotions, memories, manage our learning potential. On a physical level, they are fundamentally tiny connections between different neurons in the body (not only in the brain). You may have heard the term 'neurons that fire together wire together.' It was first used by the neuropsychologist Donald Hebb known for his fabulous work in understanding the associative field of learning. In essence, what he means is that every experience we have — all thoughts, feelings, and physical sensations — triggers thousands of neurons at the same time. These associations form a neural network, a simple pathway or groove in the road. Like any pathway the more it is used the stronger or deeper the connection becomes. As we repeat an experience over and over, the brain learns to trigger the same neurons each time.

This is a wonderful process for us and what helps us learn, store, and remember important information simply and efficiently. The good and bad news is that these neurons can be rewired to respond to a situation in a new way. This is *not* so helpful if that pathway is an unhelpful thought, habit, or belief, or if we experience something traumatic, which can change our previously good experiences into ones to be avoided.

OUR NERVOUS SYSTEM

To complete our understanding of the nervous system we need to know how it works on a physical and energetic level. It is the nervous system that creates the connection between our heart and our brain and all the other functions in the body on a physical level. Think of it as the information superhighway, continuously passing electric signals through the body. Later when we discuss chakras and meridians, which are the energetic equivalent of our circulatory system, we will see how these systems work closely together. Our nervous system acts as an antenna reading information from the outside world and sends information back out. Energetically this same function would be our meridians.

The Central Nervous System (CNS) is made up of our brain and spinal cord. It is called the central system because it receives all of the information and coordinates what all parts of our body does. In addition, we have the Peripheral Nervous System (PNS), which connects our limbs and organs back into the CNS. The autonomic nervous system (ANS) is controlled by the Medulla Oblongata and is responsible for breathing, increasing our heart rate, sweating, sneezing, goose bumps, our food being digested, blood flow, and managing hormone levels. You may have heard of the 'fight, flight, or freeze' response. This is predominantly managed by our ANS system.

MIND THE BUS

Let's look at the science of this process in action. You are walking down the street thinking about the 101 things you have to do and you step into the road. As you do, you look up and notice a bus is hurtling towards you. In that moment, your eyes and ears send a signal via to the Amygdala (the almond shaped part of the brain in charge of processing information). It senses danger and sends a signal to the hypothalamus, which controls the production of all hormones and chemicals. The hypothalamus thinks *Run!*

The hypothalamus activates the ANS by sending signals through the Medulla Oblongata to the adrenal glands. (Run quick run!) These glands respond by pumping the hormone adrenaline into the bloodstream. As it circulates through the body, it brings on a number of physical changes. The heart beats faster than normal, pushing blood to the muscles, heart, and other vital organs. Your pulse rate and blood pressure go up. You breathe more quickly, the airways in the lungs open so you can take in as much oxygen as possible. This extra oxygen is sent to the brain, making you more alert. At the same time this adrenaline is triggering the transformation of sugar and fats from storage in your body to supply more energy so you can run. All of these changes happen so quickly you miss it. In fact, by the time your visual centre has processed this, you have already jumped out of the way of the bus, shook your fist at the speeding bus driver and given thanks that you are alive.

This wonderful process keeps us out of danger. Yet it is the same process in action when we think a thought, relieve a memory, or are stuck in unhelpful emotional patterns. Your brain perceives everything as real. Many people are living their lives in stress from their energy, thoughts and emotions every day. Living on constant high alert at 'perceived threats' as if a bus is hurtling towards them at any given moment.

My question is what made you look up in the first place? Before your nervous system picked up that there was a bus bearing down on you, what happened energetically first? It was your energy, your intuition, and your aura. Exciting right! We'll explore more of this in Chapter 2.

NEUROPLASTICITY

EAM teaches us a new process or way of being. By using EAM, we readapt and create a new pathway in our brain; we literally REWIRE the brain. This process of rewiring is called neuroplasticity, and it happens throughout our life. This is how we learn, create our experiences, and connect information together on a neurological level. It was previously believed that our brain was fixed and immovable, and from a certain age it did not change. Research has now shown that our physical brain *is evolving all of the time*. This process is our brain's capacity to create new connections between events and information; in creating these changes it's also able to eliminate old connections and associations in information. Our brain is continually evolving and rewiring itself. How exciting is that!

This amazing process happens in a number of different ways whether it is individual cells rewiring themselves and creating new neural networks, or if we've received an injury, trauma, or illness that affects our brain tissue. Our brain keeps itself functioning by cleaning out the connections it no longer needs or are no longer used. It then ensures that connections which are in use are strengthened. Think of all the things you had to 'learn' as a baby, which you have long forgotten because they are no longer needed as an adult. This is a really important concept to understand, because previously we believed that the brain is the boss and that our BRAIN determines our life experiences. But what we've learned is that our life experiences and perceptions *actually change the brain*. It is how WE interpret information that influences the neural connections in our brain. As these connections develop, we learn new habits, patterns, and ways of being. Think of it as creating an automatic pilot system as a 'way of operating'. These are set points. Set points can apply to almost anything. We create mental and emotional set points and habits. We also have energetic set points. This is powerful stuff and one of the exciting parts about what we can do when using EAM. By changing your perceptions and past experiences, and by creating new experiences, you are actually rewiring your brain! The more you continue to learn, grow, and expand, the more we invite our brain to grow with us.

Our brain is
not the boss.
Your life experiences
& perceptions
change the brain.

BRAIN STRUCTURE AND CAPACITY

Through the senses and all of our body systems, we are sending over 11 million bits of sensory data per second to our brain to be processed and sorted. However, our conscious mind is only able to process around 50 bits. So what happens to the other 10,999,950 bits of information?

That is an awful lot of MISSING conscious awareness. It's what happens to this missing information and how it's processed, that gives us such different perceptions of life, situations and circumstances and why some people are able to see the good in a situation and others can't.

The electrical activity of our brain is measured on an Electroencephalogram (EEG). More recently Magnetoencephalography began using another device called the SQUID (superconducting quantum interference devices) to measure brain activity. It is a neuroimaging process designed to map brain activity by recording the electrical currents naturally occurring in the brain. It is these SQUIDS that are used by the Heartmath team. The actual energetic output of the brain is hard to measure at any distance over 1 foot away from the body. Yet our heart energy has been shown to be over 5000 times greater in magnetic energy and can be measured several feet away from the body.

From an Energy Psychology perspective, it is clear why and how our EMOTIONS are the stronger energy that is carrying our messages into the world. Most people think it is our thoughts, but our emotions are actually the more powerful transmitter.

DIFFERENT PARTS OF THE BRAIN

We have several different parts of the brain, all of which maintain various elements of our life and cognitive function. They keep us alive. These higher brain centres are the parts we use to create our experiences. Through the process of matching known patterns, sorting and sifting information, they create our perspective of reality. Studies have shown that these parts of our brain can actually monitor our pattern-matching process and can self-regulate the information we perceive by preventing certain information from actually Flowing into our brain. This means we are never consciously aware of it.

OUR LEFT BRAIN IS THE LOGIC

The left side of the brain is responsible for controlling the right side of the body. It is also great at performing logical tasks. It likes analytical thought, logic, language, reasoning, science, and maths, written work, and using numbers. It is your left brain that is reading and processing this information right now. The left brain is a serial processor. It just loves to sort and process, yet it can only manage one thing at a time, like stacking building blocks. It works on the principle that there is a process and functional order to the way things happen and the outcome or result of one thing must be known before processing the next. From an energetic perspective, we would consider the left brain to be more HEAD, more YANG or MASCULINE based in its function of making important decisions and bringing logic to situations.

OUR RIGHT BRAIN IS THE CREATIVE

The right side of the brain is responsible for controlling the left side of the body. It is designed to performs tasks that are creative, artistic, and more intuitive. The right side of the brain loves, creativity, imagination, intuition, insight, holistic thoughts, and music. In contrast to the left brain, our right brain has the ability to simultaneously sort and process incoming information from different sources, which is known as parallel processing. So instead of doing things one at a time it is multitasking. From an energetic perspective, we would consider the right brain to be more HEART based, YIN or FEMININE in its function, providing a connection to more feeling-based, intuitive, energetic connection based feedback.

MENTAL, EMOTIONAL, AND ENERGETIC SET POINTS

In neuroscience, set points are called complex somatic states, which are neural pathways that act as our internal reference. We establish set points, which then become 'default patterns' or ways of being and behaving. Once we have created a set point our brain and nervous system will work to maintain them. This is unhelpful when the set point is creating energetic, physiological, psychological, or behavioural patterns that takes us out of alignment. Yet it is a useful process when we have created an energetic, mental, or emotional set point that keeps us in FLOW. As we change these set points with EAM the brain helps to maintain them.

Physiologically and psychologically, set points are partly created by the Hippocampus in the brain, by processing memories mixed with the sensory information and emotions. Energetically, these patterns are created in the HEAD then connect energetic imprints across different auric layers. It is the ultimate recording device. Every experience we have is referenced to our current set points on that subject and others. When our current experience is matched to one of our set points, the brain thinks, *hmm, yes, this is familiar,* and we experience that feeling of comfort and safety. However, that set point can be linked to feelings of anxiety, chaos, confusion, or feeling overwhelmed. It then becomes comfortable because it is familiar. Even though the experience is clearly out of alignment.

We are creatures of habit, who want to feel safe. Our brain is always looking to create a match between our past and our new experiences. If it is unable to find a reference in our energy or neurological programming, then it is outside of our comfort zone. As a result, we feel unsafe and can get 'stuck' in unhealthy set points. It's then almost impossible to create the lasting changes we want because our energetic and neurological patterns are trying to bring us back to what it knows.

The only way to create change is to establish new set points by changing the connected information. That is exactly what we do with EAM. By creating new energetic and emotional experiences, the hippocampus can associate this new information with that set point. This also enables us to rewire the brain and energy imprints in our aura. By changing our set points, we create a happy healthy internal reference which provide safety and comfort.

Energetically, on a universal level the set point is love. It is because this set point is the ultimate emotion that we experience all those other emotions. Our natural way of being IS in FLOW = LOVE and we always want to get back to that IN FLOW state. Anything outside of that creates resistant thoughts, feelings, patterns, and emotions. This is all unconscious, yet it's what we are all searching for. Everything we do is about bringing us back to this universal set point.

NEURO LINGUISTIC PROGRAMMING

Neuro means mind and linguistic is about language. Therefore, Neuro Linguistic Programming (NLP) is about 'speaking' the language of the mind. By understanding some basic concepts of NLP, you can begin to change the way your brain thinks and some of the unconscious patterns that affect it. It is also very useful to help us understand how we interpret information from our environment. The language you speak will be continually 'speaking' to your subconscious mind. So be mindful of what you think and what you say as it plays a key part in what you manifest in your life. Within the framework of EAM we adopt some of the principles of NLP, particularly around Step 4 TRANSFORM and Step 5 MANIFEST, of the process. As you begin to understand the impact of positive language on your energy—what you create and are able to manifest in your life—it will be useful to understand how we interpret the information.

HOW WE PROCESS INFORMATION & EXPERIENCE

Our brain receives information through our six senses every second, but we are only consciously aware of a tiny percentage of it. It would be far too much to process otherwise. How do we decide what becomes conscious? We try to reference information, to match it to certain scenarios we have already experienced. In order for that information to be useful we have to filter it before presenting it to the part of us we call 'us'. Imagine it's like a postal office with lots of packets of information that need to be summarised down to one parcel. In order to do that we have to sort the information, generalise data, and delete an awful lot of input. Below is a general concept within Neuro Linguistic Programming (NLP) that can help us to understand the cognitive functions and how our brain sorts all this data. This is how it works.

- **WE DELETE.** We exclude certain information from our senses, so that we can pay attention to the things that matter to us. Although this 'deleted' information is not presented in our consciousness it is still held in our aura even though we are not consciously aware of it.

- **WE DISTORT.** This process transforms information received so that it makes sense to us. This is how we create different representations of our reality and how we can 'misinterpret' information from our environment. We use it when planning, creating projects, or envisioning our future. It is often the distortion of information that creates the RESISTANCE in our energy.

- **WE GENERALISE.** Have you ever heard someone say something like, "all men are a**holes" or "all women want money"? We know these statements are generalisations, yet they may be true for the individual. By generalising we can summarise things into a wider picture, without lots of detail. From an EAM perspective the downside is when someone draws on one experience and applies it to their life and decisions.

- **WE EXTRAPOLATE.** This is when we look at what is happening in our lives in one situation and then project it onto everything, usually what it means about us as individuals. Have you ever looked at your bank account and been broke? Then you decided you were 'bad' because of it! I know I have. Yet is that really true?

- **WE PROJECT.** Our previous experiences shape our perception of the world and our interactions with others. We project our thoughts, beliefs, and values into a situation and then think other people see the world the same way we do. Which of course they don't we can only see the world through our experience. Energetically this projection is filtered through the information held in the different layers of our Aura.

- **WE ANCHOR.** We usually believe the information we hear FIRST; even if it is not real, truthful, or accurate, that becomes your reference point. This is why that saying of making a good first impression is so important. If you hold a reference point in your energy which is unsupportive, we need to let it go, which you can do with EAM. Then we can a) receive new information or a better answer and b) create a new pattern or belief about that subject.

- **WE GROUP.** Have you ever noticed that when you want to buy a new swanky car, you see them everywhere? This is because our brain is matching information together. Grouping is a very useful process and one that comes into play with The Law of Attraction and EAM. As you become aware of it, you add that information into your energy. Then you begin to find, people, conversations, and situations that match that experience. Then it becomes your conscious experience of reality.

- **WE LOOK FOR CONFIRMATION.** We are always looking to make sure that we are right, so we can validate how we think and feel. How many times have you shared a story with someone and said, 'do you see why I feel like that?'. We will selectively look for, feel into, and listen for information that matches our current beliefs, as we get a buzz of endorphins when we are validated. Then we easily disregard new information if it fails to match.

- **WE MAKE CHOICES.** When you are able to 'choose' something for yourself, it is powerful and you are far more likely to accept it, work with it, and implement it. However, making a choice can also prevent you from seeing the downside, as you seek to prove you were correct in the decision you made. With EAM you can use the sway to enable you to make decisions. You will learn about the sway decision-making process in Chapter 3.

UNDERSTANDING YOUR FOCUS & ATTENTION

We want to understand what creates and guides our experience. Have you noticed how sometimes a thought or belief can run away with you? Allowing you to focus your time, and energy on situations which are unhelpful? Yet it is all just energy that we have allowed to gather momentum and run away with us. We have a choice about where we focus our attention.

If our brain is going through this process of sorting, distilling, and generalising information on our behalf, surely it is up to us to consciously ALLOW ourselves to focus our attention on what WE want, not what other people want and not what other people believe, think, or say we should do. It is up to US. If we give our attention and focus to things which are not what we really want to do, we are creating our own RESISTANCE, a pull between where we are and where we really want to be.

WHY IT'S IMPORTANT TO FOCUS YOUR ATTENTION

Energetically, by giving your attention to a subject you are FLOWING your energy towards it. The more energy you FLOW, the bigger it gets and the quicker it manifests.

- When we focus, we are more in control of our energy. With EAM we can change our energy so that our focus and attention can be brought back to what we want to work on.

- We feel happy because we are giving our thought, energy, and emotions to that one thing. In doing this we create a more coherent (in FLOW) state of energy so we are more positive.

- When we are focused and in FLOW with our actions, we are more likely to achieve them much more quickly, again creating a feeling of success

- We create a better connection and understanding of who we are. This helps us to feel safe and to maintain our attention and energy, which we need to achieve long-term outcomes.

- You solve problems more quickly when you are focused. You are more able to access the right ideas and thoughts. You get clearer pictures, ideas, and inspiration and information because your energy is in the FLOW state.

By using EAM you are able to keep your focus by maintaining your energy in the flow state. This process can also be instrumental in helping you change your life.

POSITIVE PSYCHOLOGY

Positive psychology is a form of science that is less focused on what is 'wrong, sick, ill, or weak' and is more focused on strength, ability, and capability. The focus is on enabling people to find and build the best of themselves, to create the life they want. It is less focused on pathology and more focused on enabling people to be fulfilled and happy.

Many self-help tools, psychology methods, and counselling practices are focused on what is wrong, the energy of which is very past-focused as it seeks to look for the root cause. That's not to say it's wrong, just that there is another way. EAM focuses on what is good, right, inspiring, and will take you to where you want to go in life. The only time you 'look back' is if something is standing in the way of your success right now.

Many experts in the field of positive psychology define a few key elements, which make this field of psychology different and are also key within EAM. These include:

- Seeing the world through the lens of abundance, which enables you to expand and build on your own resources and to find answers and solutions. This mindset helps you to recognise that you have the capacity for everything.

- To focus on building our strengths and loving the good elements of ourselves. Believing that we all have the innate ability to grow, change and develop.

- To be able to use an approach, which is working whole-istically with both the negative and positive aspects of someone concurrently.

- Our overall sense of happiness and well-being, which can be our level of life satisfaction, positive emotions and relatively fewer negative ones.

- That we want to have a lasting sense of purpose and meaning, and experience self-development as a person. The purpose is to create more positive emotions, engagement in life, a greater sense of meaning, better relationships and a feeling of accomplishment.

These are key elements you need to be able to change your life. That is exactly what I want to share with you in the rest of this book and how using the 5 Steps of EAM and the Energy Evolution journey can do just that.

THE 6 LEVELS OF OUR LIFE EXPERIENCE

As human beings, we experience our lives on many different levels. We are more than just our physical selves. It is the combination of these different levels of our life that collectively make up our life experience.

1. ENERGETIC — SPIRITUAL

This is the overarching energy that drives and creates our whole life. It is the 'unknown' or more mystical, inexplicable element of our lives. This includes things which people may refer to as spirit, energy, or acts of god. Whatever religion or civilisation you come from, these are the concepts and philosophies known by many ancient civilisations for thousands of years. These philosophies were the first explanations into patterns of nature, meaning, structures and understanding how life works before we had 'modern' science. We feel the impact of this energy yet we have only some ideas of how it works and what it can do. This is the foundation of the universe and life itself.

2. ENERGETIC — SCIENCE

The level of energy that mainstream sciences are able to track, measure, and examine is more about the physical science basis of energy. We think about the exciting explorations and data that are now proving many of the concepts and ideas previously known to ancient cultures. In our life experience this is technological advances and the impact of radio waves, gamma rays, X-rays and all of the energies we live with today.

3. CELLULAR OR DNA

Then we have our experience at the cellular or DNA level of ourselves. Remember, we are a massive community of organisms, not just one human body. There is a lot of our life experience happening on a level without our conscious awareness, yet we know when it is out of FLOW as it impacts our physical health.

4. PHYSICAL

The physical level refers to more than just our physical body. This also means the material- based physical elements of our life such as objects and people. It is the aspect we often call 'real' because it is what we see the most.

5. EMOTIONAL

Our emotional experience of life, or what we feel, is one of the most significant aspects that determine our life experience. We remember more of how we felt in a situation than what we remember or what was said. Our emotional experiences are key to our state of flow. Much of our life is experienced emotionally. We often believe it is out of our control.

6. PSYCHOLOGICAL

The level of thoughts, memories, beliefs, and patterns make up our thinking or logical mind. These mental constructs influence our life through the way we interpret information in our environment.

Collectively, these make up our individual human experience when we are interacting with people and the world. Of course, we are also part of a collective, mass or a global consciousness, the one mind, which is created by the way we communicate, see, and have experiences in our shared society.

It's important to notice these levels as we explore different aspects of our experience in relation to energy, what the effects of each of these areas being in or out of FLOW might be, and how by working with energy and using EAM you can create shifts and transformations.

I Reclaimed My Sparkle

SUNITA KOSHAL, AGE 61

I was out of work, with a shoulder operation on the horizon. It was a time of sleepless nights and stress when Yvette Taylor popped up as part of a free online study about EAM. I had no idea who she was but I knew about positive thinking... had studied, practiced, lived, and breathed it for over a decade believing that 'one day there would be a magic moment when I automatically become all these things and life would always be in flow.' It hadn't happened yet, and now Yvette was saying EAM would address the hidden saboteurs in my subconscious energy and help me release them, and then the magic would happen? *Really*, I thought, and not without some scepticism.

I signed up for the Energy Experience with EAM. Although challenged with time and commitment I started going through the program of shifting energy. Soon after, coincidences started happening. Out of the blue an agency called having found my CV online. Subsequently I started a new contract close to home, where my husband could drive me to work whilst my shoulder healed. It was a win-win on all counts, with financial concerns and travel taken care of.

I joined the Energy Evolution 10-month programme, not really interested in being a mentor, but just a couple of months in the journey, the magic continued. EAM gave me the tools to remove each single brick in the wall to break it down and move forward with confidence AND I have discovered *me* — the me I came here to be. Now my shoulder is healed and I am doing work I love.

EAM created wonder and magic in my life. By helping me to change my mindset, it put me in aligned flow and transformed challenges into the greatest gifts I have ever received.

CHAPTER 1 — WHAT TO REMEMBER

I hope you can see, from this chapter and Sunita's story, that everything is energy. Even mainstream science is yet to understand all of these powerful and magical forces within which we live our lives. As yet no one has the 'complete' answer, only pieces of the puzzle. What we can all agree on is that energy is the one true thing that connects everything. It is the foundation of life. Being in FLOW is about more than manifesting. The state of FLOW has a direct impact on your energetic, mental, emotional, and physical health. You can see how science is able to show the pivotal roles of our HEAD and HEART in creating our life experience. As you allow yourself to be more in FLOW, the quicker your life will change. We can see the effects that FLOW has on us on a physical and psychological level and later we will explore more of the energetics behind it. You'll see how EAM enables you to work on all levels of your life and experiences because it is all just energy. Your ability to change your life is a direct correlation in remembering that it is all energy, and because of this you can influence and change it.

In Chapter 2 I will show you how your energy interacts with the world.

CHAPTER 2

Our Powerful Energy

"It's not just that your purpose is joy, it is that you are joy. You are love and joy and freedom and clarity expressing. Energy-frolicking and eager. That's who you are."

- Esther Hicks

In this chapter, we'll discuss electromagnetic energy. By exploring ancient Chinese philosophy, energy structures, and the nature of qi in our energy bodies, you'll learn how your energy impacts your life and how by changing it YOU can change every area of your life to get unstuck and be more in FLOW.

In China, these energy principles form the basis of traditional medicine. Your doctor would look at you holistically and address your diet, environment, and overall well-being. He or she would then provide therapy which in addition to medication, could include acupuncture, herbs, and wellness remedies, bringing eastern and western practices together. Modern science, quantum physics, and cutting-edge research are now able measure the effectiveness of energy tools and techniques at work, helping to prove that working with energy does make a difference.

EVERYTHING IS ENERGY

In the beginning, there was chaos ... No matter which ancient mythology you refer to, they all talk about the beginning of life, the birth of creation where everything came into form from nothing. To date, no one has been able to explain the origins of our universe, yet we all refer to this time as the Big Bang! Chinese medicinal philosophy describes it as the Tao of one, or the universal order of everything which is chaos. From the chaos, the separation of everything began, some call it the heaven and the earth, or the light and the dark, it was the beginning of our polar opposites. In science, we describe exactly the same things as light matter and dark matter.

UNDERSTANDING CHINESE MEDICINE

WHAT IS QI (Energy)

In Chinese medicine, we refer to all energy as qi. Throughout this book we refer to qi as Energy, and imply the same meaning. When we are thinking about our energetic makeup there are many different types of qi. In Chinese medicine, we talk about these different types of qi and their influences because they work in so many different ways in our energy and it's also an important concept to understand.

UNDERSTANDING QI

Qi is known to describe everything from the 'breath' of air everywhere. Energetically, it describes the potential of all energy right through to the physical forms of energy. Qi covers a wide spectrum of everything that exists, just in its different forms. In Chinese philosophy, we talk about qi as movement. It is not static; it's all around you, it ascends and it descends, it transforms and it stores. Qi is also protective. It transforms things, like food and air, into you so that you can continue to exist. Qi energy holds things in place; it creates form and structure like our organs. It keeps the blood in the vessels, where it is meant to be. It warms and protects the body, and it nourishes the organs inside.

There are two types of qi. One is our ancestral qi, known as jing qi, which is inherited from our parents at birth and is created at the point of conception. In Chinese medicine, we believe this is stored in the kidneys. We talk about our jing qi being the energy that makes up who we are. It is the primary energy that is used to help us grow and develop throughout the different stages of our life. This energy can be conserved but it cannot be replenished. The preservation of our jing qi determines the length and quality of our life.

Secondly, we have acquired qi or da qi, which is created after we are born, through the food that we eat and the air that we breathe. This qi is created through a balance of energies that are produced and created in the body, which can be stored up and replenished throughout our lives. We also have a type of qi known as wei qi, which is our protective qi that helps to maintain our physical and energetic bodies from the outside world.

Within EAM we talk about the term energy, which is used to describe ALL forms of energy, the different types of Qi flowing in all ways in all of its manifestations. The overall purpose of EAM, The Energy Alignment Method, is to enable you to create a greater flow of Qi / energy and be able to direct that flow of Qi / energy in any way you choose. By doing this you can influence every area of your experience, physical, mental, and emotional. Deliberately directing energy to create changes in your environment, relationships, wealth, health and well-being.

As you work on yourself to release RESISTANCES and REVERSALS in your energy, you allow a greater flow of Qi in every area of your life, body and energy structures. Your chakras become more open, larger and more powerful. Your meridians flow qi more effectively, and your aura expands and becomes more powerful. Your HEAD energy is able to send clearer signals. Your HEART becomes an unstoppable force sending messages, and your HARA is free flowing, so you can manifest and take action more easily. The greater the flow of qi, and the higher vibration your energy becomes, the better your ability to direct energy and attract what you want in your life.

We'll discuss three things frequently: your energy, thoughts, and emotions. Whilst they are all manifestations of energy, we use them in different ways to change our life.

YIN & YANG

In Chinese theory, we take the Tao, which represents the foundation of life which is one and it becomes two, splitting into the YIN and YANG elements. These two are not finite; they are terms used to explain the interconnected relationship between two seemingly opposite phenomena. Yet in truth these two 'opposites' are connected and it is the movement from one to the other that creates the FLOW of life. For example, to describe the different times of day we would call midday, YANG and midnight YIN. They are opposite in nature — midday is bright and sunny and midnight is dark and moonlit. Yet we cannot explain one without having reference to the other.

The Yin Yang Symbol

In general, the YIN element is the more feminine element—dark, wet, down, and slow. YANG is the more masculine—light, dry, up and fast. (You can draw any jokes you like from that!). YIN and YANG define and describe the limits of our experience within which we live every day. The sun cannot be higher in the sky than at midday. The sun cannot be lower in the sky than at midnight. Nothing can be more feminine than a woman and nothing more masculine than a man.

As human beings, we live between the greatest yin (the earth) and the greatest yang (the sky or the heavens), both of which support our energy bodies. We should ensure that we are connected to YANG energy to energise and wake us up. To restore nurture and replenish us, we should have a good solid connection to our YIN energy. This means grounding resistant energies into the earth to once again be transformed into something productive. This connection and balance of energy can be affected by anything in our life, too much sleep, not enough sleep, too much food, not enough food, too much coffee, not enough water. All of these and more influence our most basic system of homeostasis or equilibrium. In the body, there are some areas which are more yin and some which are more yang in comparison to one another.

YIN	YANG
Feet	Head
Front	Back
Hips	Shoulders
Toes	Fingers
Legs	Arms
Heart	Head
Left	Right

Yin & Yang in the Body

Everything in our lives has an element of YIN and YANG. In order to be high at some point, you must experience the low. In order for it to be light at some point, you must experience the dark. In order for you to experience happiness, sometimes you need to be able to experience sadness. Without one you have no reference point, no context, and no motivation to move to the other. It is energetically impossible to be riding on a wave or place of high vibration and FLOW ALL the time. It would be exhausting.

It is time to give up that myth. Rather than feeling downhearted, what this means is you're now free to truly get in FLOW. TRUE FLOW means being able to ride the wave *between it all,* the ups and the downs with as little RESISTANCE or push as possible. **Which is exactly what you can do with EAM.**

True flow means

riding the wave

between it all,

with as little push

as possible.

LET GO OF BALANCE AND FIND TRUE FLOW

Changing your life is about working with the FLOWs all around you and listening to your FLOW to know when to be active and when to be still, when to make progress and when to reassess. There is benefit in both which is what TRUE FLOW means. It would be impossible to be in a state of expanding and developing all the time, we need to rest. By using EAM you can work within this dynamic of yin and yang and learn to listen to your own energy.

How many people are striving for 'balance' in their lives, health, and between work and play? The term 'balance' is an ungrounded philosophy. We are striving for an elusive concept which cannot exist. Balance is static, there is no movement. If you look at the Yin Yang symbol, it doesn't show balance: it shows movement. It shows the FLOW between the two, the transformation of energy from one to the other. So please apply the same concept to your life

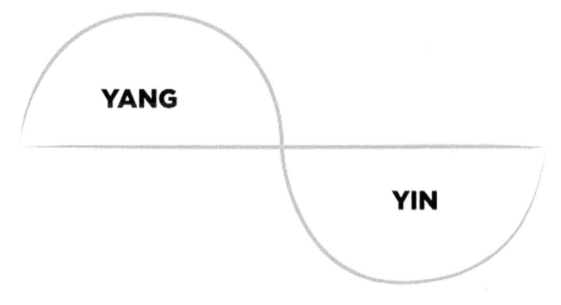

Yin & Yang in Flow

CHINESE 5 ELEMENTS

In Chinese philosophy one of the main principles is the 5 key energy FLOWs: Wood, Fire, Earth, Metal, and Water. In the same way that we work or live between yin and yang, we also FLOW between these five energies. Everything in life travels through these five phases. This understanding represents our entire life experience. The cycle of arrows on the outside represents the generation (Sheng) cycle, this represents growth one thing must feed to the next. You cannot skip these 5 stages. Inside you'll also see a star shape which represents the control (Ke) cycle, the interdependent relationship which prevents an excess of any element.

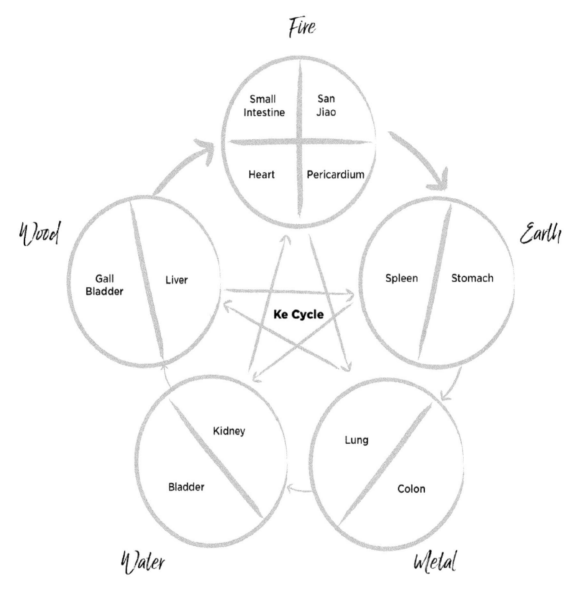

The Chinese 5 Elements and Associated Organs

- The energy of WOOD is about GROWTH, new beginnings. It is the start and the catalyst for what is to come.

- The energy of FIRE is about EXPANSION, being in full flow, at its peak of growth or fullest expression.

- The energy of EARTH is about SUPPORT, grounding, stability and transformation from one thing into another.

- The energy of METAL is about DECLINE, letting go, shedding of anything no longer needed.

- The energy of WATER is about COLLAPSE when something is at the bottom peak of the journey. Ready to return again.

These 5 differentiations of energy can be used to describe the seasons, stages of pregnancy, different parts of our body, our emotions, different sounds, food, the weather, planets, directions, different movements of energy the list is endless. In Chinese philosophy, everything can be categorised into these different energies of 5.

	WOOD	FIRE	EARTH	METAL	WATER
PHASE	Growth	Expansion	Support	Decline	Collapse
SEASON	Spring	Summer	Late Summer	Autumn	Winter
DIRECTION	East	South	Centre	West	North
TIME	Dawn	Midday	Late Afternoon	Evening	Midnight
FOOD	Acid	Bitter	Sweet	Spicy	Salty
ORGAN	Liver & Gallbladder	Heart & Intestines	Spleen & Stomach	Lung & Colon	Kidney & Bladder

Examples Of 5 Elements In Our Life

THREE FLOWS OF ENERGY

The concept of the 3 FLOWs of energy is one of the key theories of EAM. We've talked about these 3 FLOWs in physics with electromagnetic energy and when we talked about the science of the cells. This concept applies to everything in life. It will be in one of these three energetic states: RECEPTIVE in FLOW, in RESISTANCE or in REVERSAL. Remember everything is electromagnetic energy, including us. Therefore, energy is either moving in one direction from one place to another, not moving, or moving in the opposite direction.

Reversal   **Resistance**   **In Flow**

EAM 3 Flows of Energy

BE RECEPTIVE — IN FLOW

The receptive mode is the state of flow. The meaning of FLOW: if something moves somewhere, it moves there steadily and continuously without stopping. How nice would it be to experience that in our lives?

As we talk about FLOW we are discussing the more metaphysical aspects in all forms of our experience—energetic, physical, emotional and psychological. When in FLOW we are able to receive. The state of FLOW is synchronistic and creates changes in these levels all at once. These are all just different expressions of the state of our energy. You may have also heard FLOW called alignment. In EAM it means the same thing but specifically we use alignment to mean that our key energy centres HEAD, HEART, and HARA are sending a congruent message.

In the personal development space, many people talk about this state of FLOW mainly because they want to manifest external circumstances like more money, power, love, wellness or other experiences in their lives. FLOW is about so much more than only manifesting. Being in FLOW is a way of life.

The Heartmath Institute has shown that the energy wave of the state of FLOW moves in one consistent forward positive movement. If you think about energy when in FLOW, it should be travelling in one direction towards the things you want.

EAM In Flow Direction

WHY BE IN FLOW?

When you are in FLOW you experience positive emotions, thoughts, and experiences. Emotionally, most people have experienced this state as feeling content, happy, in control, and in sync within themselves and with others around them. It is the search for this state that drives most of our decisions.

Let's explore how the FLOW state expresses on the 6 different levels of our human experience we discussed earlier.

1. ENERGETIC — SPIRITUAL

You vibrate at a higher, stronger energy frequency. This allows you to attract more positive energy, it easier to manifest things you want. You create synergy in all levels of your energy structures. It enables the free FLOW of qi throughout. Your aura expands and strengthens. Channels of flow are wider, meridians are free Flowing, and your chakras are open. Energetically you are able to receive more insight, spiritual downloads, access information, abundance, and love. You are more in tune with life and your intuition and psychic abilities are enhanced. Your energetic messages sent out are much stronger, clearer and manifesting is easier. You are more connected to the wider world.

2. ENERGETIC — SCIENCE

The FLOW state creates a more coherent heart rhythm pattern. This synchronises communication throughout the body on a physical, mental, emotional, and cellular level. The effect of being in FLOW can be reflected on many levels of our physical life.

3. PHYSICAL

Flow allows our body to go into the healing phase as the cells are no longer in a resistant environment. We change our brain structure. Our hormones change as the physiological effects of stress, anxiety, and adrenaline leave the body.

4. EMOTIONAL

When in FLOW we feel love, happiness, confidence, peace, joy, empowered, and unstoppable. We experience more happiness and freedom in our daily lives. We feel hopeful about the future.

5. PSYCHOLOGICAL

You will be in 'the zone', 'on it', or 'be present'. The FLOW state changes your perception and improves mental and emotional stability. You have greater clarity, focus, and direction.

6. CELLULAR OR DNA

Your cells work effectively, processing waste, allowing filtration, openly connecting and communicating within the body as it goes about its normal healthy functions.

Being in flow also positively affects your Human Experience, overall. You are more connected to others. You shine when you enter a room and people notice you. Changes happen at a rapid speed. When we look at Society and Consciousness, communities more easily come together, and there is more positive communication. Societies work in harmony with a central drive for growth and development. We live more harmoniously with the environment and the world around us.

HOW DO WE GET IN FLOW?

We naturally get ourselves in the state of FLOW all the time. It is those moments when you are present, happy, enjoying being exactly where you are doing that one thing. This is when you are in the state of FLOW. Nothing else is on your mind and you are at one with yourself and life. You've had these moments all your life, and you can back get to them at any time. The trouble is most of us have forgotten what they feel like.

Here are few simple ways we can get ourselves in FLOW. Go out in bare feet in nature, get enough sleep, eat healthy well-balanced meals, go for a run, meditate, watch a comedy and laugh until your tummy hurts, dance like everyone's watching, or go on a roller coaster ride. Really any experience that snaps you out of your daily habits and allows you to let go of your troubles, that is FLOW.

When our energy is in a FLOW state everything flows effortlessly. You wake up feeling great, you find some money on the floor, someone buys you a coffee. You hear great news. You get a promotion and taken out for dinner all in one day. You can choose to be in that state anytime you want, which is what I want to share with you in Chapter 3 — The 5 Steps of EAM. This leads me beautifully to the next two states of energy.

IN RESISTANCE

In the dictionary RESISTANCE is defined as: a force that acts to stop the progress of something or make it slower or the degree to which something prevents the FLOW of an electrical current through a circuit. It is also explained as 'a measurement of the difficulty encountered by a power source in forcing electric current through an electrical circuit, and hence the amount of power dissipated in the circuit.' Notice the words in the definition: 'stops progress' 'make it slower' 'prevents the FLOW' 'difficulty encountered' 'forcing' 'dissipated'. These are exactly mirrored in the state of RESISTANCE, which we create in our lives. These concepts apply when thinking about RESISTANCE in terms of our energy.

In Heartmath they call it INCOHERENCE and this energy state can be specifically measured. In this state, our heart's rhythms do not appear smooth or wave like; rather, they are demonstrated in a non-uniform manner. It is erratic and all over the place, which also mirrors how we feel when in this energy state. We saw this image in chapter 1. In other methodologies or personal development circles, you may call these 'barriers' or 'blocks'. In EAM we don't use that terminology because it does not accurately describe what is happening. RESISTANCE does. If you're a fan of the Law of Attraction you've probably heard about RESISTANCE. I know for sure you've experienced it in your life — we all have.

EAM Resistance Direction

When in FLOW, energy should be travelling in one direction. When there is RESISTANCE it is usually because there is something creating a counter FLOW. This results in a two way pull of energy that creates a friction, tension, or pull which is what we experience as RESISTANCE.

WHY DO WE HAVE RESISTANCE?

Energetically, RESISTANCE is a two-directional pull of energy in your life. Say there is something you want to create in your future. Maybe there is also a contradictory thought, belief, pattern or emotion holding you back. Whilst you have this in your energy it creates a RESISTANCE as the two things pull against each other.

RESISTANCE can come from all sorts of places, including your thoughts, your words, your emotions, the food you eat, the soap you wash with, other people's energy, objects in your own energetic space, your health and energy REVERSALS.... The list is endless, and we will cover them in more detail as we work through the book. RESISTANCE can also be from a past life or lives, trauma in the womb, or during your birth, and throughout your childhood and adult life. There may be a lot of places in your life that need energy work to remove RESISTANCE. That's what we'll explore in chapters 5 through 7.

HOW IS IT CREATED?

What you experience as RESISTANCE is your HEART and SOUL telling you that there is something out of alignment. It doesn't mean there is something wrong with what you're doing, just that there is some RESISTANCE in your energy and you need to transform it to get back in FLOW. In terms of energy psychology, we experience RESISTANCE when we have two or more opposing energies within ourselves. These are two forms of energy contradicting one another. RESISTANCE can be created in many ways across multiple scenarios with a messy interwoven tangle of energy, thoughts, beliefs, memories, emotions, values, stories, feelings, and patterns.

For example, you want a different job; a part of you really wants to explore a new career and pursue something you love and enjoy. The other part of you perhaps has a belief that you aren't good enough to earn more money and it is better 'safer' to stay in the job you have because at least you have money coming in.

Pulled in Two Directions

BELIEF 1

It is safer to stay in the job I have than make more money.

BELIEF 2

I want to do a job I love and enjoy every day

Resistance

Example of Being Pulled in Two Directions

RESISTANCE could be two opposing beliefs or values about a subject that create tension, as we are pulled in opposite directions. This is what we experience as negative thoughts or emotions. In most cases this is usually a conflict between our HEAD (thinking) and our HEART (feelings); the two most powerful electromagnetic communicators in our body. This tug of war in our vibrational energy is usually what causes RESISTANCE.

HOW RESISTANCE AFFECTS US

We've all experienced RESISTANCE. It's probably what brought you to this book. When something isn't right, it feels like hard work and requires a lot of effort. Have you ever met someone and thought yuck? There was something about them that you just didn't like. What you sensed was their RESISTANCE. Something in their energy that was not a match to yours. All the energetic imprints we carry from the past show up in us, in our conversation, our outlook, our perception. Until we release them it will be hard to FLOW in the direction that we want to go. This is how RESISTANCE expresses across all 6 levels of our experience.

1. ENERGETIC — SPIRITUAL

It prevents you energetically moving forward. Your aura contracts, less qi flows, chakras close and spin more slowly. Your HEAD, HEART, and HARA send incongruent messages. Meridians get stuck. Things take effort. You feel contracted and heavy.

2. ENERGETIC — SCIENCE

Think about this in energy terms. Remember the faster and slower energies on the electromagnetic spectrum — feelings of RESISTANCE are measured in the lower, slower, heavier vibrations.

3. CELLULAR OR DNA

There is decrease in fluid exchange and poor absorption on a cellular level. Cells shut down and stop communicating as freely. DNA and gene expression can be impacted as they perceived stressors in the environment.

4. PHYSICAL

This can be acute illnesses, or short-term health conditions. The body is in a stress state with high levels of cortisol and adrenaline impacting our physiology.

5. EMOTIONAL

We feel emotions such as fear, depression, blame, shame, anxiety, guilt, anger, feeling overwhelmed, frustration, and jealousy.

6. PSYCHOLOGICAL

There are changes in our ability to think clearly. We have negative thoughts, are unable to reason or recall information, and there is a decrease in our emotional stability and well-being. We make bad decisions and emotionally disconnect from family and friends.

When we look at our Human Experience overall, everything feels like hard work and we lack a sense of direction or purpose. We feel pulled in multiple directions. On a Societal or Mass Consciousness level, when you think about the impact of RESISTANCE and what it does to us individually imagine the number of people who are living their lives in RESISTANCE and its impact on our mass consciousness and to our planet? Maybe all the chaos we're seeing in the world is RESISTANCE on a mass scale, which is affecting us on a on a physiological, psychological, energetic, and mass consciousness level?

WHY AND HOW TO LET IT GO

To get in FLOW you have to transform your RESISTANCE. Only then will you clearly see the right actions and steps to take to receive, achieve, or manifest what you want. As you transform the RESISTANCE, you easily get clarity and epiphanies. Energetically you can speed up the rate you manifest by increasing your momentum. With the 5 Step process in EAM, we TRANSFORM the RESISTANCE with STEP 4, which I explain in Chapter 3.

What if you knew the only thing standing in the way of you changing your life was the level of RESISTANCE you have in your energy? I know people will say 'No, it's because I have no money' or 'My partner is a pain in the ass' or 'You don't know what I've been through'. I hear you. I get it. What if those beliefs and thoughts were just RESISTANCE, too? When you change your energy, thoughts and emotions with EAM, you'll get yourself in the state of FLOW. Once you do, watch how easily things start to FLOW.

Releasing the Resistance in My Life

K. BEATE RICHTER, AGE 59

All my life I have felt like the odd one out. I was perceived as outgoing, confident, easy to talk to, always having a big mouth, yet deep inside I was shy and constantly afraid someone might find out that I was no good. I felt embarrassed being German and felt more comfortable in the company of foreigners. During the 7 years that I lived in Shanghai, I spent more time with international expats and the Chinese than in the German community.

Using EAM I discovered I had RESISTANCE around being German, which I had carried all my life. In my energy, I was carrying a mixture of shame and guilt related to all the bad that had come from my country. I was able to identify it and released all of it completely and fast. I aligned to being proud of who I am, and grateful for all the good things that had come from my home country. I felt much lighter, relieved, and the shift in my energy could be clearly seen by others.

Since I joined the Energy Evolution 10-month programme and embarked on my journey to becoming a mentor, I feel so much better, calmer, and stronger. I also carry myself differently whenever I meet people.

IN REVERSAL

REVERSAL is the act of changing or making something change to its opposite. This term is used in physics in relation to the FLOW of energy that is flowing in the opposite direction. We also use them in terms of energy psychology, too. Energetically energy REVERSALS are when a person's energy is flowing in the opposite direction than what it would normally be.

Earlier we described FLOW as energy flowing in one direction towards what you want. Energy in RESISTANCE is energy flowing in two opposing directions creating a PULL. REVERSALS are moving in the opposite direction to what you want. From an energetic perspective, we describe an energy REVERSAL to be like a shock or disruption in your energy. This energy can become literally stuck and prevent the free FLOW of positive energy around that part of your life, body, or a particular subject.

Imagine a REVERSAL creates a fracture or break, like a broken plate that has been glued back together. Often these broken pieces have rewired parts of your energy, thoughts, beliefs, and emotions and made neurological connections in your brain with incorrect information. These energy REVERSALS are powerful. Everyone has them, on all kinds of subjects and often multiple REVERSALS on some. Ironically, they are designed to protect us and to keep us from danger yet when it comes to energy psychology they are hidden gremlins.

EAM Reversal Direction

Unless we address the reversed energy, it is almost impossible to create change. Because there is no energy Flowing in the direction of what you want. It is flowing away from it. So, every time you give energy to that subject, it pulls it in the opposite direction.

WHY UNDERSTAND ENERGY REVERSALS?

Energy REVERSALS are often the root of most people's STUCK energy patterns, those repetitive states of living, like being broke, doing work we hate, or unhappy relationships, that never seem to go away. REVERSALS create beliefs, negative emotions, and repeating habit or behaviours, which can be self-sabotaging. They are often the reason that some more traditional forms of therapy or self-help may not work. As the REVERSAL was not dealt with energetically, it was probably only addressed on one level, for example, psychologically or, medication has numbed the effects. Until you effectively address the underlying energy REVERSAL, it will continue to affect you energetically, mentally, and emotionally.

Using EAM we are able to identify what the energy REVERSALS are even on an unconscious level. We can identify when it began and what the emotional, mental, physical, or spiritual cause is as well as what else it is affecting your energy. We then use the 5 Steps of EAM to address them. When you address it with EAM, you will feel the transformation of the energy. On the other side of energy REVERSALS are often your biggest breakthroughs, as all of that stuck energy begins Flowing towards what you want.

HOW ARE ENERGY REVERSALS CREATED?

In this context energy REVERSALS are created at a significant point in time by a group of decisions, choices, and experiences. Usually they are created when we are in situations in which we have no 'normal' coping mechanism that we have never encountered, or were shocked or surprised by the event or outcome. Physiologically this can be the shock state. At that point, we make choices and decisions and connect them to seemingly disconnected events. This creates conflicting or opposing energy. The situations that caused them don't have to be big or memorable. It was just a shock to your energy at the time. Conversely, if there have been BIG, catastrophic or tragic events, there will most certainly be an energy REVERSAL.

HOW WE EXPERIENCE AN ENERGY REVERSAL

We experience energy REVERSALS differently and different REVERSALS will affect you differently as well. It depends on which level of your energy is in REVERSAL. It's not only the moment that it's created but *any time we are reminded of that situation* (consciously or unconsciously). This is made more difficult because when our energy is 'broken', the parts it has been 'reconnected to' may not make sense. Because of this, energy REVERSALS can be highly irrational. Symptoms of REVERSAL can vary widely from mild to severe, for instance, when someone is classed has having PTSD or have been in a traumatic incident. Energetically it is a reversed energy state. That does not mean, however, that all REVERSALS are PTSD.

REVERSALS in our energy can happen in varying degrees. More frequently it is in an area of your life you can't change and you are unable to explain, either exactly what it is or why you can't change it. There may also not be any significant trauma you can remember. You may also have multiple REVERSALS that contradict one another, because of this 'broken' connection in your HEAD and energy. Or you may be in RESISTANCE with one aspect of a situation and have a REVERSAL on another.

Here is an example of how a minor energy REVERSAL may be created.

Four-year-old Lilly is at school painting a picture of her house for her daddy. She loves to paint. Her dad loves her paintings and always praises her for being so creative. Just as she picks up her brush to paint the tree by the front door, a little boy runs past, knocks over her paint pot and it covers the floor in bright green paint. Her teacher Ms. Ferguson doesn't see the boy run past. All she sees is the mess on the floor, so she shouts at Lilly.

"No! Lilly what are you doing? What an awful mess you've made."

Poor Lilly who was a moment ago happily painting her picture jumps as she is shouted at. Right then at age 4 little Lilly makes an unconscious decision that painting is bad, that her work is rubbish and she would never paint again because the teacher told her off. In that moment, her energy locks in the exact thoughts, words, and emotions she is feeling into her energy and she now has a counter FLOW of energy about painting. The reality of it had nothing to do with the painting of the house. Later in life Lilly stifles her art and creativity. She secretly longs to be a creative interior designer and architect, yet she never pursues it because she believes that accessing her creativity is bad.

Although heart-breaking, sadly, this is a relatively mild example. Here we have the other extreme.

Ivan lost his wife and child when his house was bombed in his war-stricken country. He managed to survive and rescue one child from the burning wreckage. In the disaster, he had to pull his burning child screaming from the building and helplessly watch as it collapsed with the rest of his family trapped inside. In that moment, an energy REVERSAL was created, it was such a shock to him and his energy. It was a situation he had never encountered before and had no coping strategy for. Afterwards he is still locked in the event, replaying the scene and the sounds of his family screaming over and over in his head, agonising over what he could have done differently.

Energy REVERSALS affect us on all 6 levels of our experience.

1. ENERGETIC — SPIRITUAL

Can feel like 'life lessons' or perceived obstacles to overcome. A part of our energy becomes locked at that age and we are stuck repeating the same pattern. Our aura layers can collapse, and our chakras can shut down.

2. ENERGETIC — SCIENCE

Linked to an incoherent heart pattern. Deactivation of the frontal cortex of the brain and the hyper-activity of the limbic system, in particular, the amygdala.

3. CELLULAR OR DNA

REVERSALS shut down the cell walls and prevent the exchange of fluids and foods. DNA genes can be expressed by stressors in our environment.

4. PHYSICAL

We are plagued by chronic disease, and serious or terminal illness. We may be locked into this pattern with medication. We are constantly in a heightened state of alert in the fear/stress mode. This is known as hyper-arousal, which can create neurological brain changes.

5. EMOTIONAL

We feel extreme debilitating FEAR, DEPRESSION, anxiety and hopelessness.

6. PSYCHOLOGICAL

We are overly sensitivity to the environment. We have inappropriate mental or emotional responses, and abnormal fears or phobias. We relive traumatic events and feel disconnected and isolated. Psychological studies have shown that from a neuroscience perspective, these situations can create an experience of being frozen in time.

On a Human Experience level, we become locked in situations which seem to never change. We may also repeat the same patterns for years, just with different people in your life. On a Mass Conscious level, an energetic REVERSAL is a Society at war plagued by famine, separation, and a lack of moral, social, and empathy. There is a rise in illness and widespread disease.

HOW DO WE LET REVERSALS GO?

There are ways to deal with energy REVERSALS in psychology and some energy healing practices, and of course with EAM. In my experience, until you address REVERSALS energetically they will not transform because our energy has literally shut down. By creating the change energetically in our aura and other energy structures, we allow change to happen on a physical, mental, and emotional level.

GETTING BACK IN FLOW

Now do you understand why some therapies or practices used previously may not have worked out for you? Letting go of an energy REVERSAL is powerful. When we change the REVERSAL in our energy we get 'back in FLOW'. We are able to access better choices, ideas and insight. We become more whole. Whilst you hold RESISTANCE or REVERSALS in your energy you will continue to repeat more of the same in your life. This is what stands in the way of changing your life every single time. This is why I have such a passion to enable people to raise their energy vibration with EAM, to move past these RESISTANCES and REVERSALS and create a state of FLOW. Being in FLOW means being able to ride the wave of it all. The ups and downs the highs and the lows moving between the yin and the yang.

FLOW, MOMENTUM AND RHYTHM

Momentum is another physics term, which also applies to energy transformation and refers to the quantity of motion that an object has. We use this term in everyday language to explain something that is on the move and is going to take some effort to stop. Examples include a train speeding down a railway track or a snowball rolling down a hill. The momentum of something is dependent on how much mass it has and how fast it is moving.

Momentum moves an object in the same direction unless you do something to stop it. How does this apply to your life? We can have momentum of energy in anything. Think about your thoughts, beliefs, feelings, emotions, and experiences in your life. Momentum can be helpful, for instance, if you have gathered momentum on something you want to bring to you. Can you see how momentum could also be the reason more of the same sh** keeps coming into your life? It is momentum coupled with the Universal Laws that will continue to bring you the same thing.

HOW WE GATHER MOMENTUM OF ENERGY

Energetically, the more energy we put into a situation, conversation, or relationship the more it will grow or evolve. This IS powerful for you when the repetition is positive for your affirmations and things you want to manifest. As you repeat them it creates new neural pathways in the brain, which we can rewire through the process of neuroplasticity. This is exactly what we do with Step 5 – MANIFEST.

Emotionally, we gather momentum with positive and negative emotions. Have you noticed how things seem to spiral out of control you are in a bad mood?

The same happens with our life experience too. When you fight, or push against a situation adding more momentum, it usually grows or worsens. Equally, when you let go and stop adding momentum it gets easier. As you do, you are able to get into alignment and redirect energy to gather momentum towards the things you want. Think about MOMENTUM as the speed of MANIFESTATION. The more you think or feel something, the more it will manifest. The speed of manifestation is directly related to the energy you put into thinking and feeling around that subject. It is the force of momentum empowering you. As you bring more areas of your life into flow the quicker the changes come. This is why The Energy Evolution, which I will introduce you to in chapters 5 – 7, is so successful.

In Chapter 3, I will share with you how we use momentum in EAM and in Chapter 4 how it applies to changing your life.

Finding My Momentum

JEANI HOWARD, AGE 38

For years, life had been a series of pain and trauma, PTSD, and manic depression. I was caught up a negative loop of emotions, literally wanting to die. In my search to change my life, I trained as an energy healer in EFT (Emotional Freedom Techniques), Life Coaching, NLP, Reiki Master, and in chakra therapy, yet I still struggled to cope with things that had happened in my past and with managing my 4 young children. I loved them dearly but I felt I wasn't good enough to be their mum.

I managed my emotions with alcohol, drugs, and music. Everything in life was hard, and I felt like a yo-yo — up one minute, straight back down the next, wrapped up in fear and despair. I was always exhausted. It felt like everything was getting harder. No matter what I did, more bad stuff kept on coming and I was powerless to change it. I truly believed that I must have been so bad in another life, to deserve all the pain in this one. I never felt worthy, deserving or good enough. I couldn't even take my own life.

Then I met Yvette and was introduced to EAM. The sheer speed of relief from every emotion and feeling was stunning. I used the Energy Alignment Scale to release fear, shame, guilt, and more. I was then able to release the number of RESISTANCES in my energy, Step 4 TRANSFORM.

In less than 5 minutes I was able to move onto Step 5 MANIFEST to open up and allow all of the positive emotions, beliefs, and energies that I wanted to bring in, to expand my energy.

As the negativity stopped, I was able to create more positivity in my life. Then all the good things started and have kept on coming. Now every part of my life and myself are utterly amazing, more than I could ever had imagined. I love my life, I love me.

THE RHYTHM OF LIFE

One of the things I love most about Chinese philosophy is they've understood these principles of energy flow for so many years and enabled us to put into words those things which cannot fully be explained. When thinking about yin and yang, we see there is a FLOW between the two extremes. From the yang as it grows and comes to its peak it must also then FLOW towards the yin. As the yang begins to decline it goes into the Earth energy. In the Earth, there is the energy of yin as it becomes its strongest most powerful yin; at the peak, it must also then FLOW back towards the yang. As the energy begins to push up, the yin begins to decline as it comes back into yang energy. This is the FLOW and rhythm of everything in life. This is always a wave and a peak FLOW of energy as you can see in the five FLOWs of energy yin yang diagram.

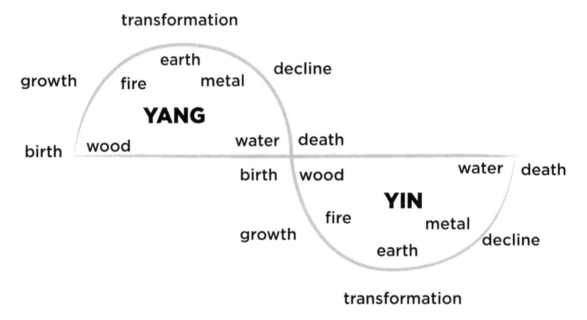

Rhythm and 5 Energies of Life

The word rhythm comes from the Greek word *rhythmos*, meaning measured motion. Your ability to successfully move forward and change your life is directly related to your ability to FLOW between yin and yang energies. You must understand how to work with the rhythms of life because everything in it goes through this process. Your journey of transformation. Your journey of healing. The seasons of the year. The cycle of the moon. The energy and sunrise of each day. Your life itself from birth through childhood, teenage years, through marriage to death and rebirth, if that's something you believe in. Everything in life goes through these phases in a consistent FLOW from yang to yin and from yin to yang.

As we start using EAM, we cannot prevent the FLOW of rhythm from taking us into a downwards pool of energy. Use these times as an opportunity to release any RESISTANCE, any negative thoughts, beliefs, and emotions that come up. By doing this as the rhythm moves upwards again you will be coming out of this phase a brand new shiny version of yourself who is able to operate on an even higher state of consciousness.

We are influenced by so many different energies, not only our own energy but also the energy of the planets, our environment, radio waves, electromagnetic waves, the pull of the Moon, the rising and setting of the sun, and even the solar flares going off in our solar system. They all affect our flow state and our ability to move through life.

WE ARE MADE OF ENERGY

We know that everything around us is made of electromagnetic energy — electro (meaning it has an electrical charge) and magnetic (which means it attracts like back to it). Therefore, whatever you send out, whether it's lack, abundance, fear, love, happiness, or sadness, comes back to you. YOU are literally a MAGNET! We know the only electromagnetic energy we can see is visible light, yet there is more electromagnetic energy in our world. In the same way, there is more to us than we can see with the naked eye. We are a powerhouse of electromagnetic energy; our energy extends and interacts far beyond our skin or the ends of our fingers and toes. We are energetic radios sending and receiving messages from the environment all the time.

What ever you
send out comes back,
you are a magnet.

THREE POWERFUL ENERGY CENTRES

We have three strong electromagnetic communicators that are constantly sending out messages into our environment and receiving information back. They are your HEART, HEAD, and HARA. They are fundamental, and we even use them in everyday language. We say things like 'I'm stuck in my head' or 'I follow my heart' or 'I feel it in my belly'. It would be useful to understand the functions they have in our lives. Being stuck in your head feels busy, it feels chaotic, like you have 101 things going on all at the same time. You've also experienced being in your heart, when everything feels peaceful and calm. You've also had those moments when you 'follow your gut', which means something feels 'right' deep inside you.

When we talk about HEART we are referring to anything which is emotional, intuitive, or in the layers of our aura. It is the part that makes us who we are. Your HEAD energy is used to describe our mental, psychological or any kind of brain activity. As an ENERGY, it is not just located in the physical brain structure also in our aura. With our HARA energy, we are referring to the processes of assimilation, sorting, creation, manifesting and our primal power force and drive.

EAM Energy Centres Your Head, Heart & Hara

Imagine these three energy centres are like the energetic power behind a broadcasting tower. The content of the messages is influenced by the different levels of your aura, which we will explore shortly.

THREE KEY ENERGIES — FORM AND FUNCTION

All these messages, from your head, your heart, and your gut, are from your energy. They are there guiding us ALL the time yet very often we ignore them. We're taught to ignore these signs and use 'logic' or 'brain power' to make decisions when our energy already has the answers. When we ignore the signs, situations go wrong; we create more stress (or RESISTANCE) and feel unhappy. The sad thing is we can spend years living our lives like this, never connecting to ourselves or realising that we had the answers all along.

It is the FLOW and function of these energy structures, which create and shape our whole life experience. The POWER of alignment comes from having the three key energy centres sending a congruent message. We need the planning, decision making, action taking energy of the HEAD. We need to be connected and guided by the soulful, peaceful, calm of the all-knowing HEART. We need the powerhouse of action taking, creating and manifesting energy of our HARA to bring things to life.

When we experience feelings of negativity, stress or feel overwhelmed it is due primarily to a mixed energy from these three energy centres. It could be that your HEAD and our HEART are out of sync; for example, your HEAD is *thinking* one thing and your HEART is *feeling* another. Or when you've made a decision with your HEAD that you know is right in your HEART and you are not taking action to making it happen with your HARA energy.

When you experience something positive, we call this state of energy Alignment. This means that all levels of our energy are congruent with other another and energy is Flowing in the same direction. It's because these three centres are in sync and are congruent in their message — your HEAD, HEART, and HARA are vibrating the same message. This is when magic happens; when these 3 powerful energy centres are working together, you cannot help but manifest anything in your life.

If you're talking, thinking, feeling and taking action in your life with LOVE, HAPPINESS, GRATITUDE and JOY, that is the message you send out which allows you to attract more of it into your life. If you're talking, thinking, or feeling and doing anything which are based on HATE, FEAR, ANGER, GUILT, BLAME, that is the message you are sending out so you will attract that back into your life. Let's take a look at how each of these powerful structures is made.

UNDERSTANDING YOUR HEAD FUNCTION

Our brain controls our nerves, our hormones, and makes decisions. It controls our psychology and our physiology and sends messages all over the body. When you are in hospital what are the two things they measure if you are on life support? They are measuring the electromagnetic activity of brainwaves and heart waves and if either one of those are not working you're considered to be dead. Our HEAD energy can influence the world around us, way beyond the reach of our skull. Energetically our thoughts project, travel, and connect to mass consciousness.

Your HEAD energy does much more than keep us alive. It is all things you would consider to be the 'logical' thinking elements and controls our beliefs, patterns, memories, traits, and thoughts. Our HEAD function is so important, think about its location on the top of the body. It is our 'lookout': it enables us to 'see what is happening around us and to 'listen' to what is going on. It enables us to read the electromagnetic and vibrational energy and decipher it into something meaningful. It is the antenna that receives energetic information, thoughts and ideas. Our HEAD is an important and powerful energy for defining our experience. Our head filters information based on previous experiences and information we already hold. If we have not experienced much of life, been exposed to new ideas, thoughts, concepts or ways of being, we are limited. This will persist unless or until we receive new information to process and access, which is what we do with EAM.

IN REVERSAL

When you are in REVERSAL, you are unable to send out clear messages about what you really want. Your brain activity would be mainly registering in the OCCIPITAL, the hind or reptilian brain. You are in the fight or flight or freeze mode. Your brain function will be re-firing neurological set points and associations, which were made at the time of the REVERSAL and maybe reconnecting them with other similar situations where that REVERSAL has been reactivated. You are not able to make any clear choices. You are unable to see any positive outcome. In extreme cases, you may have mental disturbances and flashbacks.

IN RESISTANCE

When your head is in RESISTANCE there is conflict in your energy. It is unable to send clear messages and will start 'misfiring' information. Your brain function will be more chaotic with less activity in the frontal cortex. When you are in RESISTANCE you're unable to make decisions, decipher information, or be able to think clearly. You will have resistant thoughts and beliefs, which hold you back. You would refer to this state as limiting thoughts or beliefs.

IN FLOW

When you're in FLOW and we talk about sending information or messages, it is our HEAD energy which defines the thought, belief or message. When receiving information, our HEAD energy makes 'sense' and assimilates information into something cognitive, logical or sensible. When in FLOW, your brain would be registering positive information. Your hypothalamus would be creating and sending out neuropeptides to create oxytocin and serotonin in the body. Your frontal cortex will be active and you'll have clear thinking and brain function. You experience greater insights, clarity of your vision, and have more 'aha' moments, when things come together and make sense.

You can see how important our HEAD energy is. Let's see how it connects to our HEART and HARA.

HEART STRUCTURE & FUNCTION

Our HEART is responsible for the free FLOW of blood and oxygen around the body. It is our HEART that feeds our HEAD. We already know how magical our heart can be. Traditionally we've been taught to believe that our head rules our heart. It is almost ingrained in us; people say "don't follow your heart", "you need to think that through" or "don't be so emotional, be rational" or "you're not being logical" when someone is expressing emotion. If anyone connects into their heart, they say "it doesn't feel right" or "that isn't what my heart wants to do". We have been taught to believe that our head rules the roost.

However, studies have shown that our HEART also has functions previously attributed only to the brain, such as controlling our nerves, hormones, physiology, and pathology. Think about this. There have been many tragic cases of people who are clinically brain 'dead' yet their hearts are still pumping blood around the body. This makes powerful case for the intelligence and autonomy of our heart and that maybe more of our body is not, in fact, entirely controlled by the brain.

HEART ENERGY

Energetically our HEART is one of the biggest influences in the experience of our life. It creates a field that can be measured up to 20 feet away. In energy terms this electromagnetic field is what we know as our aura. The frequency and the energy transmitted from our heart energy is also 60 times greater in amplitude than the brain.

Our HEART energy is primarily powered by our emotions. The unhappier you are the smaller and more condensed your aura will be. The happier and more love you feel the BIGGER and stronger your whole energy field will be.

In Chinese medicine, your heart is considered the seat of your soul in the physical body. It is the governor or emperor, where the ruling energy of your body lives. If your heart is unhappy the rest of the body is unable to properly function. Your heart is able to read and direct all of the other areas and energies of the body and unless or until HEART energy is free Flowing, the rest cannot circulate efficiently.

YOUR SIXTH SENSE

We have five senses — taste, sound, sight, touch and smell — that pass information to the brain. The brain processes that information and sends messages to the body to take action. We then experience the outcome of that processing through the filters we have created. Our heart and brain are in constant communication, sending information through nerves, biochemicals, pressure waves, and electromagnetic interactions. Our HEART is reading information in our body and sending it *into* the brain before our brain has registered information from the other five senses or even *before* it has been able to create chemical messages and send that information out to the body.

The other five senses are taken care of by our eyes, ears, mouth, nose and skin. If that is the case, WHAT is our heart reading? The HEART is reading our energy! It IS OUR 6th SENSE. Your heart is reading all the energy in your physical and energetic bodies as well as information outside. I get so excited about this because it challenges what we've all been taught, that the brain controls the heart. Remember in Chapter 1 we talked about the bus hurtling towards you. When we look at it from an energetic perspective, what initially alerted you to the bus was your aura. Your energy field sent the energetic signal into the body via the afferent neurons. It was your HEART field that made you look up and alerted the rest of your body.

IN REVERSAL

When your HEART is in REVERSAL, your energy is shut down. Your aura will be small. You would see the heart rate variability to be significantly out of FLOW. Physically, you would suffer the effects of long-term stress and adrenal exhaustion, chronic heart and lung health conditions, and issues with circulation.

Emotionally, you would feel overwhelming fear, depression, and feel trapped or stuck in repeating emotions. There may also be PTSD-type symptoms such as mental health issues and feeling 'detached' from life and reality. There may even be symptoms of paranoia, dementia, and bi-polar disorder. When in REVERSAL people shut down, create distance, and disconnect from others. Whilst these may sound like HEAD energy disturbances, in energy medicine these are all considered to be a disturbance of the HEART. In Chapter 3, I'll show you how you can create more FLOW and open up your heart.

IN RESISTANCE

Your energy bodies begin to contract, and you emit resistant vibrations. When measured, you would see an incoherent heart pattern. Physically, you'd have an elevated heart rate and stress and adrenaline would rush through the body. Cells would not function as freely. You'd experience emotions such as fear, anger, frustration, jealousy, anger, rage, and fear. You will send out 'mixed' messages and your experience of life will feel chaotic, hectic, and out of sync. I'm pretty sure that we've all experienced this?

IN FLOW

All of the benefits we have discussed about the state of FLOW, especially on an emotional and vibrational level, can be attributed to the FLOW state of the HEART. In FLOW, you can see the even rhythm of energy Flowing between the yin and yang. It enables the free FLOW of qi, blood, and fluid around the physical body. This also affects the FLOW of meridians, chakras and other energy structures including the HEAD and HARA energy. Your aura is big, strong, and expanded. Your body is in the coherent state; your physical health is Flowing and you will be spreading oxytocin and serotonin in the body. Cells and organs will be functioning easily. Your HEART will also be sending coherent signals and messages to the other organs in the body. You would be in the emotional states of content, happiness, empowerment, peace, joy, love, and freedom.

HARA STRUCTURE & FUNCTION

Our HARA energy, whilst it is an unknown part of the body, is vital throughout many stages of our life. You may have heard of it referred to as your lower *dan tien*, a Chinese term for a part of the body. It is an energy centre that you can locate by putting your hands on your belly button in a heart shape; it's usually just a couple of inches below where your fingers meet. It is often called the sacral chakra. Whilst the core of your HARA is located there, energetically the HARA refers to many of the functions. It describes the actions of everything from your waist, below your belly button and into your groin and legs.

YOUR HARA MANIFESTS

Our HARA energy is powerful. It is the foundation, grounding energy, which enables us to be alive. This HARA has the power to create life. Now if our body has the power and knowledge to BUILD, create and grow a tiny, perfect human being do you think it could also manifest what you want in life too? Your ability to create or manifest is directly related to the FLOW of your HARA. Think of it as your manifesting energy.

THE POWER OF OUR SEXUAL ENERGY

Many of us feel ashamed, guilty, rude, or disconnected when we talk about the power of sex. This topic — a whole book in itself — is often the root of most of our issues because we have disconnected from our HARA and therefore our sexual power, which is the foundation of all life. Sexual energy is one of the most misused energies. It is often used to control or take power over others or we shut it down to protect ourselves. It can also be depleted through over activity whether through too much sex or masturbation. In Chinese medicine and many other Eastern Philosophies or practices, we are taught to hold onto this sexual energy and life force as much as possible in doing so we heighten our spiritual practice, development and growth.

Our most in FLOW moments are when we have an orgasm. Why? Because we have let go of our RESISTANCE and go with the moment. Have you noticed that when you're stressed out, tired, overwhelmed, or overthinking, it is almost impossible to reach climax? Because your energy is in RESISTANCE or maybe even REVERSAL, and may be shut down. For some, sex is something they have disconnected from. Emotionally they are not present they're not involved.

As Dr. Andrea Pennington explains in her bestselling book, *The Orgasm Prescription for Women: 21 Days to Heightened Pleasure, Deeper Intimacy & Orgasmic Bliss,* if we have experienced trauma in our past it is quite possible that we have energetically shut off our brain's responsiveness to sexual energy. If the brain doesn't pick up on sexual cues, then there will be no electric flow of energy to the genitals. So unhealed wounds, whether sexual or otherwise, can create REVERSALS and RESISTANCE in the HARA and this can decrease erotic flow, desire, arousal and orgasm.

Likewise, if we are in our head, worried about work or busy thinking of our to-do list, we will not have a vibrant energy flow through our Hara, and we will not experience ecstasy.

If any of this resonates with you it means you have also shut down your HARA and your sexual energy, as well as your creative power to manifest.

There are many energetic functions to our HARA. It's not a physical body organ like the HEAD or HEART, and energetically does not function in the same way. Our HARA is about creativity, manifesting, grounded strength and power. Of all of these 3 energy centres, this is the most mystical, in that this energy has the power to create MATTER from NOTHING. This energy centre contains the information which has been passed down through the generations. It contains our life force energy, which develops our physical body throughout this lifetime.

IN REVERSAL

You are disconnected from life. You feel no drive or you are always exhausted. Everything feels like a struggle. You could experience chronic health issues with the womb, vagina, penis, prostate, bowels, kidneys, bladder, legs and anything from the belly button down. You may also notice signs of dementia and issues with memory loss in the elderly. The HARA is also related to issues with physical growth, development, and learning difficulties. Emotionally, you may experience depression and anxiety. You may feel withdrawn and unable to connect with yourself or other people. It may be that you are battling with family or hereditary patterns on a physical, mental, and emotional level. You will see repeating patterns of behaviour in your family.

IN RESISTANCE

You disconnect from your inner power. Life feels 'hard'. It is difficult to manifest and instead feels like more 'work'. Physically, there would be acute health issues with the womb, vagina, penis, prostate, bowels, kidneys, bladder, legs, and anything from the belly button down. Your level of arousal would be low. You would often feel exhausted no matter what you eat or how much sleep you get.

You may notice this especially after childbirth, when the HARA energy can significantly deplete our energy. This may be one of the biggest reasons so many mothers change emotionally after birth. They are not aware of the energetic impact of giving birth (especially if they have had a Caesarean section or extremely difficult labour and delivery). You will be withdrawn from people and especially partners or lovers. You may make love with hesitancy or do it because you feel you should yet remain distanced from the act.

IN FLOW

Your HARA is able to manifest and you can create magic. What you think, feel or ask for will manifest at amazing speed. You will feel driven and motivated by a force deep inside you. This is the source of our YIN in the body and its reserves must be maintained. Your body will produce more love hormones such as oxytocin and serotonin. For women, you will experience powerful orgasms and create a strong pelvic floor. Men will have increased strength and stamina when making love and be able to withhold ejaculation.

Emotionally, you experience love, feel turned on, or be in a state of arousal and are attracted to the world around you and people. You are also 'attractive' to others and they are drawn to you.

Aligning Your Hara

MELANIE COOPER, AGE 42

There is a history of abuse in my family. My grandmother's family were African-American slaves. My Granny was pretty much an orphan from the age of 5. As a mother, she was neglectful, violent, and controlling. My mum passed on these patterns of violence and neglect to me in her own belittling and unloving way, and at times I even genuinely believed she was trying to kill me. As a teen, an adult woman came into my life who filled those spaces, and before long she began sexually abusing me. I then married a stranger. He was very abusive, rejected me sexually and soon after I had a breakdown. Since then I've been treated medically for severe PTSD and other mental health issues. I've done Cognitive Behavioral Therapy, Neuro-Linguistc Programming, acupuncture, homeopathy, vision therapy, shiatsu, a TON of counselling, and everything else under the sun. I'm now happily married, have two young sons, and I have a PhD., but I still didn't enjoy sex. It didn't give me flashbacks any more, or traumatise me, but I didn't like it.

Since starting EAM, I have found the missing piece of the puzzle. I found 1,250,000 RESISTANCES in my sexual energy, and working in small batches began clearing them all. When I cleared the last one and I spontaneously orgasmed out of nowhere! I ran upstairs and for the first time in 9 years I initiated sex with my husband and it was amazing! After years of trying, we also have our long awaited baby number three on the way. We couldn't be happier!

The power of sex is phenomenal. The power of orgasm isn't the only way to get in FLOW but it definitely helps! As you read in Melanie's story, you can have great success working on your own with EAM. However, unless you have previously done the work on releasing some of the trauma and drama, you may wish to seek guidance from an EAM coach or mentor. Not because it is bad or you may not be able to do it, but because past trauma can be complex and it can be more powerful to have someone knowledgeable in the field guide you and create quicker shifts.

You now have an understanding of these three key energy centres. When they are all in alignment your structure is strong, your yin and yang energy can FLOW and you are fully supported to start expanding yourself in all directions in your life. In Chapter 3, I'll introduce you to EAM and the Sway, a powerful technique that will show you HOW to bring these energy centres into alignment.

YOUR AURA FORM & FUNCTION

Our aura is our electromagnetic field generated primarily by our HEART and influenced by our HEAD and HARA. The heart energy can be scientifically measured up to 20ft away from our physical bodies. This field is made up of energetic layers, and each of these interact with our physical body and the world around us. Have you ever experienced when someone walks into the room behind you and you can sense them without seeing or hearing them? Or have you met someone and had an instant like or dislike before you've even spoken to them? It's because you are picking up on the energy in their aura. If you could see it our aura might look like a Russian nesting doll, with different layers one outside the other, each layer corresponding to various aspects of our lives. These layers and energies are always changing. If you cannot yet see your energy or aura, then you can always have your photo taken with a Kirlian photograph. Kirlian is a method of photography which is able to show an image of the electricity when a high voltage source is placed on a photographic plate.

Our aura is also a recording device. Every thought, word, feeling, action, memory (good or bad) has been stored in our energy somewhere. Energetically, this is where we hold our conscious and subconscious information, it's a log book. If you picture your aura it is like an expanded 3d version of our entire life experience, which we carry with us all the time like a library of information all around us. Your aura is a two-way communication system; it both transmits energy from us into the outside world and receives and processes the information that comes back. If our HEAD, HEART, and HARA are the power producing broadcast stations, imagine your aura is the radio producer deciding what messages get aired and sent into the world or are filtered out.

Our AURA is forever changing; it is expanding or contracting depending on what is happening in our lives. It is the largest of our energetic structures and when you understand how it works you can choose to deliberately work with it to change your life. Everything we experience in our daily lives is an outcome of what is already in our energy; of what is sent from and communicated to us, all of which are filtered through what exists in the different layers of our aura. Whilst you hold RESISTANT or REVERSED beliefs or patterns, you will continue recreating the same patterns and experiences in your life until you shift them energetically which you can do with EAM.

Your Aura Structure When in Flow

Science has shown that our HEART sends information to the brain before it sends signals to the rest of the body. The information it is reading is the energy imprints and information held in your aura. This means that our previous experiences held in our energy influence every moment of our lives even though you are not in that situation. Our stress levels, our physiology, what we are thinking, what we're feeling, is all coming from what is held in our aura. Until we change it energetically it will remain the same. Seriously underline that bit. It may be one of the most important sentences in the book. Now that you know just THIS one thing you have the potential to change your life because you can change your energy with EAM.

HOW DOES YOUR AURA WORK

Remember, everything is energy. It cannot be destroyed, only transformed. Everything that you have experienced in your life is energetically recorded in your energy. Every word, thought, emotion, memory creates an energy imprint and these are what create the RESISTANCE or REVERSALS or in

FLOW energy. The imprints are stored in at least one layer of your energy. This is why therapies or practices which only work on one aspect of our energy, for example the mindset, may only create limited shifts. This is because you may still be holding something on an energetic or emotional level. Whilst it is there your energy is still in RESISTANCE. You are waiting for the shift. One of the beauties of EAM is that it works on all levels of your energy at once.

We talked about these filters that our brain uses to process information, deleting, distorting, generalising. You may have heard the term, 'We see the world through our lenses?' It is these energy imprints that are held in our AURA, which create the filters we use to process, delete or distort information on a conscious and subconscious level. These imprints shape every day of your life. Until you choose to recognise, shift, or change them, your life will stay the same. By changing what you hold in the layers of your energy, YOUR LIFE WILL CHANGE. It is inevitable. You only need to do the energy work.

Past experiences influence every moment of our life, until you change them in your energy.

IN REVERSAL

Your interpretation of events and energy imprints recorded in your aura will also become connected to the reversed energy. When the REVERSAL is created, or imprinted, it acts like an energy drain, a hole, or a counter current FLOW of energy in your AURA. The imprint will stay this way until you do something to work on the counter FLOW of energy.

When in REVERSAL, each layer of your aura can not only contract but also collapse, depending on the severity of the REVERSAL. In extreme cases like PTSD, many levels of the AURA may have collapsed into one another. Energetically, this why flashbacks can seem so real and take someone back to that situation in any moment because they are so close to their experience of life right now.

IN RESISTANCE

When you are in RESISTANCE your 'recording' of the energy imprint, which is stored in your energy, may not be the truth of what happened. It will have been influenced by the resistant energy and therefore distorted the real information. So, what is recorded in your AURA is based on YOUR experience of the situation. When you are in RESISTANCE and you're tired, exhausted or run down, your AURA and energy contract. This is often when people get ill because they have been stressed out, aka resistant. Their energy contracts and it is easier for them to be infected by coughs, colds, and other people's energy.

In RESISTANCE, the transmission of information through your AURA is not as clear. You will send mixed messages as it is affected by what is held in your energy. You will also find it harder to manifest things. Your filters are limiting. You are using the energy imprints from your past beliefs, thoughts, emotions, memories, and experiences to dictate your present- day life experience.

When your AURA is in RESISTANCE, or in REVERSAL, you will notice that you feel tired or drained when you are in a group of other people. Or you easily pick up other people's energy, thoughts or emotions. This is often because your AURA has shrunk and your energy is easily influenced.

IN FLOW

In FLOW, your aura expands like a balloon and each layer of your aura expands as you release RESISTANCE. As you continue to do this work, your aura naturally becomes bigger and stronger, and the energy frequency raises to those higher vibrational energies. You become a stronger transmitter of information and more aware of what you are transmitting (which is often an emotion and/or a thought). When in this state nothing can affect you energetically, emotionally, or mentally.

When you have the right beliefs and emotions to support you and you release the resistant filters, you will have more positive outcomes in life. Your neural pathways will be rewired to look for the more positive. When we do Step 5 of EAM MANIFEST, which you will learn about in the next chapter, we are literally creating NEW energy imprints and filters, which are held in your aura. We then use these to change our energy and therefore our life experience.

HOW IS OUR AURA STRUCTURED?

Each layer of our aura vibrates at a particular energy frequency. The further away from the physical body, the higher the vibration. This is why we don't experience the outer ones in our day-to-day life because most people do not operate at those frequencies like alpha and theta waves without first getting into a meditative or aligned state.

The first few levels are our earthly energy bodies and they are the ones that interact with us on a day-by-day basis. They are physical, etheric, emotional, and mental energy bodies. These are the ones we need to connect with and experience all the time. Outside of them, we have different energy levels that relate to our past lives — for those of you who believe in past lives, karma, our spirit lives and our connection to the rest of the planet, the rest of the electron field, and the rest of the universe.

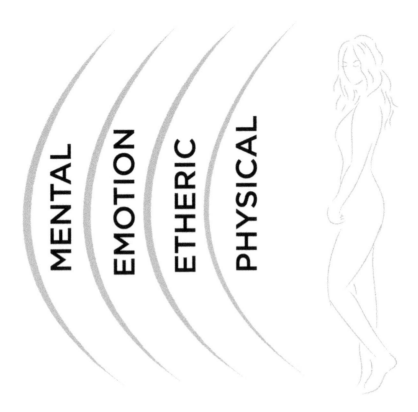

First 4 Earthly Layers of Your Aura

The first four layers of our aura are the ones which we interact with on a daily basis. These are the parts which we define as us.

PHYSICAL BODY

Our physical body is the part of our aura we can see and feel and experience easily. It is what we perceive as who we are. It is made up of our physical body, bones, organs, blood, nervous system, tissues, and cells. It is the slowest vibrating part of our energy. The healthier your physical body is, the quicker and easier your manifestation occurs.

ETHERIC BODY

Our etheric body is the next layer out. It is a representation of what is happening energetically in and around your physical body and can be measured usually 0 — 4 inches away from the body. Energetically you will often feel RESISTANCE here first, which is what we experience as symptoms before they become chronic physical conditions.

EMOTIONAL BODY

The next layer out is our emotions. It holds our emotions, imprints of past emotional experiences, as well as shocks and traumas. If this layer is vibrating feelings of fear and powerlessness it brings our energy down and therefore this layer contracts and makes it almost impossible to feel positive emotions. Conversely, if we are experiencing happiness this layer expands and so does the rest of our energy.

MENTAL BODY

The mental layer of the aura is where we hold our beliefs, thoughts, patterns, and memories. This layer is very much connected to the conscious (and unconscious) mind. It evolves as we grow, keeping a record of all past experiences. You don't 'feel' your thoughts in your physical body and that's because they are a higher vibration frequency.

The outer three layers of the aura are known as heavenly energy layers. These represent the more spiritual aspects of our lives.

ASTRAL BODY

Believed to be part of our past or other life experiences, our lower astral and upper astral levels hold our energy experiences, life lessons or 'karma'. The lower astral contains the messages of things which are actively being played out or need to be learnt in this life, and our upper astral is the record of those previous life experiences.

CELESTIAL BODY

The celestial level is a higher frequency and is said to be where your spirit guides are. If you believe in angels, gods, other ascended masters and teachers, or other non-physical beings, they vibrate at this frequency. This is often why people need to meditate and get themselves into a vibrationally receptive state in order to hear their messages. The more in FLOW you are, the more easily you hear and receive these messages.

DIVINE BODY

This divine level is about our connection to everything else — mass consciousness, the planet and the wider universe. This is where our energy merges into the connection with everything; it is the point of our energy where we reconnect as one.

It is important to understand that each level of your aura also has a set of chakras, median line (which is like a spine in our energy structure that runs from head to toe), and meridians on each level of our energy. When we meditate, our consciousness leaves our physical layer of our Aura and we travel off to explore these higher frequency levels of our energy like the astral, celestial and divine levels.

Imagine there is a boundary at which our 'human' experience ends. This is not a level of the aura but an energy layer created by a particular type of qi known as Wei qi. This is where our earthly bodies end and the point at which science is able to measurably discuss our aura. Outside of these philosophies and experience of working with energy there are another three layers, which connect more to our spiritual selves.

Energetically our aura acts like the membrane of the cells within the body. Imagine every energy flow, thought, belief, pattern or emotion is opening and closing gateways in our energy field. The information we hold in our aura creates our perception of our environment through these gateways. This is what creates our experience of life.

As you begin this journey, focus on working on your earthly bodies in your AURA. As you do, these others will naturally start to come into play. What is wonderful is that everything is imprinted in your aura. Using EAM you will be able to identify RESISTANCES and release REVERSALS within them, and in doing so, get yourself in FLOW.

CHAKRAS FORM & FUNCTION

Chakra is a Sanskrit word meaning 'wheel'. It is used to describe any number of energy centres in our physical and energetic bodies. Whilst these are not from Chinese medicinal philosophy, traditionally these are prominent in practices based in Hinduism and Buddhism, like yoga, meditation, and Ayurvedic medicine. It's important to include them here because they have meaning in the work we do with EAM. The chakras are energetic points, which connect to our physical and energetic bodies, so they can connect and interact with one another. There are believed to be 88,000 chakras within our body. Most people know about seven of them, which are often what is referred to. They help maintain the aura's physical structure, and act as a powerhouse as well as a communication system.

THE IMPORTANCE OF CHAKRAS

Chakras form part of the core of who we are. They are correlated to the different levels of our aura and our physical, emotional, and mental well-being. Their basic structures are there from in the womb as your nervous and endocrine systems grow. Once we are born these develop in cycles, seven years for girls and eight years for boys. You've probably heard the phrase 'men never seem to grow up' or 'girls mature faster than boys'. That is because every seven years women take a leap in the development of their energy one year ahead of men. So, by the time a woman is 28 she is energetically four years ahead of her male counterpart. This is also often why women are attracted to older men.

As we grow, our life experiences are essentially stored in these chakras as well as in our Aura. Different layers of our Aura align to different elements in our chakras, as we start to embody the life lessons and experiences connected with each of them. If we have issues or events, which create RESISTANCES or REVERSALS, they affect the chakras and all associated connections at that developmental stage. Until we resolve them we will see the issues reflected throughout our lives.

HOW OUR CHAKRAS WORK

Each chakra spins in a clockwise or counterclockwise direction. In doing this, they help to cycle energy up and around our physical and energetic bodies. Imagine they are like energy pumps or valves pushing the qi in the physical body and aura. The chakras in our physical body are denser than the Aura but not as dense as a physical body. They interact with the endocrine system and the nervous system. Each chakra is associated with an endocrine gland and with a group of nerves called a plexus. Therefore, each chakra can be associated with particular parts of the body, the functions controlled by the nerves and the endocrine systems.

All of your senses, perceptions and possible states of awareness can be divided into these seven categories. Therefore, chakras can represent particular parts of your physical body and your consciousness and connect to different levels of your aura. When you have RESISTANCE in your energy, you will also see a change in the associated chakra. Where you feel the RESISTANCE will depends upon why you feel the RESISTANCE.

It is through this association between our aura, chakras, and our physical nervous system that any RESISTANCE or REVERSALS in our energy can be detected by the nerves in our physical body, which is how we 'feel' our emotions or sense the RESISTANCE in our energy when we focus on certain subjects. Our nervous system reads our energy and transmits it into a sensation in the body. The information is then transmitted to the parts of the body controlled by that nerve plexus. If the RESISTANCE continues over a period of time, or there is a particular level of intensity, we can create a symptom in the physical body either acute or chronic.

The symptoms themselves often metaphorically show us what's going on mentally and emotionally, which gives us an insight into what may be happening in our energy. For example, if someone has an issue with their eyes it might be that they're keeping themselves from seeing something. If they have an issue with the legs it may be about being able to move forward. In energy medicine, we understand the symptoms are there to communicate to the person through their physical body as a last resort. Often because they were ignoring the signs and symptoms, which were there on an energetic, emotional, or mental level before. We will talk more about this in Chapter 5.

When we are in FLOW, our chakras are open, more energy is cycled to the relevant layer of our aura bodies and we expand, which means we experience greater health. The more shut down or smaller the chakra (due to RESISTANCE or REVERSAL), the more issues we'll have with different areas of our energy and physical correlations, and that level of the aura will also shrink. If you feel any pain in your chakras, it's usually because those chakras are stuck with resistant energy or shut down and they are trying to open up. You can use EAM to help you release the resistant pain with Step 4 TRANSFORM and open up the chakras to create more FLOW in the right direction using Step 5 MANIFEST.

HOW OUR CHAKRAS ARE STRUCTURED

Our chakras have a powerful energy, which seems to project out from the front and back of the body. Our chakras also form part of the structural makeup of each layer of our aura. We have a set of chakras on each level, which help to maintain the FLOW of qi in all of the associated energy structures. For example, you have a sacral chakra on each level of your aura. Because they are all interconnected by releasing the RESISTANCE at one level you will also release this on other levels of the energy body where any RESISTANCE or REVERSALS have occurred. The main 7 chakras follow the structure of our spine.

THE CROWN CHAKRA

This is the seventh chakra and represents our connection to our higher selves, higher consciousness, and connection to our divine energy levels.

THE THIRD EYE

This is the sixth chakra and it is connected to our ability to be clairvoyant, our sensitivities to energy, and our intellect and perception of life. It represents our ability to connect to vision or intuition, and foresight into the future. As your third eye opens it enables you to see greater possibilities for yourself and others.

THE THROAT CHAKRA

This is the fifth chakra and represents our ability to speak and clearly communicate our heart's truth. Speaking our truth from a place of love is like bathing the world in a healing vibration.

THE HEART CHAKRA

This is the fourth chakra and is described as the bridge between a higher energy centres and our connection to our earthlier chakras. This chakra is where yin and yang meet and where your soul is located in its physical form. Our heart energy is distinctly connected to our emotions. Our heart represents love for ourselves and others; it is our heart which enables us to connect and governs our relationships. This chakra is all about Unconditional Love, which is stored in the heart.

THE SOLAR PLEXUS

This is the third chakra and is known to be a powerhouse and represents our self-esteem, willpower, and personal responsibility here on Earth. It is one of the 3 earthly chakras. Very often this chakra is associated with our mental energy, beliefs, and thoughts and is about our ability to receive. This chakra enables us to ground, centralise, and radiate energy like the sun.

THE SACRAL CHAKRA

This is the second chakra and is often associated with the healing, creating, and sexual energies. It is a generating life force and the basis of our physical vitality. This chakra grounds our energy to the earth. The expression is pure Power in taking the right action and it's like the warrior power; strong yet humble, and flexible in our energy.

THE BASE CHAKRA

This is the first chakra we develop and it provides the foundation on which we build the rest of our life. The development of this is our connection to safety, security, and stability. This chakra represents the most material aspects of ourselves. It is connected to sexuality, self-identity, and our purely physical bodies.

The Seven Main Chakra Locations

ENERGY	AGE	LOCATION	COLOUR	GLANDS	EMOTIONS	PHYSICAL
CROWN Aura Level: Divine	48–49 Female 48–56 Male	Top of head	White	Anterior pituitary gland, cerebral cortex, cerebrum	In FLOW Connect to wider world, Wisdom, Intelligence RESISTANCE close-minded, disconnected from spirit, not care about wider world or humanity	Chronic fatigue, neurological disorders or migraines.
BROW Aura Level: Celestial	35–42 Female 40–48 Male	Centre of forehead between eyebrows	Purple	Pineal gland & cerebellum	In FLOW A clear direction in moving forward, Driven by openness, Imagination RESISTANCE Lack of direction and clarity, Unable to use vision or visualisation techniques	Conditions associated with eye, ears, headaches in the frontal cortex and sinuses.
THROAT Aura Level: Upper astral	28–35 Female 32–40 Male	Centre of neck	Blue	Thyroid and parathyroid glands	In FLOW People are able to clearly express themselves their voice, their message and speak the truth with love. RESISTANCE Shy, have issues communicating. May speak from a place of blame or fear, or be withdrawn, arrogant, or be unable to speak up for themselves.	Throat, tongue, teeth & mouth

Chakra / Aura Level	Age	Location	Colour	Gland / Organ	State	Conditions
HEART / Aura Level: Astral	21–28 Female / 24–32 Male	Centre of chest	Green	Adrenal cortex, thyroid and anterior pituitary glands Controls hormones in the entire doctrine system	In FLOW Open, expressive, loving, Love for ourselves and others RESISTANCE Depression, difficulty in connecting with relationships, Lack of self– discipline & self– love	Heart conditions, palpitations or high blood pressure
SOLAR PLEXUS / Aura Level: Mental	14–21 Female / 16–24 Male	Below the chest in between belly button	Yellow	Controls our physical and intestinal nervous system and all endocrine functions associated with our gut and pancreas	In FLOW Confident, Calm, Centred, High self-esteem, Inner strength to keep moving forward. RESISTANCE Imbalanced, Low self-esteem, Low confidence	Digestive health and abdominal conditions
SACRAL (HARA) / Aura Level: Emotional	7–14 Female / 8–16 Male	Below the naval	Orange	Adrenal glands, specifically adrenal medulla	In FLOW Confident in sexual power, Manifest with ease RESISTANCE Repressed creativity, Sexual dysfunctions, Withhold intimacy, Emotionally distant; Isolated from others; Issues connecting with and distrusting people	Reproductive issues, genital conditions, lower back pain and gynaecological
BASE / Aura Level: Etheric	0–7 Female / 0–8 Male	Base of the spine between our legs in the space between the genitals and anus	Red		In FLOW Grounded, Connected to power, Feel safe & secure in life, Untold inner strength RESISTANCE Often feel scattered, Unable to complete anything, Anxious, May live life from place of fear	Constipation, anaemia or bladder conditions

MERIDIANS FORM & FUNCTION

Scientists at Seoul National University recently confirmed the existence of meridians, a system that is a crucial part of the cardiovascular system. They found that new tubular structures exist inside and outside of blood vessels and lymphatic vessels, as well as on the surface of internal organs and under the skin. The researchers discovered that the meridian lines are not confined to the skin and are in fact a concrete duct system through which liquid FLOWs throughout the body.

If you're familiar with any spiritual concepts you may have heard about meridians. Imagine our meridians are like the energy equivalent of veins and arteries within the body. The major meridians allow qi to travel up and down our entire body system. Meridians connect our major organs inside the body and are supported by smaller meridians named nadis which act like capillaries MOVING energy everywhere in our body. There are various hotspots or points where meridians are — at or near the surface — that are known as acupuncture or acupressure points where the energy can be directly accessed. Many different complementary therapies work on meridians in a variety of ways. Some of these therapies include acupuncture, acupressure, massage, reflexology, kinesiology, EFT tapping, and a host of other practices.

SACRED CHANNELS

In Chinese philosophy, your meridians are like energetic receivers of information. These channels contain the energy FLOW of different types of qi. They FLOW the energy of YIN and YANG energy from heaven and earth through the body so it can be expressed in many ways. It is this FLOW of energy through us that creates our health and illness. These channels come into and out of the body primarily through the tips of the fingers and toes.

Each meridian has its own channel and associated organs within the physical body. It is also connected to different mental and emotional influences as well as functions on a psychological and physiological level. Each meridian relates to one of the five Chinese elements, wood, fire, earth, metal and water. For each element, there is an associated yin and yang organ and meridian in the body. It is these meridians that allow the communication between our external world and our internal organs. In addition to our chakras our meridians also enable the energetic communication of information from our aura into our physical body. These channels allow communication between all areas of the body; they create a harmonious circulation promoting of qi, which enables us to grow and protect ourselves throughout our lives.

HOW DO THEY WORK?

Our meridians are like tendrils of energy, reaching out from our physical body beyond our hands and feet, and reading information in our aura. Research has shown that electromagnetic energy does in fact loop at the end of each of our fingers and toes and back into the body. These correspond to the acupuncture points and FLOW of energy through the body's circadian rhythms and energy clock.

HOW ARE THEY STRUCTURED?

In Chinese medicine, when we think about the structure and FLOW of energy you often see a picture of a person standing with their hands in the air above their head and their feet wide apart. As you get to know the 5 Steps of EAM, you will recognise this as Step 5 MANIFEST, which enables the free FLOW of energy through our body and facilitates this connection.

Yates and Anderson (2003) believe that we also have eight extraordinary meridians. At the point of conception, it's believed that our three primary extraordinary meridians known as the Ren or Conception vessel, Du or Governing vessel, and Dai Mai or Girdle vessel are the first meridians to be created. They are present as part of the ectoderm, endoderm and mesoderm layers of developing cells in the womb. As a baby is conceived and the fertilised egg begins to split research has been shown that an energetic division takes place. These create the first of the eight extraordinary meridians. The first cell division produces the bilateral symmetry axis, which divides our yin and yang creating the Ren and Du channels detailed below. The second cell division produces the horizontal axis of the embryo; this is energetically known as the Dai Mai or the Girdle vessel. This is the only horizontal qi FLOW in the body.

You now have a much clearer picture of the different structures that make up our energy fields and how they are connected. With this understanding you will now be able to use EAM to release RESISTANCE in any of these energy structures so that you can transform the energy from a place of feeling stuck to a free FLOW of qi. Remember, you don't need to know or understand any of these correlations for EAM to work, but they may help you when using the 5 Steps to uncover new places to explore or to understand why energy is moving through your body in a particular way, or why energy may have become stuck in particular locations.

ENERGY IN ALL FORMS

Earlier we discussed Qi and that everything is energy. We've explored the flow of energy in the three energy states and how our energetic bodies are structured. It is also helpful to understand the energetic influence of our thoughts, emotions, breath and our voice.

YOUR ENERGETIC THOUGHTS

Our thoughts are also very powerful waves of energy (remember our HEAD is one of our electromagnetic communicators). You may have heard 'Your thoughts create your reality', 'You get what you think about', 'You become the thoughts you think the most'. All of them are true (when tied up with the emotions that match them, but we'll talk about that in a minute).

Our thoughts work in the same way as all other electrons, flowing in cycles, creating an electrical charge, gathering more things of a like nature together through their magnetism. As they gather, they gain more momentum. The more thoughts and focus you have about a subject the more momentum it gathers, and the more manifest it becomes. These rules apply to all of us. Whether you're thinking positive or resistant thoughts, the same things apply. If you want to perpetuate the story of what IS going on in your life right now, keep on doing what you're doing, think the same thoughts and say the same things! Things will stay the same ... nothing will change. Momentum and the Law of Attraction will bring those same vibrations back to you.

Likewise, if you want to change what is happening right now and grow into this more expanded, positive happy version of you (which I guess is why you're here), it has to begin with changing your Energy and recognising that our thoughts are powered by our emotions.

That's an important distinction.

HOW THEY WORK

Every time you THINK you send out a wave of energy. These waves influence our emotions and resonate throughout our energy bodies. Every thought you've ever thought is stored in your AURA on a mental level; some of these thoughts serve you and some do not. Whilst science can only measure our brain waves at a short distance, many studies have shown that thought form can also travel across distances and affect cells, people, or situations in physically distant spaces.

Once our energetic thoughts travel out beyond the boundary of our aura, they become part of the mass consciousness. In the same way, we can read the information in our environment, we also pick up on the energy of mass consciousness, whether it is in regard to a group of people in a room, a town, or country, or perhaps the whole planet. It's this same phenomenon in nature, which creates a spread of panic and causes a group of animals to stampede when there is a lion. Or which allows thousands of people at a concert to feel connected and become united as one. You are tapping into that energy of mass consciousness every day. By consciously transforming our own thoughts to reach a higher vibration, we are also changing mass consciousness and therefore changing the world.

Thoughts have three flows of energy. A REVERSED thought is known as a limiting belief; a RESISTANT thought is known as a negative belief and an in FLOW thought is known as a positive belief.

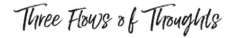

Three Flows of Thoughts

Limiting Belief   **Negative**   **Positive**

EAM Three Flows of Energy in Thought Form

With EAM you can change the thoughts that don't serve you, which means that you can change your reality! Deep right. Your thoughts are also part of your energy. They influence your life experience AND the wider world, so be aware of your thoughts.

YOUR ENERGETIC EMOTIONS

We talked about your emotions in Chapter 1. Physiologically, our emotions are created by our heart, brain, hormones, and nervous system. Here we will discuss them in the context of your energy.

We remember more about how we *felt* in a situation than we do the thoughts we *think*. So, what you experience emotionally has a lasting impact on your experience of life. Our emotions are also our MAIN guidance system as we start working through this journey. Your emotions ARE your best friend guiding you every day, use them as your signal to see if you are in FLOW or in RESISTANCE or REVERSAL. They affect your physical body and your health; your cells are listening to how you feel and your vitality will respond accordingly. Like thoughts, your emotions send information out into your immediate environment (which by the way other people can read. We're not that good at hiding our mood!). They also contribute to the mass or group consciousness and emotional state of people in your home or at work.

Our heart energy is 5000x stronger than our mind, so what you feel has a greater impact on our experience.

When you think about the three flows of energy on an emotional level, FEAR is REVERSED — all other emotions are various degrees of RESISTANCE with love being the most in FLOW.

Three Flows of Emotions

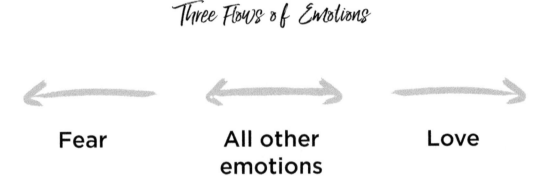

Fear **All other emotions** **Love**

EAM Three Flows of Energy as Emotions

HOW TO WORK WITH YOUR EMOTIONS

The quickest and easiest way to start consciously working with your FLOW state is to pay attention to how you feel, and your emotions and physiological experiences. Once you understand EAM, using Step 4 TRANSFORM you'll be able to use it to shift the resistant or reversed emotions, and change emotional set points in the brain and your energy. We then create new emotional associations in the brain and our energy to create a new emotion or experience with Step 5 MANIFEST.

Within EAM we have developed our own energetic model of the emotions.

EMOTIONAL SCALE

Energetic

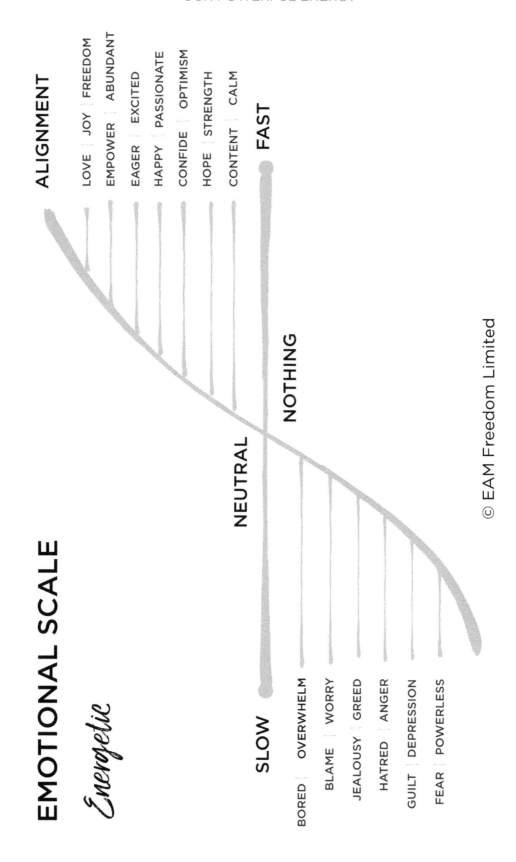

ALIGNMENT

LOVE | JOY | FREEDOM
EMPOWER | ABUNDANT
EAGER | EXCITED
HAPPY | PASSIONATE
CONFIDE | OPTIMISM
HOPE | STRENGTH
CONTENT | CALM

FAST

NOTHING

NEUTRAL

SLOW

BORED | OVERWHELM
BLAME | WORRY
JEALOUSY | GREED
HATRED | ANGER
GUILT | DEPRESSION
FEAR | POWERLESS

© EAM Freedom Limited

129

At the bottom of the emotional scale is FEAR, the lowest vibrational emotion. FEAR is debilitating; it can literally stop us in our tracks. At the highest point on the scale is the emotion of LOVE. All other emotions are somewhere on the vibrational frequency between the two. LOVE is the most in FLOW state you can be in. When you apply this emotional scale to any subject, you can only FEEL one emotion at a time. You can't be in LOVE and FEAR at the same time, but you can have more than one emotion about the same subject and different aspects of the same situation.

Your emotions are not just random things that happen to you. Each of our emotions has its own energetic vibration — its own frequency, which is sent out from your energy.

There are TWO things to know about your emotions. There is a VIBRATION and an INTENSITY — THEY ARE *NOT* THE SAME!

Our VIBRATION is like the quality of the emotion; some are a low vibration such as feelings of fear and depression. Some are high vibration such as love, freedom, and abundance.

INTENSITY — You can see at each end that the strength of these emotions is higher and therefore more intense. Towards the middle you see there is less energy and therefore less intensity.

The emotional scale goes from contracted feelings on the left to feelings of expansion over on the right. This is based on the Yin Yang cycle and FLOW of emotions, which we discussed earlier in the chapter. FEAR (deepest YIN) to LOVE (highest point of YANG). In order to manifest or live a life of happiness we want to live our lives above this point of neutral — which means we are spending time in feelings of calm, contentment, happiness, passion, love, and joy. These emotions tell you that you are in FLOW. The closer to the neutral line means there may still be some RESISTANCE in comparison to the emotions of LOVE.

We can have patterns of RESISTANCE even to experiencing love or happiness. Remember as a child how many times you were told to sit down or be quiet when you were happy or having fun? This can create RESISTANCE in our energy even to feeling happy!

If you're spending your time feeling irritation and frustration, you cannot manifest the life you want to live. You'll create more of the same. Have you ever noticed those people who no matter what they do seem to move from one drama or calamity to another? This is because they are vibrating those emotions of fear, anger, or feeling overwhelmed. They are probably talking to their friends and family, and anyone who will listen about why life is so unfair or what this person has done to them. All it would take is a simple shift of their energy to stop the drama. But most people don't do that! (For reasons we will explore more in Chapter 4 and beyond.)

Think about the strength of the emotions. STRENGTH = momentum. The strength relates to speed so the higher the intensity of your emotions that you feel every day, the quicker things will manifest for you. This is awesome when you feel love and freedom, and awful when you feel fear and powerless, because more of it will keep coming at you and quickly because the strength and momentum of that energy is so intense.

You will use this emotional scale a lot to work with EAM. By understanding which emotions, you are experiencing, you can choose to release the resistant or reversed energy and align yourself with Step 5 to MANIFEST the new emotion you want. Our overall aim and focus with EAM is to change our internal emotional set points. This retrains our energy on a mental and emotional level of our aura so that the information fed into the brain via our nervous system is something *we* would choose.

You can start by creating a habit of FEELING good; in fact, you should choose to make alignment your HIGHEST priority. The easiest way to do that is pay attention to what you feel and work your way UP this emotional scale. *You can do it on any subject, at any time.* This will make more sense in Chapter 3 once you know how to use EAM.

WHAT OUR RESEARCH SHOWS

Inside our online program, The Energy Experience, we conducted several research studies, one of which was to see if it was possible to shift your emotional set point by using EAM for seven days. You can specifically work through releasing the RESISTANCE to each of these emotions and allow yourself to get more in FLOW. The purpose of this is to change your neural pathways and the emotional set point you have in just seven days, and naturally begin to attract more positive things into your life.

The results of this have been EAMazing (yes I did just use my own cheesy pun there).

SIGNIFICANT REDUCTIONS IN FEELINGS OF OVERWHELM AND FRUSTRATION THROUGH COMPLETING THE ENERGY EXPERIENCE

EMOTIONS LAST 7 DAYS	BEFORE (878)	AFTER (297)	% DIFFERENCE	% DECREASE PEOPLE
POWERLESS	7%	3%	−4%	57% DECREASE
FEARFUL	7%	3%	−4%	57% DECREASE
GUILTY	1%	0%	−1%	99% DECREASE
ANGRY	2%	0%	−2%	99% DECREASE
JEALOUS	0%	0%	0%	
OVERWHELMED	27%	14%	−13%	48% DECREASE
FRUSTRATED	17%	9%	−8%	47% DECREASE

Research DATA SOURCE: EAM Research Study 2016

SIGNIFICANT IMPROVEMENTS IN FEELING HAPPY AND EMPOWERED THROUGH COMPLETING THE ENERGY EXPERIENCE

EMOTIONS LAST 7 DAYS	BEFORE (878)	AFTER (297)	% DIFFERENCE	% INCREASE IN PEOPLE
CONTENT	5%	9%	+4%	80% INCREASE
HOPEFUL	16%	21%	+5%	31.25% INCREASE
CONFIDENT	2%	5%	+3%	150% INCREASE
HAPPY	4%	11%	+7%	175% INCREASE
PASSIONATE	2%	2%	−	
EMPOWERED	4%	15%	+11%	275% INCREASE
ABUNDANT	1%	2%	+1%	100% INCREASE
FREE	1%	2%	+1%	100% INCREASE
LOVING	2%	3%	+1%	50% INCREASE

Research DATA SOURCE: EAM Research Study 2016

The results speak for themselves. At the beginning of our study more than 61% of people were living their lives every day in RESISTANCE! 61%! Bear in mind that most of those people are like you and I; they have an interest in changing themselves and their lives. Imagine what that is like for the general population who have never even touched a self-help book! The good news is that by the end of the study, more than 70% of people felt they were spending their days in the in flow emotions above the line like love, peace, and most significantly feeling empowered.

You can see the power of your emotions and how quickly following these steps can help you change your life with EAM. It is amazing what can happen when you harness the energy and choose to redirect it to the life YOU want to create. In Chapter 3, I'll show you how you can do that using EAM. Then in Chapter 4 and beyond we will start doing the work. If you want to find out more about The Energy Experience or more about our research studies, you can find out more here www.energyalignmentmethod.com/the-energy-experience

YOUR ALIGNMENT LEVEL

Collectively your alignment level is the overall frequency of the vibration of your energy, thoughts, beliefs, and emotions. All of them are energy expressed in different forms. By systematically working on releasing RESISTANCE and creating flow in all areas of your life, as we do in the Energy Evolution, you'll naturally raise your alignment level. This alignment level represents your ability to attract and therefore to change your life.

THE POTENTIAL OF YOUR BREATH

Your breath is one of the most, if not *the* most, important energy in your life.

Yet many of us have never learned how to breathe properly, or even pay attention to the way that we're breathing in each moment. Many spiritual practices include the power of breath work and EAM is no exception.

Your breath is vitality; it brings clean air and much-needed oxygen and yang energy into the body. Your out breath expels the resistant used energy that is no longer needed by your body. It's sent off out into our atmosphere to be transformed and recycled by the plants and trees.

In EAM we also use the power of our breath to release the RESISTANCE with STEP 4 TRANSFORM and also to breathe in and re-energise the body with the new choice, belief, thought, or affirmation with Step 5 MANIFEST.

YOUR POWERFUL VOICE

Your voice is an energy. Sound has energy and it can be carried across a room. In Chinese medicine your voice, your words, and your energy come from your heart. Your tongue is considered to be rooted in your heart. This means the words you share have power because they are energised by our heart, which is 5000 times more powerful than our brain or mind. The vibration of your voice and words carry far beyond your energy and contribute to mass consciousness.

When talking to others, your voice carries your energy more than the words that you say. Have you ever noticed that you might say one thing but somebody hears something completely different? That's because they receive the *energy* of your words, not the *words* themselves. So be mindful of your words, what you say, and the language you use. If you're angry, upset, or pissed off with someone, stop and think before you speak. Understand that when you make statements like, 'I wish you would get lost' the Law of Compensation suggests that what you give comes back to you 10 times over. So, if you speak ill, wish ill, or say spiteful words, do not be surprised if they come back to you tenfold.

The power of your voice also perpetuates drama as you give more energy to it. In the same way when you talk about what has happened before, you give more energy to the past. This will metaphorically 'hold you back' from moving your life forward. In this same way, you can use your voice to manifest the life you want. The more you voice the future the more powerful that vision and the energy of your manifestation will become.

THE IMPORTANCE OF YOUR VOICE IN EAM

Use your voice on purpose and become a deliberate and conscious speaker. Choose your words wisely and only give energy to the things you want to create. When you learn how to use EAM in Chapter 3, you'll use your words to ask the questions in Steps 1 ASK, 2 MOVE, and 3 EXPERIENCE to get clarity. By using your voice in Step 4 TRANSFORM, you'll experience a greater shift and release because the power of your voice will resonate through more of your energy field. When you use Step 5 MANIFEST, say the Step 5 affirmation out loud as often and as frequently as possible. You are retraining your brain, your energy, and your heart to send that powerful vibration of energy out into mass consciousness. This projects more power and energy to the future you want to create, voicing it out loud enables it to manifest more quickly.

The Universe is not

separate from us.

We are it.

It is us.

THE UNIVERSAL LAWS & PRINCIPLES

Many New Age practices talk about the Universal Laws. Yet they have been taught for thousands of years by different mystics and spiritual teachers. The Universal Laws have influenced everything in your life. They're not connected to any particular religion, they are simply laws, which apply to each of us. Imagine working against the law of gravity, that would be a sight!

THE IMPORTANCE OF THE LAWS

The same applies to these universal laws of nature. They work and operate silently in the background to maintain a state of harmony. They are not meant to take away free will. When you learn to work with them instead of pushing against them, you can connect to the energy and power that created and manages the entire universe. It is another way to allow your life to FLOW more easily.

- **THE LAW OF ONE (TAO).** The Law of Oneness taps back into the Chinese philosophy of the tao. This universal law is based on the principle that everything exists from the source of energy. A foundational piece of the EAM methodology.

- **THE LAW OF VIBRATION.** The most important of the universal laws is the Law of Vibration. The idea that everything in the universe is simply a vibration — everything is moving, nothing rests, it vibrates, and circles. Everything has a resonance and a vibrational frequency. This is the foundation of EAM.

- **THE LAW OF THE UNIVERSAL MIND.** This law embodies the truth that 'All is one Mind.' The universe is energetic, meaning it is consciousness and we play our part in that connected consciousness. We are all one and it is our mind, consciousness, thoughts, and energy that is the greatest communication between us all. This law suggests that when conscious attention is given to something we are able *to think things into existence*.

- **THE LAW OF ATTRACTION.** This law is based on the principle that like attracts like. Everything is a magnet attracting like energy back to it. We see this in nature with gravity. It is also working in your life. The more you have, the more will come to you. In the same way, as you think and feel more positive things — more will come. Likewise, if you focus on lack, fear, and negativity, more of that will come to you.

- **THE LAW OF CORRESPONDENCE.** The Law of Correspondence means there is a simple harmony and correlation between different areas of your life. What you see outside is a reflection of what is within. For example, if there is strife happening on a global level, such as a war, it creates fear in the world, which creates fear on a personal level. Think about the level of pollution on our planet and the correlation to the increase in illnesses. This is no coincidence. It is the Law of Correspondence.

- **THE LAW OF MOMENTUM.** The Law of Momentum is about the amount of energy or speed that something has. The greater the force and power, the faster the momentum of energy will become. This is also a physics concept and is reflected in many areas of our lives.

- **THE LAW OF POLARITY.** This law ties into the ancient philosophy of yin and yang. Sometimes known as the Law of Gender, it talks about the masculine and feminine in everything and describes the interconnection of the two — that both are a manifestation of the same thing. They are all energy but in different forms on a different vibrational level. There is an equal and opposite for everything.

- **THE LAW OF RHYTHM.** Everything has a FLOW and rhythm. We've already discussed the principle of rhythm and the importance of working with it. This universal law is about learning to ride the wave of the rhythm — the highs and lows — allowing it to carry you through your life.

- **THE LAW OF COMPENSATION.** This law often works hand in hand with the Law of Rhythm. It shows this movement between the two energies almost like a pendulum swinging in a clock. You can also think about this in terms of the energy. What you put out in the world should make a difference and not because you want to receive something back. This is the concept behind paying it forward. Whatever you give out 'good' vibes or 'bad' vibes, it will automatically and naturally come back to you.

- **THE LAW OF EVOLUTION.** This law applies to our world and the wider universe. Everything is always evolving, even the universe itself is in a constant state of self-expansion. Everything is instinctively and impulsively driven to grow and expand. That includes you and me on every level physically, mentally, emotionally, and spiritually. If we look at a human civilization, in many ways we have grown and expanded throughout our time here on Earth. In order for there to be evolution there must be a decline, a time to restructure or re-energise. From this collapse, there are always opportunities for evolution and hope we can create something new.

- **THE LAW OF CAUSE AND EFFECT**. This is also related to the The Law of Compensation, says that you are always rewarded in a LIKE manner for your energetic contribution. If you give out positive loving energy without expectation, you will receive back 10 times the amount of positive loving energy. If you are bitching, moaning, complaining, or deliberately doing things to make life difficult, you will receive 10 times the same.

- **THE LAW OF ACTION.** This law means you have to take action. For things to change, there must be some form of transformation. Most of the energy we see or interact with on a daily basis is a denser, heavier energy. Whilst our energy, thoughts, and emotions ARE powerful and do affect our lives, if you want to move things in physical form, to affect change in the world you must not only align your idea or vision, your thoughts, your emotions, your energy, but also take action.

PUT THE LAWS INTO ACTION

These universal laws apply to you and your life. What may be happening in your life is not the outcome of a vengeful god or bad karmic debt, but simply the result of the fact that you may not be living in FLOW with these laws. Like pushing against gravity, it is a pointless and energetically draining task. So, stop trying. Work with and adopt them into your life. They are the foundation of EAM and you'll see them woven into the 5 Steps of EAM and the journey that we go on to put all this into practice in your life.

PLACING COSMIC ORDERS

Maybe you're familiar with the Law of Attraction, maybe you've tried praying, wished on a star or just daydreamed about things you *really* want to do. In popular culture this can be known as cosmic ordering. My good friend Ellen Watts has written a fantastic book, *Cosmic Ordering Made Easier: How to Get More of You What You Want More Often*. In it she explains that placing an order, or asking the universe for what you want, isn't a passive process and there are many different components to it, one of which is to make sure your energy thoughts and emotions are in FLOW with what you're asking for.

Ellen explains that to prepare your cosmic order you should create your wish list and focus your language in the positive and not in the negative. She also suggests identifying beliefs that are standing in the way and making sure that you're working on letting them go. This is why I was so excited because we're on the same page and that is EXACTLY what we do with EAM. It is a brilliant book and a definite must read. EAM and Ellen's work go together perfectly. If you want to use EAM and do some deliberate cosmic ordering, I highly recommend you get a copy of Ellen's book.

In the next chapter, I'll show you how you can use EAM to place your cosmic order, or 'ask for the things you want' using Step 5 MANIFEST. I'll also teach you some powerful techniques to ramp up the energy of your deliberate manifesting.

CHAPTER 2 — WHAT TO REMEMBER

Everything is energy in one of 3 states: IN FLOW, IN RESISTANCE or in REVERSAL. To be in alignment, we must ensure that our 3 powerful energy centres HEAD, HEART and HARA are sending out the same congruent message. The flow state enables the circulation of Qi throughout all of our energy structures and therefore all the correlated areas of our life.

These universal laws apply to everything in your world. What you see in your reality and everything you experience inside, is all energy. Even that annoying boss, person, client, relationship, the fact that the car won't start or emails not arriving to your inbox — it is all just energy. Because everything is energy, we can reconnect to that energy and redirect it, which is what I want to share with you in the rest of this book.

The universe isn't separate from us. We are it. It is us. We are literally co-creating. It is a symbiotic relationship and a two-way interaction. You have the power to change it.

In Chapter 1 you learned the 'Science' and Chapter 2 I hope has filled some of the gaps in your understanding of how the science and the spirit work together in EAM. Now it's time to get started with EAM. Chapter 3 is where the fun begins and the magic happens. You're about to discover a life changing tool! Are you ready?

CHAPTER 3

The Energy Alignment Method

"When you remember it is all just energy.
You'll know once again you have the power to change it all."
~ Yvette Taylor

Hurray! We're finally here. It's time for the transformation to begin. In this chapter, we're going to discover the transformational 5 Steps to EAM. Understanding and using the 5 Steps will give you the tools you need to change ANYTHING in your life. Once you know this you have the power to change anything. Yes, really, *anything* because it is all just energy.

Sometimes in our search for happiness, peace, and contentment we will find any way to get there. We may turn to drugs, alcohol, too much TV, overeating or overspending. It could be any number of patterns or habits which in fact create more RESISTANCE. Using EAM you'll be able to take back your power and release those addictions or emotional crutches. You can have that *feeling* of FLOW anytime you want. You have the power to change your life.

WHAT IS EAM?

EAM — The Energy Alignment Method is founded in energy medicine, neuroscience research, the Law of Attraction and Traditional Chinese medicine. It includes elements of Kinesiology, NLP, Positive Psychology, and Eastern spiritual principles. EAM enables you to shift energy and let go of repetitive thoughts and overwhelming emotions. You can release physical or emotional pain, negative feelings, memories and traumatic experiences to be free from stress, feeling overwhelmed and anxiety. As you let go of what held you back, it is no longer held in your energy and your subconscious. Then you can choose to create and embody a new energy, thought, belief, pattern, emotion or experience that serves you.

We've all felt feel stuck, fearful and confused about the next steps in life. Perhaps you feel like life is passing you by or lost confidence or trust in yourself. Maybe, you want to get back on track, to feel passionate and purposeful again, or you feel you've yet to reach your full potential, and you want to know how to do that.

As you begin to tune in and master your own energy, with EAM you can instantly transform what you think and how you feel to change your life. You'll create more harmony in your relationships, find your purpose and passion, create self-belief and confidence, and experience more love, happiness, joy and freedom in your everyday life. The ultimate outcome for you with EAM is to change your energy and the way you think and feel so you can change your life.

UNDERSTANDING EAM

EAM has been described as the 'missing piece' to most self-help methods and books in our industry.

EAM IS

- A safe and powerful self-help technique, designed to find and release the energetic cause of stress and the feeling of being overwhelmed and out of FLOW.

- A powerful energy tool designed to shift your energy, thoughts, and emotions on every level so you can choose to create a state of FLOW.

- A Law of Attraction method, which specifically helps you change your energy and get in flow so you can ask for what you want and get it!

- Is designed to put you back in charge of your health. By working on the energy, thoughts and emotions first, you can prevent illnesses.

- An accredited methodology which you can train to use, learn to teach, and be able to share with others.

- A life coaching model. When you follow the steps outlined in this book and choose to work with us on the supported journeys you can change your life.

- A holistic healing therapy like Acupuncture, Reiki, or Reflexology, which can be used as a self-help technique or therapeutic practice with a mentor.

EAM IS *NOT*

- Only a mindset technique. Unlike some other practices, we work with energy. Our mindset is just one expression of who we are; by working on energy you work on it all.

- To be used as a 'quick' fix or manifesting technique. YES, it can be used for those things. YES, transformations are quick, but with EAM they are deep and lasting.

- A talk therapy or about trawling back through your past, your childhood and memories to place blame. We do not relive traumatic situations or even have to 'talk it out'.

- A predictive tool to foretell your future. It only enables you to tune in to what is in your energy and what you are in or out of alignment with.

- For diagnosing medical conditions. It does not replace, testing, interventions or advice from a qualified physician or another health care provider.

- Just a self-help technique. Rather, it is a way of life. Just learning it doesn't create the change. Using it daily, in every area of your life will.

WHY YOU NEED EAM IN YOUR LIFE

Simple. It works when you use it. If you want to see REAL life changes and not just 'quick fix' solutions, this is how. Like all things worth doing, it takes practice and dedication. With EAM we focus on the positive, what you want to have. Most other self-help techniques only release the negative thought or belief. Our focus is on aligning and replacing it with a new choice, experience or decision. You have the power to change your life. No one else is going to change your life for you. When you reclaim your power over what you think and feel, you shift your focus and energy and bring them into alignment. By using the 5 Steps of EAM in conjunction with the 10 Elements in the Energy Evolution journey outlined in this book, you will create real lasting changes in your life.

A LITTLE 'SCIENCE' OF HOW EAM WORKS

I am often asked 'what exactly does EAM do?' The simple answer is, it enables you to redirect energy. By knowing your energy, thoughts and emotions on any subject, you can assess and positively redirect it. Because EAM also works on many levels we can see the effects at different levels of our experience too.

ALLOWS MORE FLOW

EAM energetically creates new imprints and more FLOW into our aura, chakras, meridians and their associated functions. This enables us to become a vibrational match to those experiences.

CHANGES OUR ENERGETIC, MENTAL, AND EMOTIONAL SET POINTS

By creating new experiences in our energy, thoughts, and emotions and visualising with Step 5 MANIFEST, we create new neural pathways, rewiring the brain. These networks, or set points, become our new internal reference for everything we experience on an energetic, mental and emotional level.

CREATES NEW PATTERNS

Studies have shown with use of methods such as EAM, our brain literally rewires itself. We can unwire previous neural pathways, disassociating particular thoughts, memories and emotions with Step 4 TRANSFORM. We create new patterns on an energetic, mental and emotional level, with Step 5 MANIFEST.

We also create new patterns in our energy, different layers of our aura, and change the electromagnetic messages we send out. This change creates changes in our energy, our past, present and future experience too.

REPETITION CREATES NEW ASSOCIATIONS

With EAM we change our internal state, our heart wave sequence, and create positive physiological responses. Energetically, by repeating the Step 5 MANIFEST statement, we create new positive associations with the subject and gather momentum of energy.

SYNCHRONICITY BETWEEN HEART AND BRAIN

The state of FLOW has been shown to create better neurological communication between our heart, brain, and adrenals. This means your hormone levels, heart wave patterns, and stress levels are congruent. Energetically, this synchronized state is due to the prime meridian, which connects our HEAD, HEART, and HARA. When in FLOW, this is how we create positive emotions and thoughts and use our intuition. EAM works on a physiological, psychological and energetic level, to create a state of FLOW.

HOW EAM BENEFITS YOU

The purpose of EAM is to allow you to create FLOW in every level of your energy and to change anything which is RESISTANT or REVERSED in any area of your life. The overarching principle is to change your energetic, mental, and emotional set points. This allows you to create a new internal reference system. Collectively we call these set points your Alignment Level. By doing this you bring your HEAD, HEART and HARA into alignment.

So, what does this mean for you? It is all of the benefits we explored when we learnt about the state of FLOW among many things, you'll:

- create more positive emotions for longer periods of time

- reset everything in your energy

- naturally attract more

- have better mental & emotional bounce back

- become more adaptive to change

- be better able to deal with traumatic events

- power yourself through empowerment

- create more positive new experiences

- reduce adrenal and cortisol levels and create endorphins

- resolve stress phase & promote healing phase

CREATING A PRAYER STATE

It has been proven that saying positive affirmations and prayers out loud actually creates a coherence in our energy. Whilst it is not a religious practice, by using EAM and affirming our new positive intentions, we create a prayer-like state. In Step 5 MANIFEST, we engage our senses and that energetic information is sent out into mass consciousness / universe. The energetic power of our voice to transform our energy by creating the new statement is a declaration of our intention, like a prayer. In the same way, resistant beliefs are imprinted when we speak, we can also choose to create new ones using the incredible power of our words.

THERE IS NO RELIVING THE SITUATION

Studies show we do not need to have cognitive awareness of a situation to change or process it. In fact, our cognitive experience doesn't know the difference between what is now and what is past. By reliving past experiences, we reinforce old neural pathways and can re-experience past events and energies. With EAM, there is no need to 'talk it through' or relive past situations to process them. We use the sway to specifically identify what it is then work on it with Step 4 TRANSFORM and 5 MANIFEST.

HOW EAM CAN HELP YOU

In this chapter and the following pages of this book, I will introduce you to just a few of the key ways you can use EAM to start changing your life. You'll also see how EAM has helped to transform the lives of so many people as we share their stories in the following chapters. It doesn't matter who you are, what has happened in your past, or what is happening now. Recognise that everything is energy, and by changing your energy, thoughts, and emotions with EAM you can change your life.

Our experience of life
is filtered through our
interpretation of the
world.

WHEN SHOULD YOU USE EAM?

The answer is simple ... all the time, all day, every day. There are some really simple clues that tell you when you need to. Remember it's not just about releasing RESISTANCE. Use it when things are good too to create more FLOW. When you use it you feel better about life right now and in the future. By getting in flow today you are creating the future you want. Why would you NOT want to use it every day? This is where the magic of EAM lies.

Here are a few clues that it would be good to do EAM

- If your energy is low or you're in a bad mood.

- When you notice resistant thoughts or feelings.

- When you hear yourself say or write down beliefs that need working on.

- If you feel sick, ill, tired or run down.

- If you feel stuck or lost or like you have hit a wall.

- You are judging yourself or others.

- If you are dragged down by other people.

- If you feel confused and need clarity.

- When things feel they are going wrong and you feel you can't change it.

- When you have decisions to make and don't know what to do.

- When you notice behaviours that are self-sabotaging your happiness.

- If you are pushing to change things or people outside of you so that you feel better.

- If you want to give up or want to end it.

- If you find yourself in pusher, puller or protector roles (we will talk more about these in the next chapter).

- When you want to create or manifest something in your life.

- When you are in a good mood and want to feel better.

- As part of your daily routine like brushing your teeth.

These are just a few of the hundreds of ways you can recognise it is time for you to sway. Get in the habit of asking the sway questions when you feel RESISTANCE. You will know there is something to release by the feeling then instantly clear it before it grows into something more.

The easiest answer is to pay attention to how you feel in every moment. If it feels out of FLOW do the 5 Steps. If it feels in FLOW do more of Step 5. You'll soon feel the magic and you get addicted to using it yourself!

HOW EAM DIFFERS FROM OTHER PRACTICES

Most other therapies and modalities rely on a third party to mediate your conversation with yourself. Other practices can bring negative energy to the surface and don't actually present a way to transform it. Instead of me explaining, I asked our clients what they would say. Here is what they shared about EAM.

- It is a powerful and simple process.

- Enables you to tap into the subconscious in a simple and painless way.

- Can quickly release things and works faster than other methods.

- Creates lasting change.

- Is more than a method. It's a way of life.

Please know this doesn't mean that other therapies are wrong or even that we are right. Sometimes they work for people, sometimes they don't. In the same way, EAM won't be for everyone either. This is another opportunity for you to change what is happening in your life and energy.

LIMITATIONS OF EAM

Whilst I know EAM is a powerful self-help method, which can enable many shifts and changes, I see it primarily as a preventative tool to stop you from getting to critical points in your physical, mental or emotional health. I believe that we are responsible for ourselves, our life and our health. However, there are times when I would recommend you seek professional help, support and attention.

EAM is not to be used when there is a medical emergency, which requires attention from a physician or other health care provider. In such cases, please contact the relevant services. You can use it to help manage the pain and symptoms but you should also seek medical help. If someone is feeling suicidal, whilst EAM can be used to help release the resistant thoughts and emotions you should still seek help from the appropriate people. This does not replace those services. If someone is having a psychological episode, such as a mental or nervous breakdown, you should work with the appropriate medical service providers.

Whilst this is a powerful tool and method, your use of it is your own responsibility and EAM cannot take any liability or responsibility for your actions from reading this book.

From Pain to Peace

LISA JONES, AGE 49

Following two bereavements within the space of one year, I found myself absolutely devastated and brought to my knees. The emotional pain was never-ending; I felt like a zombie. My life was running on auto pilot and I was going through the motions and faking happiness for loved ones and friends. I had resigned myself to living life as the depressed version of me. I felt like I was under water, barely getting enough air.

I was already a qualified hypnotherapist, and I'd tried so many ways to try and force myself out of this state ranging from counselling to running. I trained as a Mindfulness and Meditation trainer, I became a Reiki Master ...but nothing really worked. Then I discovered EAM and even though I was just doing the online self-study version, it was hard to ignore that it was actually working. I slowly started to notice that my base level of emotions was rising up the scale. So much so that I felt like I had to learn more about it to really start understanding and using it on a deeper level.

I worked with a mentor who helped me use the sway to transform my feelings, from a place of excruciating emotional pain to absolute joy and peace. For the first time in two and half years I felt true happiness and inner peace and more like the old me again. I NEVER thought that it was possible. I now get to live my life in the new paradigm. The transformation was so amazing that the feeling remains with me, months later. I've even taken the leap myself to becoming an EAM mentor. How could I know this and not want to share it with the world?

YOUR POWERFUL SWAY

The sway is a form of muscle testing and is primarily used in Applied Kinesiology. It is also a key part of EAM. It's a simple biofeedback method to determine where stressors or areas of RESISTANCE are in our body and lives. Through muscle testing questions and monitoring of the answers, we can easily get information from our subconscious. To sway, you must stand with your feet hips width apart and ask simple yes or no answer questions. Your body will usually sway forward for a 'yes' answer and backward for a 'no'.

The sway is powerful because it can show us where strength and RESISTANCES are by creating a change in the physiological state of our muscles, which can be seen and felt. This is known as the Ideomotor response to unconscious thoughts, emotions and energy, which is then shown in our physiology.

Our body is adjusting your physiology all the time. When you are embarrassed your body goes all hot and sweaty. You don't think, *oh yes, better start sweating*! Your body does this without any input from your conscious mind. Your body is constantly responding to your 5 senses. The sway is reading your 6th sense, which taps into the layers of your aura and intuition.

THE IMPORTANCE OF THE SWAY

In EAM we use the sway because we get real time feedback on what is happening in our energy. By using this we can understand subconscious information, which would otherwise be inaccessible to our conscious awareness. The sway is used in multiple ways throughout the 5 Steps.

Why use the sway and not just go with what's in our head? The sway enables us to bypass conscious thinking to identify unconscious thoughts, beliefs, and energy about any subject. We may THINK things we don't consciously admit to, for example because they may be perceived as not right, polite, or proper. Our ego would say, 'I'm not jealous. That's not me. I'm too nice to be jealous. Yet, there are unconscious hidden feelings which say otherwise. If we only used our conscious thoughts we would limit our transformation and we edit it based on our awareness, beliefs, and filters. By asking the sway you understand what is true in our energy, you transform the REAL issues, which we are unaware of.

Why do we not just use a pendulum or another dowsing device? Because you have all of the answers you need inside of you. Why use something external when your body is giving you answers all the time? Using the sway is something you can use anywhere. I have found the sway to be more accurate than a pendulum, which can be easily influenced by your thinking.

Using the sway as opposed to a pendulum allows you to FEEL your emotions and what happens to your energy, so you begin to notice when you are in FLOW or out of FLOW. We already have all of the messages in our body, for example when you feel a positive or negative emotion. If you were using a pendulum you have no physiological or emotional feedback to help you connect to what is happening. The direction of your sway also gives you important information.

HOW DOES THE SWAY WORK?

The sway is a physiological response sent via tiny nerves which create a sympathetic micro-muscle movement. On a physiological level, we are working with our Autonomic Nervous System that controls the electrical input and output of messages. This system knows what is happening everywhere in our body all of the time. It is this system that monitors information from the inside (our body) and the outside (our environment) and responds accordingly.

In this case, it creates a motor (physical muscular) response to what we are thinking, feeling, or picking up energetically. By using the sway with EAM, we can get a YES or NO response to what is happening on every level of our aura.

5 IMPORTANT STEPS OF A GOOD SWAY

If you are familiar with kinesiology you test for a strong or weak response from your body. As you use EAM, you will notice that not all sways are the same. Sometimes you have a strong pull forward (a YES response) or backward (a NO response) and sometimes the sways can be gentle or imperceptible.

If your sways are not strong to begin the more you use EAM to free up your energy the stronger your sways will become. The strength of the sway can tell you how 'true' or 'false' a statement is to you. It may make you fall forward or throw you backward sometimes, so please take care!

So how do we get a good sway?

1. **BE IN THE RIGHT SPACE.** Your sway can be affected by many different sources in our environment, which can stop a 'good sway'. Unknowingly to you, they can put your body into a weak, reversed, or resistant state. It's not just your sway they can affect; imagine what they do to your energy *all the time*.

   Here is a quick (but not exhaustive) list:

   - Being tired

   - Medication

   - Alcohol

   - Sugar

   - Caffeine

   - Food in your diet

   - Computers and tech

   - Personal hygiene and cleaning products

   - Particular environments

   - Other people

   You can ask the sway if any of these things are affecting you. Ironically, they may stop you from getting the answer! I'll show you what to do with that shortly.

   When using the sway make sure you're fully hydrated. It is better if you are barefoot and if possible outside in the grass or at least on the ground floor of your house to earth any resistant energy. If you have any trouble swaying jump up and down, go for a little run, dance or sing to reset your energy.

   These are not necessary, but they can be helpful when first starting to use the sway.

2. **HAVE THE RIGHT STANCE.** If you're holding your body locked, with a tight clenched first, a stiff back, your shoulders up around your ears, and the back of your knees locked, does that feel open, relaxed and ready to receive? If you're holding tension in your body, it will prevent you from

getting a clear answer from the sway. To start, close your eyes, and take a nice deep breath. Consciously relax the back of your knees, and hips, and open your hands so they are by your side.

3. **REMAIN OBJECTIVE.** Yes, you can force your sway forward or backward if you choose. With EAM try to remain objective, with your only intention to get a truthful answer from your energy. Often we are invested in getting a particular answer, then feel disappointed when we get another.

You'll begin to know when you have a real sway, as it has a different feeling. The push or pull comes from inside without any thought or conscious awareness of the question you're asking.

In the same way if you keep asking the same question you may get different answers at different times, remember your sway is a 'messenger' telling you what your energy is vibrating. If you change your thoughts or emotions about something, the sway will change.

4. **BEING SPECIFIC & ASKING THE RIGHT QUESTIONS.** The words and meanings you use can determine the outcome of your sway, so be specific with your questions. For example, in response to the question "Am I feeling angry?", the sway might tell you no, because right now no you're not really that angry. If you ask the sway "Do I feel angry when I think about what Bob did to me last week, when he said my bum looked big?" then you might get a different answer. Your sway is influenced by your beliefs. If you ask, 'Do I believe I *should* take this job?' and you sway YES forward. If you ask the question, "Do I *want* to take this job?" you may sway backward. Similar question, different answers. You may believe you 'should' take the job because it will provide safety, security and money. Inside you know taking the job would break your heart and destroy your soul because you're not following your passion. Do you see how important it is to be specific about the questions?

So, leave words like 'should' and 'ought to' out. Instead ask, "Do I want...?" or "Would I like...?" or "Is it for my highest good?".

Be specific with your questions. This helps you understand what to release with Step 4 TRANSFORM and what to align to with Step 5 MANIFEST.

5. **PRACTICING YOUR SWAY.** Now, up on your feet. Let's start you using your sway. You need to learn to trust your sway. Here are a few things to

help you get started; use them 2 or 3 times to see what answers you get. Make sure you have followed the steps above for a good sway.

Try picking up different foods or items in your home. Things to which you have no emotional attachment. Ask "Is this good for me?" and see if your body is pulled towards or pushed away from them. If you find a product which makes you sway backwards you can ask for each individual ingredient. See which ones you go forward and backward on.

Once you have confidence on inanimate objects try asking yourself simple yes or no questions. Say these statements out loud then try saying the opposite; for example, I would say 'My name is Yvette'. I would expect to sway forward. Then if I said 'My name is Frank', I would expect to sway backward.

Try these both ways, with truthful and untruthful statements:

- My name is…

- My date of birth is…

- My mother's name is…

- My father's name is…

These questions are really helpful as long as there is no energetic attachment to those subjects. For example, if you didn't have a good relationship with your mum, when you ask her name there maybe something which affects your sway. If you've tried all of those and it still hasn't worked sometimes you just need to sleep. Your body works on the circadian clock and it may be that you are using the sway during a time in the day when your particular energy FLOW is at its lowest.

WHAT TO REMEMBER ABOUT YOUR SWAY

- **YOUR SWAY WON'T WORK.** In his brilliant book *Power vs Force*, Dr. David Hawkins discusses the use of Kinesiology alongside the map of consciousness. It is explained that those who are operating at a frequency below 200 on this scale may be in survival mode. Energetically this is the REVERSED energy state, which means you may find it more difficult to sway. You can still use EAM to help you. To get the sway to work you would need to begin exploring what created this reversed state. This can be difficult to do as your sway is not providing clues where to look. It may take several sessions to raise your energy. This is where the help of an EAM mentor would be highly beneficial.

- **USING YOUR SWAY TO MAKE DECISIONS.** I hear this from people a lot, "well my sway says I should or shouldn't do it". Your sway is JUST an indication of what is in your energy right now. If you hold fear or a negative emotion about something, that is what your sway will tell you. To get a clear sway when making choices you must first release the RESISTANCE, otherwise it is influenced by what is in your energy. When you are in FLOW and ask the question, the answer will be truthful and you'll get a clear YES or a clear NO. When you do, it means your energy thoughts and emotions are in sync so you can use them to guide your actions.

- **IT ALL CHANGES.** Let me briefly clarify, a sway forward is usually a YES and backward is usually a NO. I say 'usually' because one of the clearest signs we have an energy REVERSAL, is that our sway suddenly becomes difficult to read. The answers often change position meaning your 'YES' becomes backward and your 'NO' becomes forward. Argh!

- **STANDING STILL OR GOING IN CIRCLES.** This reason you're having trouble could be failure to ask the right question. It can also be another sign of REVERSAL, so follow the steps outlined for reversals. It is also a REVERSAL when you sway from side to side, or if you move in a circle instead of swaying clearly backward or forward. This can get a bit confusing. Is it a 'real' yes? Or a 'fake' caused by a REVERSAL? You'll get the hang of it. A simple way to check is by asking what is your name (assuming you have no REVERSAL around your name). It is often quicker to just follow the steps and release the RESISTANCE anyway.

- **SWAYING BACK AND FORTH.** Swaying back and forth is a sign your body is moving energy. You may sway in one direction as you say statements. You may sway before you have verbalised the question. As your energy knows before you become consciously aware.

- **SWAYS FROM DIFFERENT PARTS OF THE BODY.** You may notice that the sway doesn't always come from your heart or between your shoulders. It may come from your stomach or solar plexus or below your belly button. All of these are normal, so just trust that it is a YES or NO sway.

- **SWAYING SITTING OR LYING DOWN.** When your first learn EAM we teach you to use the sway standing. It's one of the easiest ways to muscle test because gravity helps you move, so you get a clearer signal. Your sway is just a movement of energy, when we stand it pulls us forward or backward. It is not the only way to sway. You can sway from anywhere that has a pivot.

If you can sit, try swaying from your hips. You'll feel the same push and pull of energy between your heart and shoulder blades. Once you master this you can use EAM anywhere, whilst travelling, sitting on the sofa or even on the loo! If you are unable to sit unaided, you can also sway from your neck and use your head. You'll nod forward or backward so long as the back of your chair doesn't limit the movement of your head. You can also sway lying down! This is a great one to master; it feels like a pull upwards or that you're being pushed down if you are lying flat on your back. These are particularly helpful for people with health or mobility issues, who may lack strength, or are bed-bound. Try these for yourself so you can use EAM any and everywhere.

The Reassurance of the Sway

CAROLINE A, AGE 52

Before EAM I was pretty desperate. I was overwhelmed with anxiety and fear and saw this as a lifeboat passing me while lost at sea. I was feeling physically very poorly; pins and needles all over, numbness and burning sensations in my body, heaviness of limbs and sometimes feeling so weak I could barely stand. Needless to say, this was getting in my way of really enjoying my horses. I was spending a lot of time indoors just sitting or lying down focusing on how awful I was feeling. Despite the fact that I am a therapist I had lost my way and was now scared I had something seriously wrong with my central nervous system.

As soon as I joined the Energy Evolution 10-month programme and met all the wonderful people I realised things were about to change. My priority was to establish whether my physical symptoms were purely emotional and the sway consistently said yes which was a massive reassurance to me that I could get this sorted with EAM and I would be feeling better again in the foreseeable future.

I have recently been to see a Neurologist who agreed that the symptoms are purely stress-related and there is no further exploration required. I didn't need confirmation of my sway yet I came away feeling very pleased. I am pleased to say I have sat back on my horse for the first time in 4 months. I am spending more time outdoors (where I truly belong) and have rediscovered an inner peace I have not felt in a long time. This is only the beginning of the journey and I can't wait for what's to come...

THE 5 STEPS OF EAM

Now that you understand the sway, it's time for me to *finally* share the 5 Steps of EAM with you. (I bet you thought we would never get here!)

The 5 steps will allow you to explore any situation, issue or challenge you may be facing. You'll see there are multiple ways to approach any subject to change resistant or reversed energy into the flow state. The purpose of everything we do within EAM is about bringing your energy into alignment, which we do with Step 5 – MANIFEST.

STEP 1 — ASK

Think of a subject you would like to explore. In Step 1 we ask ourselves (our energy) a question that is best said aloud. The questions you ask here help us understand whether our energy is in FLOW, in RESISTANCE or REVERSAL, about that subject. By asking our energy we are asking the question to all levels of our energy systems, structures and functions all at once.

With Step 1 we get clarity on our issue through questioning. This helps us bypass our conscious awareness and access our subconscious. The questions help us to identify the connected elements and different manifestations of it all at once.

By saying it aloud we engage the energetic power of our voice. Because our voice comes directly from our heart, you get a more truthful answer from your energy. This is more powerful than if you ask silently in your head.

HOW TO ASK THE RIGHT QUESTIONS

Stand with your feet hip's width apart, knees relaxed, eyes closed, hands by your side. Take a deep breath and relax. Then ask yourself a question that can give you a simple 'Yes' or 'No' answer.

Keep it simple when you first start working on an issue. You can approach it in one of these 3 ways.

1. WHAT IS HAPPENING TO YOUR ENERGY?

When you think about the issue, what happens in your energy?

Describe the experience of it energetically.

Does it make you feel heavy or light? Does it make you feel like you are walking in mud or skipping on air? Does it make you feel like you've been pulled back? Or pushed forward? This is about recognising what happens to your energy, and it will give you clues to where you are in FLOW or in RESISTANCE.

Then you can start Step 1 with a question like:

"Does it make me feel heavy and pulled back when I think about _____?"

Or

"Is this heavy and pulled back feeling related to _____?"

2. WHAT BELIEFS OR THOUGHTS DO YOU HAVE?

If the issue you ask about doesn't give you a physiological response, try looking at the thoughts or beliefs you have about something. It may help to write them down. For instance, do you hold a belief that you are not good enough to get that job?

Then you could do Step 1 with a question like:

'Do I believe I am not good enough to get that job?'

Or

'Do I think I will fail at that interview?'

3. WHAT EMOTIONS DO YOU FEEL?

If the subject, you are thinking of is not a belief and not a feeling you experience in your energy it may be an emotion. These are different to the energies as described above. Emotions are the ones you recognise quite easily. Examples are anger, anxiety, happiness, love and sadness.

Then you could do Step 1 with a question like

'Do I feel angry that Isabelle didn't do what I asked her to?'

Or

'Do I hold any emotions of anger when I think about _____?

WHAT TO REMEMBER ABOUT STEP 1

I'm often asked, do you have to ask the questions if you already have the RESISTANCE or negative energy that you need to transform? In short, can you just do Step 4 and transform? I would suggest the answer is no, because what you THINK is the issue may be different in your energy. If you skip this step, you will miss the specificity and clarity on exactly what you need to work on. This is part of the power of EAM. By asking the right questions, you discover the real RESISTANCE in your energy. Which means at Step 4 you can transform the actual underlying reason. It is because we can get to this level of specificity by asking the questions in Steps 1 and 2 that people report such rapid shifts with EAM. Of course, you can skip Step 1 and 2 if you know how you feel. However, the 2 seconds it takes to find the answer will be more productive to make sure you are working on the right issue. The exception to this is if you are experiencing something intensive or emotional. In those circumstances, forget about Step 1 or 2 and just do Steps 3, 4 and 5. You may find yourself asking several questions, cycling between Steps 1 and 2 for clarity before you can move to Step 3, 4 and 5. That is perfectly normal and part of the process.

Be aware that sometimes it may not be appropriate to say things out loud. Perhaps you are in the room with the person you're swaying on! Or perhaps you're standing in a supermarket queue. In such cases, it's okay to whisper it quietly or say it silently inside your head.

STEP 2 — MOVE

In Step 2, your energy bodies respond by using the sway. We are sensing the information in all possible places, in our HEAD, HEART, and HARA, our AURA layers including our physical body, chakras, and meridians. It is reading our thoughts, emotions and other imprints in our energy. This information from the energy structures is fed back through our nervous system, to create the Ideomotor and neuromuscular response, which we know as the sway.

We use the sway at Step 2 to tune into the exact issue. You don't need conscious awareness of every RESISTANCE to transform, although at times it helps to piece together a puzzle which may have been invisible. When our conscious mind feels as if it has the answer, then it will be 'quiet' because it knows. This means we can get to the real work.

The sway allows to get a deep insight into your energy also known as your intuition. By using the physiology, you can see and feel what is happening and get conscious answers to RESISTANCEs, issues and imprints which would otherwise remain unknown.

UNDERSTAND YOUR SWAY IN STEP 2

This is usually the point at which you may identify an energy REVERSAL with your sway. If you identify an energy REVERSAL, follow the amendments at each step to adjust for it.

Usually, one of the following things happen:

1. BACK TO FRONT SWAY

   You get a backward sway for something, which should be a yes and forward for a no.

2. SIDE TO SIDE

   The side-to-side sway or round in circles again tells you there is something else going on.

3. A NO SWAY

   If you don't sway it can mean a couple of things. It can be that your body is in an energy REVERSAL, which can create a frozen or locked state of energy. It can also mean you need to refine your original question asked at Step 1. When you first start using EAM you may just need to be patient, as your body may be slow to respond.

CONFUSION & DOUBLE ANSWERS

You may ask a question that is both resistant AND reversed at the same time. Usually this will happen because you've asked a question on a big topic, like "Do I have RESISTANCE to money?". That is a huge subject with many different elements. Be more specific with your questions and explore them with clarifying questions at Step 3.

If you have a REVERSAL, your sway is confusing and not giving you clear answers. In those cases, skip the sway and do Steps 4 to release the RESISTANCE or REVERSAL. At all other times, use the sway.

NO RESISTANCE

If you ask the question and find there is no RESISTANCE to something you want to manifest, check a couple of similar questions with Step 3 just in case it is the wording. If nothing comes up, you can move to Step 5 and align. Once you have a clear YES to something which is a RESISTANCE or REVERSAL which you need to address then you can move onto step 3.

STEP 3 — EXPERIENCE

Step 3 is when YOU experience. The purpose is to assess what is happening to your energy right now, in relation to that subject There are a few ways to this step. It varies depending on the issue, and how you learn or communicate.

Some people are Kinesthetic, which means they like to feel or touch. These people may be very visual and see pictures and images. They may be logical and like to use numbers and systems. It is not always about your learning style; it also depends on the RESISTANCE you are working on.

Step 3 gives clarity on what is standing in your way. What is your current experience or level of RESISTANCE on this subject? We all interpret energy differently, which means RESISTANCES may show up differently for us too, so we need multiple ways to approach them. Remember your voice is powerful. By verbalising at this step, you tune into the frequency and give words to something intangible. We want to define what is happening in our energy right now. This is a marker of the RESISTANCE or REVERSAL before doing Step 4. This helps us to assess that we have created a full transformation.

By exploring what is happening in to you energetically, you gain a greater understanding of how it may affect your energy and life experience. You may find clues to the origin of the RESISTANCE and get more specific descriptions to use at Step 4.

This helps to account for the different sensory styles, as well as give common language to explain RESISTANCES and REVERSALS so we can let them go.

5 MAIN WAYS YOU CAN USE STEP 3

Step 3 gives conscious awareness and an opportunity for you to explore your energy and connect to your feelings. By describing your energy in physical forms such as size, shape and colour, you will be better able to connect to your energy and give language to intangible feelings connected to the RESISTANCE. By using the numbers method outlined below, you can make intangible beliefs, thoughts, and patterns easy to measure to know what you have or that still needs to be transformed at Step 4. Use the sway at Step 3 to ask further defining questions about the RESISTANCE, REVERSAL or statement. These questions help to identify the source of the imprint, RESISTANCE or REVERSAL to gain clarity and specificity about the RESISTANCE to be transformed at Step 4.

Below I outline the 5 key ways to explore Step 3: Energy, Thoughts and Beliefs, Emotions, Ask Clarifying Questions, and Visualisation.

STEP 3 — FEEL THE ENERGY

The easiest way to use EAM is to describe what happens to your energy when you think about the particular subject. This is always the first question I ask: "What happens to your energy when you think about ___?" In the same way, we explored the questions in Step 1, what happens to your energy? Does it feel heavy or light? Does it make you feel tired or drained? etc. There are lots of ways your energy can affect you. Describing the effect it has on our energy means it will be easier to transform with Step 4.

WHY WE WORK WITH ENERGY

The body is sending you messages all the time; these are what you sense in your energy. It is a valuable tool. By recognizing what is happening in your energy is a great way to work on intangible thoughts or emotions. What you are feeling as sensations in your body IS the RESISTANT or REVERSED energy that you often cannot name or describe.

The reason we begin with energy is because many people have disconnected from their body. As a society, we have learnt to ignore or push aside these very clear signals that something is going on. Tuning into your energy enables you to gain a greater sense of awareness. As you grow with EAM, you will begin to notice your energy *before* it gets out of FLOW.

Remember what you feel in your energy is one of the biggest indicators of what messages are being sent out by our HEAD, HEART, HARA and AURA. So, make sure to use this often.

HOW TO USE ENERGY IN STEP 3

Close your eyes and think about the situation, memory or person that you feel you need to work on. Pay attention to what is happening in your body; you may be able to tune into the feelings straight away. Or you may need to work methodically from your head down to your toes. You may feel as though it is energy inside or outside of you. Notice where you feel pressure, heaviness, tension, holes, gaps or RESISTANCE in your energy. It helps to describe the RESISTANCE as an inanimate object so you have a definition of what it is like.

You can identify it verbally or ask the question of yourself or the sway

- What colour is it? Can you see one in your mind's eye?

- What size is it? For example, is it the size of a tennis ball or a rugby ball?

- What shape is it? Can you describe it as a square circle triangle or a weird blob?

- Where is it in location?

- Does it feel like another object, for example a knife or spear?

- Is it hard or soft?

- Is it still or moving?

- Is moving fast or slow? How does it move?

- Is it inside or outside of your physical body?

The answers to these questions will help you to formulate a statement to release with Step 4 of the Energy Alignment Method.

WHAT TO REMEMBER

It helps to describe the resistance you experience as an object. For example, if you are feeling stressed out about work, when you close your eyes it might feel like there's a hard, spiky, tennis ball inside your stomach. The tennis ball feels like it is spinning and it's half inside and outside of your body like it's bursting to get out. I would then use this description in Step 4 to help with the transformation step.

E.g., "I am ready to transform this hard, spiky, tennis ball which feels like it bursting to get out of my stomach, when I think about work. I release this from my energy in all forms, on all levels, at all points in time."

STEP 3 - THOUGHTS & BELIEFS - THE NUMBERS

Numbers are very helpful when you need to quantify something you cannot feel. They are especially useful when working with our thoughts, beliefs, or patterns, because we do not feel our thoughts. Let go of attachment to the amount of numbers you discover with this step. All they represent is the number of times you have thought, felt, experienced, believed or repeated a specific thing.

WHY DO WE USE IT?

It is often difficult to describe something that happens on the mental level of our energy. This is why we use the sway to help us define the actual number. It is very empowering to get a definitive number and be able to see when you have cleared it down to zero. This is also helpful for those who are more logical and may find it hard to clearly describe feelings or energy in their body.

By using numbers, we are able to quantify many different thoughts, feelings, or beliefs at once. We can release them all very quickly with EAM and measure how many you need to transform with Step 4.

HOW DO YOU USE NUMBERS?

Using the Number of Beliefs

There are lots of ways you can work with numbers in EAM. You can use the numbers by asking the Sway:

"Do I have more than 100 beliefs that (Insert the belief, thought or pattern)?"

The sway will give you a YES or NO.

If it's a YES, go up in number.

"Do I have more than 1000 beliefs that _____?" (Insert the belief, thought or pattern.)

This time the sway may say NO which means you know it is less than 1000, so ask if the number is more or less than halfway between that number and the previous

"Do I have more than 500 beliefs that _____?" (Insert the belief, thought or pattern.)

Keep using this process up and down until you get in the region of the number you have. You do not always have to be specific.

If you are going up in number and it keeps saying yes, then it is easier to count up like this:

More than 100.... more than 1000.... 10,000 more than 100,000.

Then as soon as you a get No, drop back to more than half the last number and keep working in this way.

You then use this same process to release the RESISTANCE with Step 4 and count back down the number of RESISTANCES until you get it down to 0.

WHAT TO REMEMBER?

I am often asked, "Can I release all of this RESISTANCE at once?" The answer is YES and NO. Think of all the resistant energy you may be carrying. If it all changed its state at once it would create such an influx of energy, your physical body may not be able to cope. Also, when you release RESISTANCE you go into a healing phase. If you released all RESISTANCE at once then your healing phase would look like a coma.

When using numbers, you will see it may take more than one or two rounds of repeating to release it. Sometimes an issue may be complicated. The numbers help us to see what we have released. Use them as a measure or guide to know if you need to repeat Step 4 of the process. Say for example. You find 1000 beliefs; you use the steps and bring the number to 100 the first time you complete Step 4. So, you repeat Step 4 again. Then you ask the sway and the number of beliefs has reduced to 50. You repeat and bring it down to 10. If it then gets stuck and doesn't change, this may mean you have an energy REVERSAL. By using the numbers, you are able to identify how many are energy REVERSALS and specifically go in and work on each individual one, to clear Step 4. The numbers allow you to be specific and ensure a complete release.

If we had tried to say, "I'm ready to release this RESISTANCE all at once." the shift may not have been complete. We may have released some but that one statement may have got it to the first 100. This would mean we have left RESISTANCE in our energy. By using the numbers, we can be clear that all the RESISTANCE is gone. We go slower in order to go fast. It's more important to release RESISTANCE completely with Step 4 than trying to speed our way through for the sake of moving onto something else. It is an extra couple of minutes which has the potential to change your life and make you finally free of this RESISTANCE. Take the time to use the numbers to ensure that it is clear for you.

Try not to compare yourself to others. You have millions whilst they only have 100's. People process information in different ways; the numbers are irrelevant. They are simply a measure of what you hold in your energy. Either way it only matters that you get it down to zero.

STEP 3 — THE EMOTIONS — USING THE SCALE

We explored our emotional scale in Chapter 2. It is a powerful tool, which will enable you to work through particular situations or how you feel about other people. Think of it as your reference guide; the scale enables you to explore other emotions connected to these feelings.

THE POWER OF THE EMOTIONAL SCALE

This is a very simple yet powerful way to work on emotions. Often, we are unable to name emotions we experience about a situation. Our thoughts can be clouded and emotions muddied by our experience. They can be confused by the way our neural networks have been bound together. We may want to hide the emotions we feel consciously, or deny we have them.

By using the emotional scale, we can see where our emotional frequencies are on that issue. Remember your heart is 5000 times more powerful than your mind. As a result, your emotions have a greater impact on your life experience whether you're consciously aware of them or not. Your emotions are the messengers in that carrier wave of our energy.

Your emotions are the messengers in the carrier wave of your energy.

THE ENERGY ALIGNMENT METHOD

HOW TO USE EMOTIONS AT STEP 3

Have a copy of the emotional scale to hand. Ask the sway which emotion you feel when thinking of the situation or person you are working on.

Start at the bottom of the scale and ask questions about each emotion like:

"Do I feel fearful of _____?"

The sway will answer YES or NO.

If yes, you can also ask "How many fearful emotions do I feel about _____?"

There are two ways to then use this. Either use the energy method above e.g. what does it feel like in your energy or use the numbers e.g. how many times have you repeated that emotion.

Again, you would use your findings here to formulate the statement for Step 4.

Your Step 4 statement may look something like this:

"I am ready to transform these 473 feelings of fear when I think about my new job. I release it from my energy in all forms on all levels at all points in time."

Or

"I am ready to release this dark, heavy bubbling feeling of fear in my HARA when I think about my new job. I release it from my energy in all forms, on all levels, at all points in time."

WHAT TO REMEMBER

We can also feel RESISTANCE to positive emotions like empowerment, happiness, confidence or love; it's not only emotions below the neutral line. These can be connected to any subject or person for example RESISTANCES about showing love to a particular person.

You'll find yourself cycling between Step 3 and Step 4 of the process discovering RESISTANCES and transforming them. You may choose to complete Step 5 after each transformation or work on all the RESISTANCE then do a really orgasmic step 5.

If you would like an A4 sized poster of the emotional scale you can come and download one on the website here along with a host of supporting goodies to help you complete the elements of this book. (LINK)

STEP 3 - ASK CLARIFYING QUESTIONS

You can have a lot of fun asking your sway all kinds of weird and crazy questions. This is helpful to find when something began, or when it is not an emotion, or when you are unable to define it with numbers but you know it is an issue in your life. These questions also help to get specific when working on a REVERSAL.

HOW TO USE THE QUESTIONS

The list of possible questions is endless, so let's start with simple ones. Try to avoid getting bogged down digging in the past. Just use the questions to get specific; once you have the answer move on and transform it with Step 4.

These questions will help you to find the specific RESISTANCE or start point. This will help to resolve all of the connected RESISTANCES which follow after that. It could be from this life, from your time in the womb or a past life (if you believe in those).

Some questions which may help you

- "Was it this life?"

- "Was it in the womb?"

- "Was it a past life?"

If this life (or a past life), "What age was I?"

This is similar to the numbers process we used above. Use the sway to identify your age at the time the RESISTANCE or REVERSAL began. So, you would ask questions like

- "Was I younger than 10, 20, 30?"

Your sway answers YES or NO. Then work up or down accordingly until you find the age. When you get a YES, you may want to explore some more questions.

For example, if you were 5, you were not at work probably going to school. You may remember something at that age or a significant life event. It does not mean that it was connected to that, but you could ask the sway:

- "Was it when _____?" (Yes or No)

If not, you could ask:

- "Who else was involved?"

"Was it my mum / dad / brother / sister / aunt/ uncle / teacher/ friend?"

The sway will give you yes or no answers to these questions to get clarity. This may lead you on to more questions like:

- What it something I / they heard?

- Was it something I / they said?

- Was it something I / they did?

- Was it something I / they believed?

For example, if you had been working on a belief that "I am not good enough" you could then ask:

- "Was it that I heard my mum and dad talking about me and I believed that they thought I was not good enough?"

Your Step 4 release statement would look something like:

"I am ready to transform the belief that I am not good enough, created at the age 5 when I overheard my mum and dad talking about me in the kitchen. I release it from my energy in all forms on all levels, at all points in time."

You can usually skip this level of detail; just by identifying the age you where you can transform the RESISTANCE that way. You can always ask the sway:

- "Is there anything else I need to know about _____?"

If it was in the womb you can ask which month of pregnancy it was months 1 - 10 using the numbers method above. Yes, there are 10 lunar months of pregnancy not 9!

You can also ask:

- "Was it something my mum heard / said / felt / thought / believed or experienced?"

- "What it something I heard / felt / thought / believed or experienced?"

Then work on releasing it with Step 4. Your statement would look something like this:

"I am ready to release this feeling of fear that my mum had, when she was 3 months pregnant with me. I release this from my energy in all forms, on all levels, at all points in time."

If a past life you can explore some questions like:

- Which past life was it? For example, 5 past lives ago.

- Were you a woman / man / girl / boy?

- What age were you?

- Where you married / single / a child?

- What other important relationships did you have?

- Did something happen to you or someone you love?

- Did they get hurt and or die?

Then maybe explore the circumstances of what happened.

Your Step 4 statement may look something like this:

"I am ready to release this energy REVERSAL from 5 past lives ago, when I was a man, aged 35 and my wife was kidnapped and I never saw her again. I release this from my energy in all forms, on all levels, at all points in time."

I'll be honest these questions may seem a bit 'out there' when you first begin, especially if this of work is new to you. The intention is not to conflict with your belief system, especially if past lives isn't a fit for you. However, having worked with thousands of people I know that many of our biggest challenges are in these areas. It is all just energy and another line of questioning, which may enable you to uncover different RESISTANCES and REVERSALS that are holding you back right now. We will explore this more in Chapter 4.

STEP 3 — THE VISION OR VISUALISATION

Some of us are more visual. For Step 3 you can also use pictures, which you may see in your mind's eye or imagination. Close your eyes and ask the sway if you have RESISTANCE or REVERSAL to that particular topic. If the sway says yes, you may be able to bring to mind a visual representation of what that RESISTANCE or REVERSAL is like for you. Describe the picture.

For example, you may feel trapped by life. When you close your eyes, you see that you are in a prison and it is surrounding you on all sides.

So, your Step 4 statement would look something like this:

"I am ready to transform this picture of being trapped inside a prison on all sides. I release this from my energy, in all forms, on all levels, at all points in time."

WHAT TO REMEMBER

So those are a few ways that you can explore Step 3. These are the main approaches to using EAM to account for all learning styles and ways of reading or interpreting information in our life. As you learn more about EAM you'll discover more ways to approach situations.

Now you have done Step 3 and assessed your energy, what it is, and why and how it occurred. You are ready to move to Step 4.

The Power of EAM

CATH STOCK, AGE 55

Anxiety and panic used to occupy a massive space in my heart and chest. It felt like a large, hard lump, squeezing so tight, my insides would churn creating a knot in my stomach. My heart would pound; hands shake and I found it difficult to breathe. I would take deep breaths and tell myself I would be ok.

I joined the Energy Evolution 10-month programme and on my first day of the live event I felt sick; the anxiety in my chest and stomach completely took over me inside. I was shaking and just wanted to cry and escape as quickly as possible.

Thankfully, I had the support of everyone who was there. I worked one to one with a mentor until they helped me to create a huge shift of the negative energy I could not release on my own. As I sat quietly afterwards on the window ledge enjoying the peace and the light watching the world go by...I realised...after 20+ years, my anxiety and panic had gone. The space where anxiety used to live in my heart was empty and ready to be filled.

Now, I am an EAM mentor. I no longer break down with anxiety or find myself crippled by panic. Instead, I get healthy, happy butterflies and excited about life's journey and everything it brings.

STEP 4 — TRANSFORM

In Step 4 we transform the energy from a RESISTANCE or REVERSED FLOW to an in FLOW or free flowing energy. So, that we can direct it towards the things we like. It is always the same simple statement which will enable you to transform the energy. You can vary the wording depending on the subject you are working on.

In Step 4 we transform the energy. Most other energy or healing modalities fall into one of two camps. Either they focus on the release and do not include a positive manifestation step. Or they only focus on the positive step and do nothing to release. Both are vital. If you only focus on the release you go into a low energy state, as your body goes into healing. If you only focus on manifesting without releasing, you are pushing against your energy. The words we say at Step 4 change the way we think, feel, and anything that may be held in our energy structures.

HOW TO SAY THE RIGHT WORDS AT STEP 4

You've already seen the Step 4 transformation statement.

"I'm ready to transform / release this _____ (Fill in the blank with what you found in Step 3). I release this from my energy, in all forms, on all levels, at all points in time."

We repeat this statement 3 times to talk to the three main levels of our experience, HEAD, HEART and HARA. The statement works by sending a command to all elements of our energy at once. Saying the words out loud overwrites existing imprints, patterns and beliefs, subconscious thinking, and declares our intention.

CHECK THAT ALL RESISTANCE HAS GONE

When you complete 3 repetitions of the transformation statement, check your sway to make sure all RESISTANCE has gone. This gives us conscious confirmation of the release. You also feel empowered as you shift your energy from what you found in Step 3 to what you released in Step 4.

You can do that by simply asking a question:

"Have I released all of this RESISTANCE about _____?"

You can also check by going back to the energy that you felt at Step 3.

- Energy - What does it feel like now in your body? Does it need a new description? Has it changed size, shape, location?

- Numbers - Reassess the number of thoughts, beliefs, and patterns that you have. Use the sway to define the new number that may still be left.

- Emotions - Check with yourself and ask do I still feel _____ emotion or use the emotional scale to ask which emotions you have about that subject now.

- Clarifying Questions - Do I still have the RESISTANCE or REVERSAL about _____?

- Vision - Check in and see if the picture has changed.

If there is any remaining RESISTANCE, even if it's moved, changed, or reduced, repeat Step 4 until you have released all of the RESISTANCE / REVERSAL on that subject. Amend your Step 4 statement each time you repeat it, and be specific about what you are transforming in your energy. The more specific you are, the quicker your transformation.

WHAT TO REMEMBER ABOUT STEP 4

Always make sure you've released the RESISTANCE or reversed energy about that subject before you move on to Step 5. Otherwise you're trying to MANIFEST whilst there is RESISTANCE so you're still PUSHING against it. If you complete Step 4 a couple of times and the RESISTANCE has not shifted, shrunk, or moved, it is usually an energy REVERSAL. Follow the steps for that above.

If you notice the sensation moving around your body or have a physiological pain after completing Step 4, it's perfectly normal. This includes headaches, backaches, toe ache, nausea, dizziness or any other form of sensation. It's likely energy moving from RESISTANCE or REVERSAL to FLOW. If you still feel something, it means you've not cleared the RESISTANCE. Repeat steps 1 - 4 and work on the pain. Follow it through until you feel it has gone and confirm it has gone by using your sway.

You may complete Step 4 and a new feeling appears, which feels positive. Check your sway and ask "Is this a feeling that I need to keep?" If yes, use that to manifest on Step 5. If not, it could be another RESISTANCE you need to transform, so repeat Step 4.

Once you've completed this stage of the process you're ready to work on Step 5.

STEP 5 — MANIFEST

Step 5, allowing yourself and your energy to be ready to receive, to manifest, and create what you want in your life is what EAM is all about.

- **GET YOUR ENERGY IN FLOW.** Step 5 is important for many reasons. It enables energy to be in FLOW, in all forms on all levels at all points in time. We can command our energy and physical body in the same way we did with Step 4 to transform. We also address the 3 levels, Head, Heart, and HARA, and rebalance our meridians, and chakras for a free FLOW of qi. This creates new thought forms, new emotions and an overall coherent state of FLOW. Because we do Step 5 in EAM, we transform the energy that was previously stuck from Step 4 into something positive.

- **MANIFEST YOUR VISION & PLACE ORDERS.** You can also use visualisations to create a picture of your future. By visualising what you want when you are in the FLOW, it becomes quicker and easier to manifest in your life. When in the Step 5, state you're ready to place universal orders to specifically ask for what you want.

- **BRINGS ENERGY LEVELS BACK UP.** When you release stress on any level, physical, mental or emotional, you will naturally go into a healing phase that can feel low in energy. Your body wants to sleep so it can rest, repair, and heal itself. When you do Step 5, you bring your energy levels back up. It fills in the gap left as you release RESISTANCE or REVERSALS.

- **REPROGRAMS YOUR AURA.** The same way that your aura has always been recording and listening to everything you think, feel, say and do, by completing Step 5 you are imprinting new information into your aura so it becomes your new reality.

- **BALANCES YIN & YANG.** The Step 5 pose is designed to connect you to yang energy from heaven which is more energising. As your arms are open you are able to receive. With your feet placed on the ground you're also grounding that energy into the yin, gaining strength and support which help create balance in your body.

- **ACTS LIKE AN ANTENNA.** The stance is also how energy FLOWs into your body through the meridians. Your hands act like little antennae as your meridians reach out from the end of your fingers, extending into the different energy levels of your aura.

- **STRENGTHENS YOUR AURA.** Being in the manifesting state and even the pose itself expands your aura, allowing a stronger structure. It also helps you to 'bounce back' or let things roll off you like water on a duck's back. It also naturally 'protects' you from other people's energy.

- **EMPOWERED TO MAKE THE CHOICE.** You are also empowered to make a new choice, by putting yourself in the driving seat and making a clear declaration out loud about what you choose to think, feel or experience in your life.

- **OPENS UP YOUR HEART.** The position opens up your heart, lungs, chest cavity, diaphragm and internal organs which creates a greater free FLOW of energy in your whole body. It strengthens the heart and lungs, so you are more open and ready to receive.

HOW TO POWERFULLY MANIFEST WITH STEP 5

You've seen how to do Step 5 already. It's a version of the statement we said at Step 4. The best way to do this is to stand with your arms in the air, above your head, connect to the yang energy above you. Stand with your feet hips width apart allows you to ground your energy to receive into your body. Close your eyes and think about what it is you want. If you're visual, try to see a picture in your mind's eye. This is THE most powerful way to manifest.

A Powerful Step 5 Stance

A really good way to do Step 5 is to create a statement using the same questions we had at Step 3.

- What colour is it?

- What size is it?

- What shape is it?

- Where is it in location?

- Does it feel like another object like a heart or cloud?

- Is it hard or soft?

- Is it still or moving?

- If it's moving is it fast or slow? How does it move?

- Is it inside or outside of your physical body?

Imagine the sensation expanding to fill your physical body. Let the colour or feeling fill each layer of your aura. Then say:

"I'm ready to allow / receive / feel _____ (Fill in the blank with what you would like to think, feel or experience instead) _____ I allow this into my energy, in all forms, on all levels, at all points in time."

Again, for the same reasons we repeat this statement three times to speak to our HEAD, HEART, and HARA.

- **REWIRING THE BRAIN.** Our subconscious is always listening. By tuning into the emotion you want, becoming an energy match to it at the same time repeating the statement three times, we are rewiring the neural pathways. This allows the amygdala to connect thought, emotion, and experience together in a new way to create a set point, which shapes your new experience

- **USE POSITIVE LANGUAGE.** When doing your statement for Step 5, make sure to use positive language. Instead of focusing on what you don't want to happen, for example "I am ready to remain safe, protected and keep negative people away from me". We want to manifest the positive, so focus on asking for what you do want. "I am ready to allow myself to be free and happy with everyone I spend time with."

- **ALIGN TO ANYTHING YOU WANT.** People often get stuck at Step 5, because you can ask to receive anything. They wonder what words to say or what to ask for. You can align to anything, a new belief, new feeling, greater FLOW of energy, a new emotion, a new experience. Even world peace! Literally anything you want. Because IT IS ALL ENERGY. (Surely you must have got that by now).

- **GATHERING MOMENTUM.** As you repeat the Step 5 statement, it gathers more energy due to momentum. As you use EAM you can repeatedly create a particular state or feeling in your body with Step 5. The more you connect with the state of flow on different subjects, the quicker things will come because it has momentum and is gathered by the Law of Attraction.

WHAT TO REMEMBER ABOUT STEP 5

You may notice at Step 5 that you sway forward a lot! This is a good sign, as it means you're in alignment with your statements. As you speak the words, they manifest into your future and pull you along the path.

- **USE IT TO ALIGN YOUR ENERGY.** There are lots of different ways to align your energy with Step 5. You can work on your general energy levels in simple ways. Here are a couple of ideas for statements for Energy, Thoughts and Emotions. As you get used to it, you'll find your own ways.

  "I am ready to allow myself to be 100% in FLOW… I allow this into my energy, in all forms, on all levels, at all points in time."

  Or

  "I am ready to allow myself to FLOW freely through life…. I allow this into my energy, in all forms, on all levels, at all points in time." Or "I am ready to allow my chakras to be open and spin in the right direction. I allow this into my energy, in all forms, on all levels, at all points in time."

  Or

  "I am ready to receive a FLOW of abundant energy. I allow this into my energy, in all forms, on all levels, at all points in time."

- **WORK ON THOUGHTS & BELIEFS.** You can align to new beliefs, patterns or anything which you would associate with your mental awareness. Here are a few examples of statements you could use (but we encourage you to get creative).

  "I am ready to allow myself to believe that I am awesome. I am more than good enough. I deserve everything I want to receive. I allow this into my energy, in all forms, on all levels, at all points in time."

  Or

  "I am ready to believe that life is meant to be good, it is meant to be fun, and I love everything about it. I allow this into my energy, in all forms, on all levels, at all points in time."

  OR

  "I am ready to allow myself to create a pattern of seeing the good in everything. I allow this into my energy, in all forms, on all levels, at all points in time."

- **CHOOSE YOUR EMOTIONS.** Almost everything you want to experience is because you want to feel the emotion you will have when you get it. You can align yourself to any emotion you like. Remember the power of our emotions. Get yourself connected to the emotion. What does it feel like in your body? Where would you locate it?

  "I am ready to allow myself to receive love, freedom, peace and joy into my life. I allow this into my energy, in all forms, on all levels, at all points in time."

  Or

  "I am ready to allow myself to feel happy when I think about going to work. I allow this into my energy, in all forms, on all levels, at all points in time."

  Or

  "I am ready to allow myself to feel this warm glow of happiness in my solar plexus whenever I think about my life. I allow this into my energy, in all forms, on all levels, at all points in time."

- **DEFINE NEW EXPERIENCES.** You may want to create a new experience or attract something. To do that, change the way you get connected to the feeling of HAVING it. Let it fill your energy. Then say:

  "I am ready to allow myself to connect to this feeling of happiness, empowerment, and excitement when I think about _____. I allow this into my energy, in all forms, on all levels, at all points in time."

- **CHANGE RELATIONSHIPS WITH PEOPLE.** This one I love — we have a WHOLE Element devoted to working on relationships. This might be my favourite work to do with EAM. (Actually, all of it is.) I love seeing the shifts in relationships as people understand how to change themselves and in turn see the change in others. An example of what that may look like is this.

  "I am ready to allow myself to be kind, thoughtful and loving towards _____ (name). I allow myself to feel love, peace, and connection when in their company. I allow this into my energy, in all forms, on all levels, at all points in time."

  The statements can be as long and creative as you want.

- **MANIFESTING SOMETHING SPECIFIC.** The good news is you've already done the hard work in manifesting. Most people ask for something from a place of lack or not having something. But you have now done the work, and all you have to do is ask for it. Remember to be very specific and that it is best to write this down. Remember to make sure you're in a step 5 FLOW state, adding in "for the good of everyone concerned." Then repeat it at least 3 times. This is important as it will help to ensure that however this happens it is a win-win for everyone. If you use EAM to manifest specific things, I suggest you say those magical words "for the good of all concerned" too.

Often I get asked, "If I can feel the positive energy Flowing at Step 5, do I need to ask my sway?". The answer is both yes and no. Remember we can still have RESISTANCE to experiencing positive emotions, so just check with the sway first to see if you have any. If you are ready to go, then go for it.

Please also remember that this step is about aligning our energy. Everything we have done is to allow us to get our energy in FLOW. So, don't just 'skip' this bit. Even if you struggle to find the right words to align to a new energy state, thought, or emotion, you can always come back and do Step 5 again and add to it. After a good swaying session, allow yourself to acclimatise to the new level of energy. Take a walk, have a night off. Enjoy a bath, be gentle with yourself, eat healthy food, and drink plenty of water. Then wake up in the morning and do it all again.

You are already a master manifestor.
You manifest every day by making something happen.

MANIFESTING

Manifesting is the act of consciously creating something. We all have the beautiful gift and ability to manifest anything, except it isn't a skill we are often taught. Whatever you want to call it your journey of awakening, empowerment or alignment, it is about waking up this skill we all have and putting it to good use. When we think about manifesting, we usually think about a physical thing, like a car or house or money. The truth is you manifest everything every day. *Manifesting is the ACT of making something happen.*

We are natural manifestors. We are BORN to manifest. We manifest everything, even if we are doing so unconsciously. We can choose to manifest consciously by becoming aware of our energy, thoughts and emotions. Have you noticed your mind is constantly trying to get somewhere or achieve something? It is always dreaming something up, painting a picture or imagining something happening. You are manifesting all the time. Even when you sleep. So make it your choice what you focus on.

WHY IT'S IMPORTANT

The art of manifesting consciously is something that you can develop. Manifesting happens through the focus, attention, energy and action you give to a particular situation. Most people are mis-manifesting their lives, because their energy is distracted by everything else. Their energy, focus, attention, and actions are usually directed to 'firefighting' the things they do not want. Or they focus on what they do not yet have, which creates more of the same, instead of giving positive energy and focus to what they are asking for. In addition, this creates more RESISTANCE and REVERSALS which then stand in the way manifesting what is wanted.

HOW TO SPEED UP MANIFESTING

I'm always asked, 'how can I speed up getting what I want?'. The answer is simple: get in FLOW and get intentional about it as quickly as possible. It is not about TIME as most people tend to think. It is about YOU. It is about how ready YOUR energy is to receive. The Law of Vibration means you have to be a vibrational match to the what you are asking for. You can speed up the process by being in focused alignment (meaning matching energy which has gathered momentum) that you FLOW at that subject (and others). It is about deliberately and systematically cleaning up your energy, so that you can become a vibrational match to the things you want. That is exactly what we do with The Energy Evolution journey.

HOW TO MANIFEST

With EAM we talk about these five key pieces of the puzzle that you need to have in place. Yes, you can create what you want without them in place, but I can guarantee almost every time that something will go amiss if you don't follow these steps. Your only job is to figure out WHAT you want and leave out the HOW it will happen. Below are the 5 key components to manifesting.

1. CREATE YOUR VISION

First you need some direction; your visualisations and intuitions will often be the inspiration for what to do. This is not a thought. Accessing your vision is like accessing the global consciousness and your future. Reaching into the unknown.

2. ENERGY & VITALITY

Then you need to make sure your energy is as in FLOW as possible. This means all of the energy structures and layers of your aura, including your physical body and vitality, should be open and ready to receive and allow what you want into your energy.

3. THOUGHTS & WORDS

You then need to align your thoughts, beliefs, and communication which will support you, change your neurology, and shape your experience so you have an abundant mindset to create the life you want.

4. FEELINGS & EMOTIONS

Next you must deliberately get yourself in FLOW with the positive emotions you want to experience about that subject.

5. ALIGNED ACTION

Now it's time to take action and move in the direction of what you want. Remember the Law of Action. As you take more action in the direction you want magical opportunities, happy coincidences, and the right people will fall into your path. Together your energy, thoughts, and emotions define your energy alignment set point. The purpose of which is to raise your vibrational energy.

The only thing that stands in the way is us. By putting RESISTANCE in the way or by taking away any of these pieces of the process. When you have these 5 key elements in place, keep yourself in FLOW with EAM and raise your energetic set point you cannot help but manifest the things you want.

Be intentional with your manifesting, and be conscious of what you think, say and do. As you become purposeful with using EAM watch your life change as you become more in FLOW with yourself and raise your alignment level. That is when the magic begins.

TRUST IN THE PROCESS

Manifesting works both ways. Often people in the 'spiritual' community believe money is evil or manifesting material things is unspiritual. If everything is energy (which it is) does it matter what form that energy arrives in? I believe that all gifts are spiritual. Manifested knock on wood things are allowed! Just because you have yet to manifest a car or a house be just as excited that you deliberately manifested a state of well-being. If you catch yourself judging the spirituality of someone else's manifestation, that is a great opportunity for you to use EAM to work on those beliefs.

5 STEPS OF EAM | ONE PAGE GUIDE

A simple quick reference guide for you to keep nearby when working through the 5 Steps.

STEP 1 | ASK

This step is to give you clarity on what you need to shift. Ask your energy a simple question about the subject to see if it is something you need to work on. Example: "Am I holding any RESISTANCE or worry when I think about making more money?"

STEP 2 | MOVE

Your energy body will respond and give you the YES or NO answer to the question you asked. Forward is usually YES and backward usually being NO. If it sways another way check for energy reversal.

STEP 3 | EXPERIENCE

This step is all about assessing what is happening in your energy when you think about that subject. For now, let's look at 3 ways for you to do this step. Choose which is appropriate for you.

1. What happens to your energy? Describe the size / colour / shape / location etc.

2. How many of something do you have? Use the sway to identify the number

3. Which emotions do you feel? Use the emotional scale to see

4. Explore clarifying questions. Ask further questions to get more detail

5. What do you see in your mind's eye? Describe the visual picture

STEP 4 | TRANSFORM

"I am ready to release (whatever the subject). I release it from my energy in all forms, on all levels and at all points in time." Repeat this statement at least three times or until you can no longer feel it.

STEP 5 | MANIFEST

"I am ready to allow / receive / experience / think / feel (whatever the subject). I allow this into my energy in all forms, on all levels, at all points in time." Repeat this statement three times or more until you can feel it and you have a sway forwards.

EAM ANYTHING - WORKING WITH BUBBLES

This is a simple and clarifying technique to get thoughts and beliefs out of your head and onto a sheet of paper. Let's use money as an example. Money can be a very complicated issue to work through for some people. On a piece of paper write money in the middle and draw a circle. Then draw five other circles and connect them like balloons to the middle.

- In one circle write the word ENERGY. Around the outside describe what this subject does to your energy; for example, heavy, drained, light, expanded.

- In one circle write THOUGHTS AND BELIEFS. Around the outside write down all the thoughts and beliefs you have about that subject. Use the numbers method to find how many of each you have.

- In another circle write EMOTIONS. You can use the emotional scale or perhaps you can name the emotions you have about that topic.

- In another circle write SITUATIONS. List any significant life events or memories you have connected to that or you believe will be impacted by it in your future. You can also find how old you were and check if there are any RESISTANCE or REVERSALS.

- In the last circle write PEOPLE. Write all the names of people you attach to that topic. You can add how you feel about them, and things they have said or done.

Once you have the lists you can draw lines between the different thoughts, emotions, topics, timeline, and people that are connected. Now of course energy REVERSALS and past lives associations may come up here. You can keep adding details or notes to it as you work through to help build the picture. Make a note of the positive statements that you use when working through, so you can align to those more in the future.

For each of these bubbles systematically work through each issue you identified using the 5 Steps of EAM. You can ask the sway which one to start with and which one you need to do next as you work through.

IS EAM REALLY THAT FAST & SIMPLE?

The short answer is YES. It can be that fast. You can let go and align quickly too. We have been conditioned to believe that letting go of stuck energy, thoughts, beliefs or emotions is complicated and takes time; for many people that is true. This is because they're using practices or methods that do not deal with the true underlying pattern or everything, which is ENERGY as we do with EAM.

IT MAY GET WORSE BEFORE IT GETS BETTER

When using healing modalities like EAM, what you work on may seem to get worse before it gets better. Sometimes it may feel like the RESISTANCE is coming back. It's not; believe it or not, this is a sign that EAM is working.

There are three main reasons why this happens:

- One is the way energy transforms. Whilst energy cannot be destroyed it does shift, change, and it can move like a wave. Say for example the RESISTANCE was held on the etheric level of your energy. As it transforms it sends a tsunami of pent-up energy through the different layers of your Aura out into your life experience before the tide returns and brings back what you've been asking for. It's perfectly normal, for instance, to have arguments with your partner when you've been working on relationships. Or to lose money when you've been working on having more. Just know that change is on the way.

- In Chapter 2, we discussed the yin yang transformation cycle which correlates to the 5 flows of energy in Chinese medicine. This is the process which everything must go through in order to change. When you release the RESISTANCE, what happens next depends on which stage in the cycle this situation was already at.

- In the healing phase, there is a spike in the journey where you are 'tested' on that subject. Use EAM to work through the healing phase; it will transform faster and you'll 'pop' out the other side into the new FLOW state far more quickly.

When manifesting with Step 5 we do not know how it will be delivered. Part of the journey to change your life means learning to surrender, so you can allow the things you want in. Maybe not in the way that you had imagined, but always for your greatest good.

NOT ALL TRANSFORMATION ARE THE SAME

You may notice that as you're releasing or allowing energy your body may begin to move in weird and wonderful ways. Then you might sometimes feel as if nothing has happened at all. Not all transformations are the same It depends where they are and how long you have held them. Just trust that a shift has occurred.

WORKING IN THE RIGHT ORDER

You'll see in Chapter 4 and beyond why there is a particular order to approach changing your life. We are beautiful and complex beings with different life experiences, interlaced with emotions, beliefs, patterns and memories. If you try to approach changing your life in a haphazard way with EAM whilst you will experience significant relief, it is not as profound. However, if you're really ready to change your life there IS a systematic way to do it. The shifts are compounded and speed up your momentum of change as you work along the journey. As tempting as it is to want to tackle your BIGGEST issue, I would suggest you start with something small. Focus on what is happening to your energy right now. Get used to using EAM with simple things. Get practice and feel shifts in your energy, strength and mood.

COMMON SIDE EFFECTS & HOW TO OVERCOME THEM

People have many different experiences with EAM and they are all normal. Everyone experiences shifts differently. Because everything is energy; we never know how it might manifest. That said please take care and take responsibility for yourself. EAM is a very powerful process. In all the years, I have shared this process with thousands of people, there has only been one case which concerned me as she experienced the side effects of a healing cycle. As we worked through it with EAM it lead to a HUGE healing experience for her. She let go of trauma and memories which she didn't even know about and been hidden from her subconscious.

HEALING PHASE – SLEEP – SNOT – POO – WEE – BURP

As you work on releasing RESISTANCE you will naturally go into a healing phase. If your body has been in stress / RESISTANCE or you've felt overwhelmed for some time, your body must go through a healing process to rejuvenate and get well. The healing phase looks like, low energy, tiredness, headaches, exhaustion, the flu, a cold, or a build-up of mucus, and yucky things leaving your body, poo, wee, burping, tooting or anything else you would rather not share with the world. It's all a sign of release and your body is in the healing phase. Luckily with is EAM you can transform the symptoms using the 5 steps and move your way through the healing phase much quicker.

I KEEP ON CRYING!

If you are crying it means that you are releasing the RESISTANCE, which is FAR better than holding it all inside. You can use the 5 Steps of EAM to transform what you are crying about. If you can then use the sway to help you explore that the RESISTANCE is about. If you are deep in the emotion just focus on the feeling. Use the 'what is happening in your energy' steps of EAM to release it. Or shorten it to, "I am ready to release this from my energy. I release it in all forms, on all levels, at all points in time." Repeat this statement until you feel the emotion subside. Then explore it with the sway. If it is something that intense that is usually a sign of a REVERSAL, so then follow the normal steps from there.

Tears are good; use them as a sign that there is something for you to work on. Use the 5 Steps to work through anything you experience.

INCREASED PHYSICAL PAIN OR OLD SYMPTOMS RETURN

This is good news, believe it or not. If using EAM has given you a new pain or made old symptoms seem worse, this means you are shifting stuck energy. If it was more than only energy, why would it get worse from saying a few words? The RESISTANCE has moved from the original place of being stuck, which may have been at a deep cellular level or hidden inside one of your organs, bones or tissues. You are now feeling the energy that is stuck on a physical level, which you can shift. Use EAM with Step 4 to release the physical symptoms and align to more free Flowing energy with Step 5. That said IF the pain is alarming, you are concerned, or have signs of a serious medical condition please seek appropriate medical attention. EAM is not to be used when there is a medical emergency, which requires attention from a physician or other health care provider. In such cases, please contact the relevant services.

COMMON POSITIVE SIDE EFFECTS

Aside from the short list of negative side effects, we've talked about all of the benefits of being in alignment and what it can do for you. I wanted to share a few of the other amazing benefits that can happen as a result of using EAM.

REPORTED EFFECTS OF USING EAM

- You may feel lighter and taller. This is because they have stopped being held down and heavy because they have transformed the RESISTANCES. They feel taller because their aura has been able to expand.

- You may experience subtle changes to your emotional response and no longer overreact or become upset or emotional. You may become calmer, more open and softer towards others.

- Your thoughts may be more positive and memories that once troubled you are now changed or no longer hold an emotional charge or may even be forgotten.

- You may attract more opportunities and positive 'coincidences' because you are more connected to your intuition and are able to access new information and have inspired ideas.

- By changing how we feel about ourselves or how we feel about other people we may see 'magical' shifts in how people respond to you and how we behave when with them because of changes in your energy

- You'll see many changes in your life which happen quickly because you are freed from limiting thoughts or emotions. You are empowered to make positive changes and take more action.

- You may look younger and your skin brighter. Your wrinkles may disappear, and you'll glow from inside. (It's known as the EAM Halo!) Your eyes will sparkle. You may lose weight or shift where you were carrying it. You may change the way you hold yourself and stand. I have seen people's posture literally change in front of my eyes as they release years of carrying the emotional baggage.

- You may even notice changes in physical health conditions even though you haven't worked on them directly. As your body gets more in FLOW your cells are able to shift and repair. Organs can properly function and your body can return to a place of wellness.

- You are more positive and empowered. You may feel that no matter what everything IS going to be okay for you.

- Your charisma and magnetism may increase. You'll have a new sense of presence about you.

WHAT TO REMEMBER ABOUT THE 5 STEPS OF EAM

Now you really know how to use EAM. These are just the basics but certainly more than enough to get you started. You've explored the SWAY, why we use it and how it creates this powerful connection. You've learnt what makes EAM different and you know how to use the 5 Steps of EAM every day. Now it's time to get ready to change your life.

PART TWO

The Inner Work Begins

CHAPTER 4

Get Ready to Change Your Life

"So many of us choose our path out of fear disguised as practicality. What we really want seems impossibly out of reach and ridiculous to expect, so we never dare to ask the universe for it."

~ Jim Carrey

ARE YOU READY TO CHANGE YOUR LIFE?

This is where the work begins. Now you understand your energy from the science and spiritual aspects, and you've got EAM to start putting it all into practice. This is where it starts to get real. There may be a few common themes that get in the way of you changing your life, which we will take a look at now. Ironically these RESISTANCES are probably the reason you bought this book. They are what you need to transform so you can move forward!

I've something important to tell you. You may want to sit down for this because it's big, important news. I am saying this right here right now because most people I meet are stuck in this very place. Are you ready? Here it is ... Wait for it ... I mean this with love. Stop f***ing around! There is NEVER a right time to change your life. No one else is going to change it for you. YOU HAVE TO DO IT. So please stop putting it off! I'm here with you. Now is the time. In this chapter, we get you ready to let go of the beliefs, patterns, and stories which are holding you back from living your most epic life. In the Introduction, I mentioned the 6 biggest myths that led me to EAM below I break down myths 1 — 5. I discuss Myth 6 Setting SMART Goals, later in the chapter.

THE BIGGEST MYTHS

MYTH 1 — TO CHANGE YOUR LIFE JUST THINK POSITIVELY ... SAY YOUR AFFIRMATIONS.

THE TRUTH

You HAVE to let go of the RESISTANCE or negativity first. You HAVE to let go of the resistant energy thoughts, beliefs or emotions BEFORE you do the positive thinking and affirmations because your ENERGY is saying something different to the words you are using. YES, affirmations, positivity, and focus are important, but you must release and TRANSFORM (Step 4) the RESISTANCE before you can MANIFEST (Step 5).

MYTH 2 — THE LAW OF ATTRACTION IS QUICK. YOU ALWAYS GET INSTANT RESULTS.

THE TRUTH

This myth has led to a world of people looking for a quick fix solution to changing their life. When what they are trying to attract hasn't arrived in 24 hours, they give up on themselves or think they are wrong or broken. They then change their focus and give attention to it NOT being there. Which manifests more of the same! I've seen people release issues with EAM, which would take years or months with other therapies, in minutes. When they are gone, your ability to attract can be fast; however, sometimes things are meant to take time. Maybe other pieces of the puzzle have to fall into place, timing has to be right, or you need to be ready to receive all you're asking for. It is during that magical space when it's being created that your faith in yourself has to stay in FLOW.

MYTH 3 — IT'S ALL ABOUT AN ABUNDANT MINDSET.

THE TRUTH

Being in FLOW and changing your life is about more than your mindset. You must understand ALL the key elements of the manifesting / change your life / personal development puzzle. I've heard people say things like, "Just write your gratitude journal" or "Just meditate" or "Just think positively". Then it doesn't work and no one tells you WHY ... These practices are only tools to enable you to harness your energy and they work brilliantly when you are in flow. But they only form PART of the picture. Everything is energy and energy can only be in one of three states. For these to work you need to know which of the three energy states it's in before you can use these tools to enable you to change it. Because we address all three states in ONE simple technique with EAM you can use it on EVERYTHING. It works wonderfully alongside these tools too.

MYTH 4 — JUST ASK AND YOU WILL RECEIVE.

THE TRUTH

The Law of Attraction is seen as this mystical magical principle which will just pop a £Million in your lap. Without you having to do anything. It kind of links back to what that quick fix mentality. It's also this underlying belief that *If I just sit back and do nothing it will be brought to me.* However, the Law of Attraction is not a passive process. YOU have to get involved in it to make it manifest. It's not just something to do when you want something; it's a way of LIFE. What determines the answer you receive is really the vibrational question you ask. But what you attract is rarely in the form you expect. Here's the thing. The guidance you receive is often more subtle. It may be a chance meeting, an intuitive nudge, finding a book, meeting a person, or hearing from a friend. People believe manifesting only means receiving the THING they asked for. We are manifesting and receiving all the time. We do get an answer; we just often miss the message. You have to take action. Otherwise you'll never find the answer you've been asking for.

MYTH 5 — YOU HAVE TO 'DIG' FOR THE ROOT OF YOUR UNHAPPINESS OR TALK IT OUT.

Many other self-help methods or traditional forms of therapy require that you relive the past. You may be invited to a session to talk with a total stranger, who will ask you questions about things which happened in the past. It can feel uncomfortable. For some people, it is helpful. For some it is painful. By re-energising past experiences, we put ourselves back into the energetic state we were in at the time. You can release, transform and let go of things in your energy, without the need to 'dig', 'find the root' or 'talk it out'. Whilst it IS important to find the point at which something began, by using the sway you can remain objective. You can get clarity on things without the pain. By releasing the energy of the situation, you also create change across multiple levels of your experience at all once.

HOW TO CHANGE YOUR LIFE

When we think about our life, most people have a mindset like this: When I have the successful business or career and the money that I want I can live my dream lifestyle and I'll be happy in my relationships. I'll be able to buy the home that I want, have the time to look after my physical health, to eat the right food, and do my yoga and exercise. I'll have the time and freedom to finally be happy. Then I will have abundant positive thinking, and I can go and sit on my spiritual mountain and do my yoga and meditation whenever I feel like it.

Most people who want to make lasting changes in their life fail before they've even started, because they approach it in a haphazard way, without a system, process, or structure. They also try to solve the right problems in the wrong order. When they don't get to where they want they think that they're a failure. With EAM you align with the FLOW of energy, and systematically work your way through each area of your life. Step by step, you allow yourself to create more FLOW and momentum. This is how we create true and lasting change.

We often get so focused on our biggest challenge and try unsuccessfully to wrestle it to the ground. Or we never complete a significant transformation in any one life area before moving on to the next. We often think, "if I can solve this *one* thing, then my life will be sorted". That might be a relationship, money, your career, business or your health. When we identify one thing it is just a tiny piece of the puzzle. You are NOT one thing. Your life is not one thing. On the flip side, if you try to change your whole life all at once it will be overwhelming. How do you know what to do first or where to start?

THE ENERGY EVOLUTION

This is why I created The Energy Evolution, a WHOLE-ISTIC step-by-step guide to changing your life that REALLY works. It's a simple, systematic way that works with the FLOW of your energy and not against it. Working through each area systematically, you approach one subject in your life at a time. As you begin working on each area of your life, you create more FLOW. It's a cumulative domino effect, which multiplies the energy. This extra FLOW of energy means that situations begin to change more rapidly for you. As you unstick each consecutive area the momentum of energy speeds up the change at increasing rates. You feel more empowered as everything is easy because you have more energy Flowing in your life. How do you begin to change your life? Well, we have to look at your life in three main areas: we call them YOUR SOUL, YOUR LIFE, and YOUR WORK.

THE ENERGY EVOLUTION

These areas are the foundations of the Energy Evolution 10-month programme. Each area has a collection of elements that are in a specific order. We work in this way because it works with the way your energy systems are structured.

YOUR SOUL

A collection of four elements of your life which only you ever experience. Your spiritual or energetic makeup, your thoughts and beliefs, your emotions, and your physical health. These four areas of your life you do not share with anyone. These are the elements which make you, you.

YOUR LIFE

Then there are areas of your life that you share with people close to you. This includes your home or physical environment and your relationships and connection to others. Your lifestyle is about enjoying your freedom, the things that make up your life which are not about work.

YOUR WORK

What we mean here is how do you express your soul's life work in the world to make money, live abundantly, connect with your passion, discover your purpose, and make your impact in the world. By working this way and by bringing all the areas of your life into FLOW first, you THEN you have the power and capacity to make a real difference to others.

Chapters 5 — YOUR SOUL, 6 — YOUR LIFE, and 7 — YOUR WORK, will guide you through each of these three life areas and give you an in-depth understanding of how to change each area using EAM.

WHY THE ENERGY EVOLUTION WORKS

We begin by working on the outer levels of your aura and systematically work our way in. We start with the outer layers of your aura, then we move onto the mental, emotional, and physical. As we release the RESISTANCE in each level, our energy is able to expand and your energy becomes stronger. This makes it easier for the RESISTANCE from the levels to transform more easily.

In Chapter 2 we talked about our HARA needing to be in FLOW to manifest. We also need our physical body to be healthy and in FLOW. If your body is sick, you're not vibrating at your highest level. To change your life, you need your physical body to be at optimal health.

We are unable to make changes in our physical health unless or until we have changed our energy, thoughts, and emotions first. By releasing RESISTANCE your body becomes strong enough to work through the transformation process.

Once your physical energy is healthy, we start working out through the levels of our aura looking at the other elements including, for example, your physical environment, your relationships, and your lifestyle. Then we can expand past the levels, connected to our earthly energy, we have the power strength and support to use our energy to influence the world around us so we have a greater impact. Ultimately, there is no one 'thing' that will change your life. It is a systematic cumulative effect that will create the biggest shifts, which is why we work this way within EAM.

Separate from the
story of your past
so you can create a
new narrative.

TIME TO RELEASE THE PAST

So many people define themselves and their lives by what happened in their past. As if it somehow explains or defines our future. We've all had life experiences that have shaped our way of living or being. Think about the logic of this for a second. BEFORE it happened, did we use it to define ourselves? How could we when didn't know it would happen? Until you experienced that situation you did NOT define yourself by it. You were alive, weren't you? You woke up and enjoyed your life? What changed? There was a shift in your energy, your perspective, and the story you held onto.

What if you could let go of that limiting story from your past that you are using to define who you are years later. What if you could shift the emotions and beliefs you hold about your past instead of allowing it to colour your life experience now? To move forward we must separate who we are now from the story of our previous life, the story of what was. Only then can we create a new narrative.

DEALING WITH THINGS OTHER PEOPLE HAVE "DONE" TO YOU

What should we do when someone has 'done' something to us? I mean *really* hurt us, either physical, emotional, or mentally? How do you find it in yourself to do the energy work when the pain inside you is so deep? Some of us have been in situations or relationships where we have experienced abuse or traumatic situations. Those will undoubtedly create RESISTANCES or REVERSALS which are stuck in our energy. You may feel angry, fearful, depressed or alone. It may feel as if no one understands you or your pain. I get it. Believe me, I really do.

When I meet a lot of people who have been in situations like rape, attack, or abuse, they say "I don't understand how I attracted that" or "the Law of Attraction doesn't work". No one consciously invites an attack. These situations can however, be 'attracted' on a subconscious level, below our conscious awareness. We attract what is in our energy even if we do not know it. It could be that on some level you did not feel worthy, or you may have felt useless or alone, or even attacked in some way? It could be a pattern from a previous or past life? It could be a pattern passed on through the family lines. Resistances come from many places.

This does not place the blame on you. We cannot control other people in our life. If something does happen, whatever the reason, the only thing we can ever be responsible for is our response to it. When something traumatic happens, we have two choices. We can let it define us for the rest of our lives or we let it go and become all the stronger for it. I am sure you can guess which one I will suggest.

HOW TO LET GO

What happened to us was a set of energetic circumstances, which will have impacted our energy. Now if we REALLY believe that everything is energy (which it is), we can choose right now to change our experience of what happened. This is one of the most powerful practices of EAM. It is a phenomenal way to change our experience of trauma on many levels. Depending on how far down the quantum physics rabbit hole we want to go, by doing the energy work you can actually change that experience throughout time, for you and everyone else involved. We can get stuck with holding on because it feels like we're letting the other person off the hook for what they did. The truth is the person you are letting off the hook is *you*. We want to get to a place of alignment towards this person. It does not mean absolving them of their wrongdoings. It's about raising your vibration. Shifting it to an emotion, which is somewhere above the line, even if you can get to the neutral point towards them. This will do wonders for your energy. If something has happened to you and it is still influencing your life, I'm sorry to say the only person being impacted by it is you. Not letting it go is hurting you much more than it is hurting them.

Imagine what it will feel like to be energetically, emotionally, and mentally free from your past. By releasing the energy, recurring thoughts and memories, heavy emotions, RESISTANCES and REVERSALS, and trapped energy from that situation, which have been stored in our aura, you can literally change your experience of it and your experience of life. You have the power and the tool now to heal the impact it has had.

What Happened in Your Past

EXERCISE

Imagine you are meeting me for the first time. You've had a bottle of wine or two and you're in full on story mode giving me the unedited version of your life. Write the answers to these questions in your journal.

- What is the story you would tell me about you?

- Who else is involved?

- What did they say?

- What did they do?

- What did you believe about it?

- Who was to blame?

- What did it stop you from doing?

- What did it allow you to do?

- How has it affected your energy?

- What beliefs do you have about it or yourself?

- How does it make you feel when you think about your past?

- What emotions do you carry about it?

- How has it affected you and your life since then?

- What does it stop you from doing?

- If you could go back and wave a magic wand, what would you do differently?

- Anything else you feel you need to get off your chest?

Now using the 5 Steps of EAM look at what happens to your energy when you think about these things. What are the thoughts and beliefs you see in there? What emotions do you feel? Now, work on each of these to align yourself using the 5 steps of EAM to a new story free from resistance.

WORKING THROUGH TRAUMA

I worked with a client over 3 one-to-one sessions. He had been brutally attacked. Before the incident he had been such a happy, empowered and confident man, successful in his work. He was disfigured during the attack and had several operations to repair the injuries. Now months on, he felt the physical pain like it was yesterday. He was living every day in this recurring nightmare of what had happened and was unable to leave the house, work or even care for his children. Every time he closed his eyes he would replay the incident, leaving him feeling fragile and exposed. He felt like he was trapped in a cage, watching life go by without being truly present. He was on numerous amounts of medication from the doctor, some to manage his mental health and some for pain management. He was petrified with worry of his children leaving the house and was stuck in a state of constant fear.

Energetically the reason this incident kept replaying is because his energy was in a reversed state. We worked through releasing this feeling that he was disconnected from his life and his body and we were able to start working on releasing the energetic pain that was still trapped in his body too. So even though the physical body had healed the 'pain', the reversed and resistant energy was still trapped inside him. We worked on releasing the pain in his back and stomach, where he had been kicked repeatedly. This was then something he was able to go away and continue working on between sessions.

At the end of the session by following the 5 Steps of EAM we were able to undo the REVERSAL, which stopped him from replaying the images. We had changed the constant replaying of the event in his mind. He was also back in his physical body, able to experience life from within. As well as significantly lessen the pain in his body after the first session he was able to reduce some of the medication for pain management, too.

At a time of shock, your body holds onto the pain energetically. This happens so frequently in traumatic situations where we literally 'detach' ourselves from the physical level. We've all heard stories of out of body experiences when someone is on the operating table or near death. In this type of life threatening situation (when faced with near death and the same with PTSD), exactly the same thing can happen.

Because the most impactful parts of the trauma (for example, the trapped sensation and repeating memories) had been dealt with in a session, he was able to start managing his emotions, working daily on the physical pain. He regained his confidence to start going back outside and finally being able to walk his children to school again. After two more sessions, we worked through many of the emotions he felt around feeling powerless at being able to protect himself and his family. We even managed to move him to a place of letting go of the anger and resentment he felt towards the attacker, which was a huge step for him.

YOUR PATH IS YOUR OWN

If you've experienced trauma or been affected by what someone else has done to you, please know your path is your own. You have two choices: you can either let it hold you or take back your power by reclaiming yourself energetically, emotionally, mentally, and spiritually. I believe you owe it to yourself. Your life is far from over; you have so much more to live. So, live it. You can start today. No matter what has happened in your past you still have your future. Using EAM you can claim it back for yourself.

WHERE YOU ARE TO WHERE YOU WANT TO BE

We've taken a look at where you were; now let's see where you are, what may be holding you back, and what you need to change to move past this point and allow the future that you want to become your present experience. Do you have situations or people in your life that drain your energy? We have to change that, otherwise you'll never have enough time or energy of your own to get on with doing what is important to you.

In the previous chapters, we talked about the Law of Correspondence: what is happening outside is also within. When you look at your life right now what is it telling you? What is the message you need to hear or receive? If your boss is being a rude, obnoxious pain in the arse are you being a rude obnoxious pain in the arse to someone else in your life?

BE TOTALLY HONEST

Look at your life right now. What is going really well? What is not going well? What makes you happy? What makes you sad? What areas of your life or people do you avoid? What topics have you buried away? What could be better? What really needs to change? These are some important questions to address because these things create RESISTANCE in your energy. If you have

RESISTANCE about something you will find it hard to change your life. Not just about that subject but everything. It is ALL energy. In the next exercise, we can take a look.

WHERE YOU WANT TO BE

To change our lives, we often look at what is happening around us right now and wonder how it could be 'better'. I know you already have a REALLY long list of things you want to change. We often dream of how we want life to be. To change our lives, we have to close that imaginary gap between where we think we are and where we think we want to be. Before now this reality of where you think you want to be may well have been eluding you. That's because the journey to change your life and close the gap is an energetic one.

The big question to ask yourself is "Is this REALLY what you want?" Do you know for sure the future you want is really yours? Or is it a construct of what you THINK you want? Is it *your* dream, or what society, family, or friends have said is right or led you to believe will make you happy? Is it possible that you have taken on a plan to change your life that may not be your own?

We often push and struggle to create a life that we think will make us happy, only to wake up and realise that what we are giving our time and energy to isn't what we really want. Or we push and sacrifice everything important along the way to attain a dream that is not ours. We also think that we have to 'get somewhere' in order to change our lives. We put ourselves on this endless journey to a destination changing circumstances outside of us, relationships, work, money, car, house. We think that those exterior things are what needs to change when it is ALWAYS an inner game. If you know the future you are creating is not yours, please stop. To change your life, you must WANT IT with every inch of your soul, otherwise how will you remain committed enough to create it? It also means you're out of alignment with it too, so it will never come to you. This is ultimately a good thing if it isn't what you really want, but it's a bad thing if you keep giving energy to it.

Where Are You Now?

EXERCISE

Look at the 10 key areas of your life outlined here. Look at the questions I asked above. Be truthful with yourself and make a note for each thing. You may want to recreate this in your journal. This is just a checklist of what we need to do so4 you can see where you are right now and what you would like it to be

ELEMENT	WHAT IS IN REVERSAL?	WHAT IS IN RESISTANCE?	WHAT IS IN FLOW?	WHAT WOULD YOU LIKE IT TO BE?
UNIVERSAL CONNECTION				
THOUGHTS & BELIEFS				
EMOTIONS				
PHYSICAL HEALTH				
PHYSICAL SPACE				
RELATIONSHIPS				
LIFESTYLE				
ABUNDANCE & WEALTH				
PASSION & PURPOSE				
MAKING AN IMPACT				

You can use the sway to allow you to see what is in REVERSAL, in RESISTANCE or in flow. When you've written something look at the message in each area for you. What does it mean? Use the 5 Steps of EAM to just work on how you feel about any of these. We will explore each in more depth in the next few chapters.

GOING ON THE JOURNEY

When we begin a transformational journey, we think the change will happen in an instant. However, there will be days when you want to give up, and you may wonder if you've changed at all. You may find friends and loved ones who are no longer a match to you energetically moving away or leave your life. This is because of the Law of Vibration. You may see things which you once held dear collapsing entirely around you; again, this is the Law of Evolution at work. There will also be days when you feel on top of the world, like everything in your life has transformed in an instant and you'll want to shout from the roof tops how awesome your life is. You'll meet new people who you have an instant synergy with. It will feel magical. Like electric goosebumps and you'll see things grow, develop and manifest in your life faster than you ever imagined.

SLOW AND STEADY ...

We have been led to believe that everything in our society should be fast and instantaneous. If we haven't achieved something we set out to do straight away we tend to give up or try a new direction or the next fad promising a quick answer. Whilst EAM is quick and the energetic transformations can be fast for one issue, there is a process of adjustment as you bring the changes into your life. The truth is changing your life IS NOT a quick process. It is a continual journey of changing your energy, the way you think, communicate, and act. Changing your life is about the cumulative effects of doing this every single day. You have to put these internal shifts into action and live in a different way. We will always be somewhere on that transformational journey and often transitioning on multiple levels, on multiple subjects all at once. So, things can feel chaotic and a little messy. Remember that in order for things to change we have go through the chaos first.

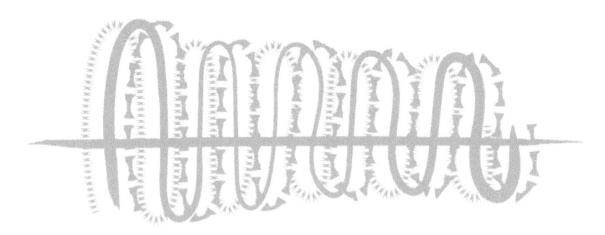

Issue 1

Issue 2

Issue 3

Roller Coaster Journey Working on Multiple Issues

THE STRESS PHASE AND HEALING PHASE

In the transformational community, we talk a lot about the stress and healing phase. This healing happens on every level of your energy, energetic, mental, emotional and physical. When you have been carrying a RESISTANCE or REVERSAL, you are in the stress phase this is a YANG type of energy. Our body has endured a lot of tension, and anxiety and is filled with stress hormones. When you resolve the issue, either by the stress being removed or the use an intervention like EAM your body there is a transformation point before you go into the healing phase. This phase looks comparatively low in energy and more YIN in nature. During that time, you need rest and relaxation and you may get physical symptoms or your life will seem to get worse.

In this healing phase, everything gets worse before it gets better. This is the most YIN of YIN. This is the bottom of the cycle and the only way is up from here. You may wake up one morning and feel that you have crashed! All your emotions will be the opposite of what you've felt. Your insecurities and beliefs will be challenged. You may feel that you've lost your self-esteem, confidence or self-belief. You are just in the process of transformation. So, hold on and be patient.

In this phase, you can use the 5 Steps of EAM to work through whatever else is coming up for you. It is being shown to you for a reason. By doing this you enable yourself to change much more quickly; you get through the healing phase and bounce out the other side. At the same time, you are reducing the pressure on your energy system to do what it will do naturally anyway, you also shorten the time frame it takes to heal. Your only work is to EAM the pants off of everything you experience. Be gentle with yourself during this process, and at the same time keep moving forward.

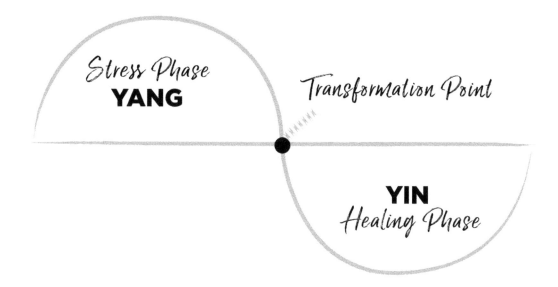

Stress & Healing Yin & Yang Phase

Your life will change
at the speed you
make aligned choices
& take action.

THE POWER OF CHOICE & MAKING DECISIONS

Have you ever been stuck in making a decision? You're not alone. We often believe that we're unable to choose what we want. That we're trapped by our life circumstances and have no choice about what to do. Or we have a decision to make and we sit on it for weeks, or months or years, waiting for the circumstances to change, without changing the way we think or taking action to change it. The other version of this is that we give away our power to make choices. We let OTHER people make our decisions for us! When we talk about the old paradigm and the new, giving away the opportunity to make a decision for ourselves is one of THE most disempowering things we can do. We are then upset because the decision which was made for us isn't the choice we really want. Remember what we learned about Neuro Linguistic Programming (NLP), 'speaking' the language of the mind; the power of making a decision means that we are more likely to complete the action and make the changes we want.

Perhaps you have to make a choice about moving. You've seen a beautiful house, which you know is your dream home. You want to go and move into it but you're worried that your partner won't want to move, or you'll be uprooting the kids from their school, that you'll be too far away from your partner's mum. You may be worried about the expense of moving or that you're too busy. So, you do nothing. Yet, if you'd release the fear, let go of those beliefs, and made a real decision about what you want, things could be different. Your partner might love to move because it *is* further away from Mum. In fact, Mum had a whole bunch of money set aside as inheritance, which she wanted to give you early. The school near the new house is in an excellent school district and the neighbourhood is filled with children offering your kids a wider circle of friends.

Indecision by its very nature is resistant because our energy, thoughts and emotions are being pulled in opposite directions. Your energy is immediately in a RESISTANT or even in a REVERSED state. When we're stuck making a decision, it's usually based on fear of getting it wrong. We then hold off doing what can change our life, all the time we are sitting in fear the lowest vibration emotion. How can any choice made from that place lead you where you want to go? When you are in fear you are physiologically incapable of making clear choices. Your body is running wild with adrenaline and cortisol, which inhibits our brain function; we are *literally* unable to think clearly.

Now, I am not advocating making rash decisions. I understand that sometimes before making a choice you need to gather information to have a full understanding. I also understand that decisions you make may have huge implications for others. However, there is a difference between actively working to understand a situation and waiting for it to magically resolve itself. The truth is, even if you make the 'wrong' choice, you always have the power to make a new one. Your life will change at the speed you make aligned choices. The quicker you make them and take action the sooner your life will change.

◐ EXPAND YOUR ENERGY WITH EAM

There are two ways you can use EAM to work through the RESISTANCE around making choices. As you release the beliefs, emotions, patterns or memories you will release everything attached to that one decision and clearly see the right action to take. Use the bubbles method to work through it all with EAM and align to making the right choice for you.

Once you have released the RESISTANCE, you can use the sway to ask the questions about what you want to do. When you hold resistance, such as a fear about something, the sway will reply to the fear that you hold. Once it is gone you will get a TRUE YES or NO from the sway. Then you can make an aligned decision.

Recognise indecision. You have the power to make choices by aligning yourself to your decision and then taking action, the universe (which you co-create) shapes, moves, and shifts to enable what you are aligned with to come to you. You just have to align and allow it.

Making Aligned Choices

CEZA OUZOUNIAN, AGE 34

Moving from London to Glasgow to be with my boyfriend was a big step. When I moved, I had trouble finding work; I had no friends and he was really unsupportive. I was trying to fix my relationship, start a business, and was stressing about the lack of money. I felt lonelier with him than when I was alone. I had lost my self-esteem and confidence and myself. I didn't realise how much was missing from within me. I was unhappy, and I never really spoke about what was going on. Instead, I just bottled it up and ignored it.

Before 6 months were even over, I broke up with my boyfriend but decided to stay in Glasgow. I was able to EAM my way through the break up; working on myself I let go of the resistances I felt. The anger and frustration. I was able to communicate from a place of love when I split up and it was as amicable as it could be. I worked through my old patterns of keeping quiet.

I worked through it with an EAM mentor and released everything that was holding me back and affecting who I was. I was able to finally open up. A lot of EAM followed, working on all areas of my life. I aligned to being myself and manifesting those things.

Now I feel myself again after about 11 years! I feel happy, calm, excited and know where my life is going and what I want. I have total clarity and my intuition is stronger than ever about choices that are right for me. I have the independence I was craving when I was in London. I've also manifested an amazing guy who is almost everything I said I wanted in a man and relationship when I wrote my manifesting list!

I know I wouldn't have got to this point without EAM. And I know I always have EAM with me for when things get tough.

THE POWER OF YOUR WORDS & COMMUNICATION

In Chapter 2, we discussed using the power of your voice to attract what you want. Your voice is your heart energy. Your energy is powerful and people FEEL the energy of communication more than they listen to the words you use. This also applies to telling the truth. Every time you tell a lie you create more RESISTANCE in your life and your energy. Lies create a separation in connection and communication between you and the other person. Most people can sense the energy of a lie.

⃝⃟⃝ EXPAND YOUR ENERGY WITH EAM

Avoid telling lies to people; if you find lying then it is time to explore. What is it that you are afraid of by telling the truth? What do you think or believe will happen? Use the 5 Steps of EAM to work through the fears, overwhelm or angst. And align to giving a more truthful response.

NEGATE NEGATIVITY

If you give power to what you do *not* want you will create more of it, by saying it out loud. I know how perfectly valid it feels to explain your circumstances to everyone who will listen. They are true. I know they are. But when you give more power and energy to them you will create more too. By using negative words in your language, you are creating more RESISTANCE in your life. Imagine every negative word or sentence is putting another brick in the invisible wall in front of you. Some people have built giant great skyscrapers of negativity in their lives just from the way they talk. Then we wonder why we find it hard to move forward.

Have you noticed how many times you use the word NO? Especially if you have children, we say it all the time. Think about your own childhood. What did you hear more, YES or NO? Studies have shown by the time a child is 17 years old they have heard the word NO 150,000+ times and the word YES only 5000! Only 3.33% of the instructional language that children hear is in alignment. Only 3.33% of the words they hear are inspiring them to take action. 96.7% of our insight from parents and caregivers is about what *cannot* be done rather than what we can. No wonder we struggle to move forward.

COMMUNICATE WITH LOVE

This is a powerful principle especially when in a tense situation. When it comes to communication you must own your energy and your words. Make sure that what you say is what you mean and that your communication comes from a place of alignment. This is the new paradigm way of communicating without fear, shame, blame, or guilt without pointing the finger of what someone did or did not do.

☼ EXPAND YOUR ENERGY WITH EAM

If you know you have a 'conversation' to have then use the balloon or bubble method and the 5 steps of EAM to work on whatever it brings up for you beforehand. Release the RESISTANCE, the beliefs, the stories, the finger-pointing and the blame; get yourself in FLOW and communicate from a place of honest loving truth.

MANAGING YOUR EMOTIONS IN COMMUNICATION

How often have you reacted by exploding in a fit of rage, pointing fingers, and blaming other people for their actions or behaviour? Imagine your most painful conversations. What if you had taken the time to release the energy, thoughts, beliefs, and emotions instead of unleashing that energy on someone else? How could that conversation have gone if you had been able to better articulate what you wanted to say? What would be happening in your life now if that conversation had happened in this way instead? Even though a situation or conversation has happened in the past you CAN change the energy of it *now*. By using the 5 Steps of EAM to work through those past conversations and release the resistant energy you can change the energy of what happened in the past for everyone involved so you can be in alignment today.

WHAT TO REMEMBER ABOUT THE POWER OF COMMUNICATION

When you are able to release the RESISTANCE then ALIGN yourself, the energy of the conversation changes. You will communicate clearly and they will receive the energy of your words, even if the content is not what they would want to hear. When you can communicate without blame or shame, people open up. They will receive your communication and therefore hear what you need to say because their defensive barriers are down. The payoff is huge. Situations will smooth out and relationships transform as people respond to your communication differently.

YOUR 'ATTRACTIVE' VISION

This is about you knowing where you want to go. I was first introduced to the power of your vision by a wonderful friend, Tamsen Garrie, author of *The Act Of Attraction In Business*. In it she describes vision in the following way: "A vision is a mental image produced by the imagination and it's usually a long-term view of the future. Many people have a vision; however, not all visions are effective when we talk about Attraction. It is about creating an attractive vision."

The source of your vision is from our subconscious tapping into our energy field. It is a wonderful expansion, way beyond what you THINK or believe is possible. We are tapping into that bigger all-knowing source of energy, which transcends our experience of time and space. When you connect to your REAL vision, it is often far bigger than you could ever imagine.

THE POWER OF VISION

When you know your vision, you know how your energy needs to feel, what thoughts and beliefs you need, and what the emotion of living life that way will feel like. You'll also know what actions you need to create your vision too. Your vision is your guide to changing your life; use it to create your step-by-step plan. It helps you to make decisions too. It's really simple. If something you are doing in your life does not match your vision, you need to find a way to change it. You have to work hand in hand with it to bring your vision to life. The reason we want to attract things in our life is ALWAYS because of the sense of peace, love, freedom, or joy we think it will bring us. The irony is to bring them into our life we have to already have those feelings.

BRINGING YOUR VISION TO LIFE

To bring your vision to life is to let go of thinking about it being *someday* and make it *today*. Whilst we think about it being a 'possible future' and rather than our actual life it will stay in possibility. I know what you see around you today may be different from your vision; what you can change today is your energy to make it match the life you want. You can live with the sense of freedom and find a way to live it now. To connect to your vision, you need to allow yourself to get into a meditative state. By doing so we bypass the limitations of our conscious awareness. Energetically we are able to almost rise up out of our body and visit our future.

When I work with my clients I lead them through this powerful visualisation where you step into the future version of yourself. I specifically lead you through the 10 key areas of your life and ask powerful questions, which enable you to connect to those aspects of your future. It is an extraordinary meditation that shows you how to tap into a life which is even bigger than anything you ever dreamed possible. The more you use EAM to release RESISTANCE in your energy, the clearer your vision becomes. Over the months and years that you use this process you'll notice your visions and intuition become clearer.

Everyone who works with us in our 10-month program The Energy Evolution, begins the journey with our one-day Attractive Vision workshop, where we work through the visualisation and I show you how to create a powerful vision board using EAM. Your vision is the start of the whole process. Your vision is constantly evolving, and everyone is invited to revisit their vision at least once a month. To begin you may only see colours or snippets the first few times you do it. The more you align and expand your energy, the more pieces of the puzzle become clear. Once you know pieces of your vision speak it out loud as often as possible. Our words have power, and the more you speak of it the quicker it comes into your reality. When people ask what do you do, share your vision. Talk about what you are creating. This makes magic happen. The right people, places, and opportunities will be presented to you. This is how you manifest because people are inspired by the future of what is possible.

WHAT IS YOUR VISION?

The first time you do connect to your vision it's not unusual to see nothing. You may only have a sense of something. Perhaps you'll see only colours or a few words. That's okay, keep working with it. I remember leading one of our vision day workshops with the group and Kerry O'Sullivan, one of our awesome EAM mentors. After I led the group through this powerful exercise, everyone awoke from the meditation and started furiously scribbling notes. But Kerry looked upset and walked out of the room. When I caught up with her she was p***ed off. She told me, "I didn't see anything in that vision. It was all just darkness. All I could see was myself running through the forest. I didn't see anything of my future. This is a load of crap."

I asked her, 'What is it about yourself that you don't want to see? Where do you feel you're hiding or can't see the forest for the trees?'

Embracing the Real Me

KERRY O'SULLIVAN, AGE 38

I had kept myself so busy all my life. Other people were my focus. I worked hard, played hard; I never stopped because when I did, I felt uncomfortable. I've never been connected to me, not truly anyway. I always had low self-worth. I had protected myself to the point of being numb and never allowed myself to receive love.

On my first weekend of the Energy Evolution 10-month programme, we did a vision mediation. At the end, everyone was writing frantically about what they saw. I was sulking as all I saw was a little girl in the woods lost with her hands stretched out trying to find her way. Little did I know then that this visual was so significant and it was the start of my transformational journey.

One of the elements of my life that I worked through in a 121 session with Yvette, was my two sides; one I had kept very much under wraps. Since I started meditating, I was having wild dreams and fantasies about all sorts of things and felt so much sexual energy. We explored this more with the sway and discovered I had experienced sexual trauma when I was younger. I had no memory of this and in the days that followed, my memory started to come back. I was able to use EAM to work through it. I had never told a soul about any of this and it had been suppressed in my memory all these years. Thanks to the sway I was able to find it and let it go. My journey with EAM has really helped me to find the real me and most importantly, love the person I've found.

PUTTING YOUR VISION INTO ACTION

If you'd like to try the guided meditation, please pop over to my website and download the powerful visualisation and accompanying workbook. It is a 40-minute visualisation which you can download and put on your phone. The more frequently you listen to it the quicker your vision will become clear and you will see more pieces of the puzzle starting to drop into place.

This visualisation is specifically tied to the 10 key areas of your life. Download the meditation for EAM from the website or if you specifically want focus around your work and business vision, book a VMA session with Tamsen Garrie (you will be so glad you did) You can download the visualisation here www.energyalignmentmethod.com/tush-freebies

TAKING ALIGNED ACTION

Aligned action is one of the five powerful principles and an important one to master if you want to change your life. It's different to just taking action. People talk a lot about taking 'massive action' but what is the point in massive action unless it is guiding you in the direction you want to go? What usually stands in the way of us taking action is those incongruent thoughts and beliefs. When you use EAM your energy, thoughts, beliefs, and emotions will be in sync with what you've asked for. When it arrives, your work is to take the action and follow it through.

To create change and transformation on a physical level, we have to take physical action. This action is aligned to your vision, energy, thoughts, and emotions. When you want to manifest a situation or effect change in your life, make sure your ACTION is congruent with what you say you want. If there is RESISTANCE in your energy then you can EAM the resistant thought, belief, energy or emotion which is in the way of you taking the action.

For example, your vision has shown you a wonderful new partner who is aligned to your values and an incredible romantic partnership. You say that you want to meet someone, but you stay at home all the time, moaning about being alone and how awful your ex was. You gripe about "never being able to find someone" and how "they are all the same". Your friends invite you out to meet their friends and you decline every time because you'd rather stay home to wash your socks. Does that sound like aligned action? What if you released the RESISTANCE and took ALIGNED action by going out with your friends and you happened to meet the love of your life who is a perfect match whilst out!

ALIGNED action should be about aligning your energy, thoughts and emotions first before you do it.

BE PART OF THE NEW PARADIGM

To really be ready to go on your journey, you need to understand a few key principles which will transform your life as you start to adopt and live them every day.

Live your life in the new paradigm. A paradigm is a model, a way of seeing something or being. A paradigm is an entire construct with ways of being that is made up of our energy, thoughts, beliefs, patterns, experiences, emotions, family, friends, society norms, and media influences. In any subject there is always the 'old' and the 'new'.

Let me give you an example of the old and new paradigm ways of being.

OLD PARADIGM	NEW PARADIGM
GROUNDED IN FEAR This is a life where you are operating from a place of fear. Trying to control things, people and situations because of fear of what may happen. You communicate from fear.	**GROUNDED IN LOVE** This is a life where you believe in the best. You allow things to be as they are. You enable freedom of choice for the people and situations in your life. You communicate from love.
LACK This thinking comes from a believe or paradigm that there is a limited source of everything. Love, money, peace, freedom, happiness, resources.	**ABUNDANCE** A way of thinking that everything is possible. That there is a unlimited and abundant source of everything. That there is more than enough for everyone.
THE 3P ENERGY TRIANGLE The Pusher – The Puller & The Protector A relationship and communication triangle of power and control. Used blame, shame, guilt to influence situations.	**THE PLACE OF POWER** A place of self-responsibility being in your own power, and communicating and living from that place in your interactions with others.
I AM WHAT I DO So many people create their status in life based on what they 'DO' for a living. Or we communicate and react to others based on what they DO.	**I AM and I DO** This way of living is about knowing WHO someone is. Where they come from as a person. In yourself it is about knowing WHO you are first and separate to the work you DO.
FALSE SELF 'STUFF' ESTEEM This is when our self of self and self-worth is based on the things we HAVE or things we have DONE. External manifestations of success where our sense of self-esteem comes from the applause and appreciation of others.	**REAL SELF ESTEEM** This is the inner self esteem which comes from being conscious of the person you are. Knowing who you are inside. So you are empowered regardless of the external circumstances. You only need appreciation of yourself.

AT 'EFFECT'
This is about a way of living your life and viewing the world where you feel you are affected by things in your external world.

AT 'SOURCE'
Where you know that you are the beginning and source of everything you see happening in your life. It is YOU who is affecting the world.

REACTIVE
You live life and react to the situations you see outside of you. It is like constantly fire-fighting.

CREATIVE
You live your life from a place of consciously creating the life you want. By managing your energy, thoughts and emotions and taking aligned action. You create by choice.

THERE IS SOMETHING WRONG
A world where there is always something wrong. Whether it is yourself, others or situations. The focus is on what is wrong.

EVERYTHING IS ALRIGHT
A way of thinking and living which enables you to know things are all ok. Whether yourself, others or situations. Your focus is on what is right and easy.

BLAME, SHAME, FAULT & GUILT
A paradigm where people try to point the finger at someone else for what is happening, without accepting responsibility for their input.

RESPONSE – ABLE
A paradigm where you are able to be responsible for what is happening. Accept your part and do something about it.

I AM NOT GOOD ENOUGH
A paradigm where often people who not feel good enough about themselves, so they look for things and people to change or valid them. Or they try to put others down in order to make themselves feel better.

I AM MORE THAN ENOUGH
A paradigm where you recognise that you are perfect, whole and complete. You have everything you need inside you. You recognise the power in everyone.

A SIMPLE SHIFT IN CONSCIOUS AWARENESS

The lists could be endless as you try to compare them all. Throughout this book I've already shared old and new paradigm ways to approach things. It is simply a shift in conscious awareness of what you think, say, do, and how you behave. You can see from the outline above that the old paradigm comes from a place of RESISTANCE or REVERSAL. These are ways of living which will often keep people stuck in those same patterns, beliefs, and habits, which prevent us from making changes. These constructs can be complicated and multi-layered as they have been created through many different situations in our lifetime.

The new paradigm way of living is about being in FLOW. It is the application of many of the principles we have shared with you. When you live your life in this way you can be free from the need to control others or try to make others change, and from the need to let others control you. You are able to create your life and respond to whatever happens in life from a place of love.

How do you live in the new paradigm? Everything in this book is about bringing yourself into this place. There are also some key practices you can do.

• **IT'S ALL JUST ENERGY.** It comes back to realising what I've been banging on about in this book, *everything is energy*. When we recognise and TRULY live this the FEAR drops away. When you recognise that everything we see has been created energetically, you can then choose to change it. At any time.

• **TAKE RESPONSIBILITY.** This only comes by taking full responsibility for yourself. This means owning what you think, how you feel, what you do, and how you communicate because we always have a choice. By living like this you create a more profound experience and empower yourself to live a life of freedom. You are no longer affected by what other people say, think or do. Truly living this means allowing other people to be responsible for themselves too. We'll talk more about that shortly.

• **RELEASE THE FEAR.** Anytime you find yourself in a place of fear, stress, feel overwhelmed or anxious, recognise that there is a belief, a pattern, or something which is holding you back. Is that coming from a place of FLOW? If we want to live in the new paradigm it means coming from a place of love. By releasing fears and all other resistant emotions you are able to clearly see or feel what is really going on. You have clarity to do the right thing.

- **MAKE ALIGNMENT YOUR TOP PRIORITY.** In EAM terms that means focusing on *you* first and getting yourself and your life in a place of alignment. It means being a little selfish in the most loving way. If you want to give to others unless you are in a place of FLOW, you really have nothing to give them without depleting yourself. If you are supporting others from the old paradigm, is it really helping? Or are you contributing to the problem?

- **STEP OUT OF THE DRAMA & INTO YOUR POWER.** You can live in the new paradigm by stepping out of the drama. It's a choice. You can choose to let others suck your time, energy, and attention into their stories or situations. You can also choose how and with whom you spend your time and energy. You do this by being empowered and coming from a place of love. We'll talk more about this shortly.

- **FIND FORGIVENESS.** I could write a whole book on this. The power of forgiveness. Forgiving someone does not mean that what they did was right. It does not excuse them or diminish your experience. By holding onto the pain, thoughts, experiences, and not letting them go the only person who is still affected is you. If only for yourself, find forgiveness and let it go. EAM the things that happened so they are no longer in your energy.

- **BE COMPASSIONATE.** Everyone is on their own journey; find a way to be compassionate about someone's situation. It means you can understand without having to jump into the drama with them. Find the place of love for them and yourself in a way that serves you both.

These are all just ideas. You'll find many ways of being. As you go on this journey you'll see that the old paradigm will start to fall away and the life you want will start to emerge. The new paradigm just becomes the new normal.

- **RECOGNISE YOUR GREATNESS.** So many of us have hopes for the future tinged with fear. We often find allowing in the abundance and positivity harder than releasing the 'bad' stuff. You may recognise the greatness in others or be able to tell them how awesome they are but often may not see the greatness inside yourself. This is your work. The list of ways

RESISTANCE can show up is endless. EAM can move you into that place of love, freedom, peace, and joy. Now that you know how to recognise your own RESISTANCE, your work is to apply the 5 Steps of EAM every time you see it showing up.

- **BE SELF RESPONSIBLE.** The secret to success on this journey comes back to SELF-responsibility. We can achieve this by paying attention to what is happening in our energy, what we think, what we say, how we feel, and what we do. As we saw in Chapter 1, we filter our own experience of life based on what is already in our energy. One of the biggest challenges we face when we make a choice to CHANGE our life is that we set a GOAL, or an INTENTION to we go into our HEAD, we overthink things, try to use logic and take action to make something happen. Ironically, this drive and push is the main reason that MOST people don't achieve their goals: they create RESISTANCE. If you're pushing to DO something it usually means you're pushing AGAINST something else. That something else is usually ourselves and the natural FLOW of life and the universe.

Most of the time we have created the NEED or DESIRE for the outcome from a place of lack or fear or a belief that we can only be happy when we have it. Whether it is losing weight, giving up smoking, eating better, drinking less alcohol, or earning more money. If you apply this energy of PUSHING, then you will be manifesting MORE of what you don't want. You'll be unable to lose weight, give up smoking or drinking and you won't earn more money because you've created RESISTANCE. The easy EAM way is to allow yourself to create from a from a place of joy, passion, or belief! As always work on the energy, thoughts and emotions and ALIGN YOURSELF TO ALLOWING those things to manifest in your life.

The power is yours

in every moment.

You can choose to be,

do or have anything.

LET GO OF SMART GOALS

In the Introduction, we discussed the self-help myths that led me to create EAM. Setting SMART goals is the 6th myth. This may be the only self-help book ever to ask you to let go of GOALS! By that, I mean let go of GOALS in the way that most people set them. Goals are about a point in the future. They are focused around achieving a certain specific thing in a certain timeframe. Usually with the intention to PUSH yourself to achieve it. This is an old paradigm way of thinking. Goals take you away from living in the moment and you get so focused on the future that you forget the present.

Most goals come from a place FEAR and LACK. We usually set the intention of the thing we want to achieve because we feel it will give us something. Ultimately the 'thing' achieving our goals will give us is a *feeling*. This hidden meaning we attach to the achievement of those goals creates RESISTANCE. For example, you want to hit a certain target at work because you'll get paid a bonus. You want to be paid the bonus because you REALLY need the money. You have no money and you are on the brink of having to move out of your house if you don't achieve it. So your drive for achieving that goal is coming from a place of FEAR. Creating anything from this place will never bring the outcome that you want.

There is an acronym about setting S.M.A.R.T. goals. They must be SPECIFIC, MEASURABLE, ACHIEVABLE, REALISTIC, TIME BOUND. This model has been used in many coaching, leadership, and mentoring programs and I once used it myself. I feel the premise of it is an old paradigm way of thinking.

- **SPECIFIC.** I agree with being specific, that allows you to have clarity, which is important.

- **MEASURABLE.** this is outcome focused. If something is measurable are you defining and possibly limiting the outcome before you begin? Measured against what? Past performance? Someone else's experience? Your own expectations?

- **ACHIEVABLE.** If something is only 'achievable', are you allowing yourself to expand to your possible full potential? Or is this you or someone else limiting your intentions before you even begin?

- **REALISTIC.** Realistic on whose terms? Why would you want to define what you want to do by what someone else has done or not been able to do?

- **TIME-BOUND.** By focusing the success or attainment of that goal on a specific point in time. Does that mean we have failed if it is not within that time period?

It is not my intention to push buttons. I am inviting you to look at the RESISTANCE that is built into the way that goals are created. These ways of thinking feel limited to me. What would happen if we allowed ourselves to set our intentions without limitations? Where in any of that has anyone mentioned, be aware of your energy, what you think and how you feel? It is all focused on the ACTION part with no alignment of ourselves in the process.

HOW TO SET REAL S.M.A.R.T. *INTENTIONS*

What if instead of setting goals we set intentions? Let's try a new way to apply SMART to our intentions and manifest from the new paradigm.

- **SPECIFIC.** You want to have clarity on what you want to create. Being specific can help you with the creation as you manifest. This gives you clarity about where you are focusing your energy.

- **MANIFEST.** Get into the space of creating it by shifting your energy, thoughts, and emotions to the things you want to have. Become the thing you intend to manifest and be clear about what it is you're asking for.

- **ALIGNED ACTION.** Be in alignment with the intention and take the right action towards your intentions. As you take action you give energy, thought, and emotion to the situation and you allow it to manifest. The aligned energy allows it to come to you.

- **RECEIVE.** Be ready to receive what you are asking for. What do you need to shift, change, or let go of in your life to allow space for this to come in?

- **TRUST.** Trust that the right people, situations, opportunities, will happen at the right time, when you are ready. Your only work is to keep yourself in FLOW.

The 5 Steps of EAM are perfectly set up to allow you to set your SMART intentions. You can use the sway to allow you to align to the right times to call this in. To know when you need to start projects or go to certain places in order to manifest this. Use EAM to set your intentions. Allow yourself to be in the right energy. Get yourself into FLOW and take the aligned actions towards what you want. As you do this you will exceed any SMART GOALS you would have set. You become limitless and with that so do the possibilities for your life.

WHAT STOPS YOU CHANGING OUR LIFE?

Very often (in fact almost every single time), *we* create the RESISTANCE. We BELIEVE that things stand in our way. Everything in our way is our creation in some way. When you think about where you are and where you want to go, there is usually something we believe we have to 'overcome'. I see this ALL the time. It usually starts with "Oh I can't do that because_____" (Fill in the blank with a story, excuse, or fear.) We unknowingly put things in our way all the time. For all the reasons we've explored, every time you share that story you make it more true for yourself. If it is a repeating pattern, then you know it is something that is stuck in a reversed energy state.

You may call them excuses, stories, patterns, or fear. Whatever way they are showing up, for you it is usually self-inflicted RESISTANCE and REVERSALS. Ouch! I know that's hard to hear. I can say that because I have been there so many times myself. I allowed my stories to get in my way. If we're changing our life by stepping into a new paradigm and taking full responsibility for ourselves including everything that has happened to us, then WHO is really responsible for still allowing these things to affect our lives. Us or them? Is that stuff really true or is it something we could choose to let go of?

These patterns can express in 101 ways. It could be self-harming or sabotaging patterns of putting others first and yourself last, keeping yourself busy, being too stressed, having poor boundaries, lack of commitment, procrastination, comparing ourselves to others, focusing on materialistic outcomes, ruining our success, not asking for support, patterns of anger or any repeating emotion, feeling helpless, overwhelmed, powerless, allowing people to treat you badly, giving others control of your life, getting in debt, ignoring or pushing away love... The list goes on and on and on.

FEAR = RESISTANCE

I'm going to invite you to let those patterns, stories, and beliefs go, because the cost to you to keep holding onto them is way too high. This is your life at stake here. YOUR LIFE. No one is going to come along and change it for you. It's up to you to do it. We hold onto these stories because there's a payoff.

They keep us 'safe' and give us a 'valid' reason for keeping our lives as they are. We can let go of responsibility, stay in our comfort zone, and maintain the status quo. Remember, one of our primary needs is to feel SAFE so anything that makes us feel unsafe will result in FEAR, which is RESISTANCE or REVERSAL.

Those patterns we have and beliefs we hold are just stories we tell ourselves. When you work through this pattern or belief with EAM and let it go, the way you think and feel about it is never the same. So how can they be true if what you feel about them changes? Does that tell you that it's all just energy? But where do these RESISTANCES come from? Everywhere. Here are a few ideas.

- We are influenced by the cycles of the moon, the sun and the planets. We are influenced by the movement and actions of the forces which are in our solar system and the wider universe.

- Our past or our energy from past lifetimes are still influencing us. Whether you believe in them or not.

- Generational patterns, fears, memories, and beliefs can be passed on through families.

- In the womb, you experience every thought, word, emotion, and conversation your mum has and they're imprinted in your energy. What happens at or during our birth can create imprints, which impact our whole life experience.

- What we learnt at a young age through our parents and caregivers influences us, as do experiences we had with our friends at school and our family. Our own perceptions of life events throughout our childhood and teenage years can create resistances we carry throughout our life.

- Maybe your current physical health is not where you would like it to be or something happened to you in the past has affected you. It may be your diet, exercise or personal care.

- The energy of the places where you spend time, what is in your environment or the energy of the buildings, space and surrounding landscape, also influence you.

- It can be patterns or beliefs we created from our previous relationships, whether those are issues from childhood or grown up relationships. It is the things we have learnt through co-dependent, emotionally, and physically abusive relationships. Even sexual experiences we've had and our partners can create resistance.

- It could be any type of grief, loss, shock or trauma, like losing your job or business, divorce, the loss of a loved one, or partner.

Do you see how all of these experiences, whether they are something you recognise and use as your story or something you do not even know, can hold you back and prevent you from attracting and creating into the life you really want. Whilst we hold them in our energy we are more likely to attract more of the same!

If you recognise any of these patterns, traits, or behaviours and you feel hesitant about letting it go consider: what is it costing you in terms of your energy, capacity for clear thinking, or your levels of love and happiness? What is the cost on your relationships, time with loved ones, and lost days of your life? Is it worth it? Or could you choose to let it go? I hope you said let it go. You did. Didn't you?

CHAPTER 4 — WHAT TO REMEMBER

This chapter was about preparing you from the journey. You've taken a look at your life. We know where we are, where we want to go. We've used EAM to let go of some of our limiting beliefs and patterns. We've outlined the key elements of the journey we're about to go on. Now it is time to look at YOUR SOUL, YOUR LIFE, and YOUR WORK in the next three chapters. This is the next steps to evolving you and your energy and ultimately changing your entire life. Are you ready?

Clearing the Way Forward

HUGH MCDONALD, AGE 58

Throughout my life I have been plagued by procrastination. With EAM I discovered that this was really masking a deeper pain of fear and hurt that started when I was around 2-3 years old. All my life I had been telling stories to a) justify myself, who I was and my actions, and b) to protect myself from the things my parents said and did. This storytelling was a way to protect myself and make excuses for why my life was no different and I carried it on into adulthood.

When I joined the Energy Evolution 10-month programme I didn't really know what to expect and believed I had a lot of baggage. I gradually worked through the first 3 Elements of the program releasing negative thoughts, emotions, beliefs, and ideas about myself. Within a few weeks' people were complimenting me how much lighter I seemed.

I could feel the difference in myself as I was no longer weighed down and held hostage by those negative thoughts and doubts. It was so empowering to feel and believe what people were saying and yes, I was so much more at ease with who I was. Since releasing these patterns I have very much been at peace with no need to justify myself to anyone.

CHAPTER 5

Your Soul

"Your soul tells you when it's time to move on."
~Oprah Winfrey

We're now going to explore some ways you can bring your soul into alignment. We've explored the theory in chapters 1 and 2. Now it's time for us to do some work and put it into practice. In Chapter 4, I introduced you to The Energy Evolution, the step-by-step journey to changing your life using EAM. This journey begins with YOUR SOUL, which is all of the elements of your life that make you, you. YOUR SOUL is the pieces of your life that you can never share with anyone. Only you experience your spirit, your thoughts, beliefs, emotions, and your physical health.

Our understanding of our inner and outer worlds is constantly expanding. We once believed that the world was flat. We did not know that we are part of a giant interconnected universe. Our connection to energy and our understanding of it all is still evolving. Yet right now we know that YOU are the key. You are the power behind what is happening.

Your Soul Phase Of The Energy Evolution

Universal Connection & Energy

ELEMENT 1

Let's take a look at the first Element in the journey of your Spiritual or Universal Connection. This relates to the outer layers of your Aura the Astral, Celestial, and Divine. We begin here in aligning your energy as best we can, so that there is nothing which will energetically hinder you as you go on this journey to change your life.

YOUR ENERGY AFFECTS EVERYTHING AROUND YOU

This energy doesn't just influence our perception of the world, our thoughts and feelings, and our physical body, it affects everything you come into contact with. Have you ever walked into a room when someone has just been told some wonderful news ... the air is electric, you can FEEL the happiness! Likewise, you've certainly been in a closed space with someone who is in a bad mood and you can FEEL it like a heavy weight. Your energy is always influencing other people. Before you shake hands with someone your energies have already met, you are literally standing in the soup of someone else's beliefs, thoughts, and feelings!

Your energy affects everything in your world, your relationships, your communication with others, what you say, *how* you say it, even what you're thinking. People don't have to be psychic to pick up on what we're vibrating about them; we can sense it through energy.

THE UNIVERSAL LAWS

In Chapter 2 we explored the Universal Laws and the importance they have in our lives. You can use EAM to help you be in alignment with these laws. Whilst the laws themselves are ever present, our energy can be out of sync with them, which creates RESISTANCE in our energy.

०:० EXPAND YOUR ENERGY WITH EAM

Using the 5 Steps, explore whether you're in alignment with each of the universal laws. This will help you to make sure you are working with them and they are supporting you on your journey.

BALANCING YIN & YANG

Another super simple way to check that you are in flow is to check your energy is balanced between yin and yang. We explored in earlier chapters that our flow of energy must be able to move between the yin and yang. If we have too much or too little of each then the flow of energy gets out of sync and it becomes harder to remain in flow.

◊:◊ EXPAND YOUR ENERGY WITH EAM

Check in with yourself regularly to see if your yin and yang are balanced. This will help you to flow through life with ease and work through the ups and downs that life will throw at you.

YOUR HEAD YOUR HEART & HARA

In Chapter 2, we explored your HEAD, YOUR HEART and YOUR HARA. Here is another super simple way for you to explore and keep yourself in flow. By regularly checking in with yourself to see if these 3 energy centres are in alignment.

◊:◊ EXPAND YOUR ENERGY WITH EAM

Ask the sway is my HEAD, HEART or HARA in flow. Ask the sway about each individually then you can use the 5 Steps to align yourself to bringing them back into sync. This will help make sure your electromagnetic energy centres are working at their optimum flow.

YOUR ENERGETIC CHAKRAS & YOUR AURA

We explored your Chakras and Aura in Chapter 2. You can align your energy by checking in with each layer of your Aura. Are they in flow and aligned? The bigger and more expanded our aura is, the more open and functioning our chakras are, and the quicker you can create change in your life. Stay in flow by checking in regularly and make this part of your morning routine.

◊:◊ EXPAND YOUR ENERGY WITH EAM

Use the sway to check in what is happening with each level of your aura or chakras. Use the 5 Steps to keep them open and aligned. By doing this you make sure your energy is open, your structures are strong, and your aura is intact.

YOUR CHILDHOOD AND TIMELINES

Energy REVERSALS can impact us energetically; they are usually linked to experiences in our lifetime, especially situations we experienced as we grew up especially during those first 14-16 years as we establish ourselves and our energy. Remember a REVERSAL is created by a situation we had no coping strategy for.

It is important to know that the way you perceive your timeline can affect the way you behave in the world and the FLOW of energy in your life. Our perception of time is shaped by our experiences, our own thoughts, beliefs, and feelings about the past, the present and the future. Using EAM you can change your timeline and the way you journey through life. When you think about the past, it takes you back there energetically. When you imagine back over your life you picture these BLIPS in your energy along the way, often significant HIGH or LOW events. When you think about the future there may also be situations you anticipate loathing or are looking forward to.

Some people experience the past as behind them while the future is in front; for others, the timeline runs from one side to the other. How you experience time can also be a clue to where you may be stuck and something else you can explore with EAM. For example, if you see the past in front of you, energetically you will see everything through the experience of your life before.

☉ EXPAND YOUR ENERGY WITH EAM

Using the 5 Steps of EAM, explore some of the significant life events you have experienced and things you foresee in the future. Work through releasing any RESISTANCE you feel connected to them. This will allow you to 'let go of the past' and align to a brighter future.

YOUR TIME IN THE WOMB

During our time in the womb, everything you mother experiences is imprinted in you. During that time when you are learning about the world; your only sense of the world is purely based on energy and learning to read the environment around you. You pick up on everything she thinks, says and does. Every emotion she experiences and every conversation or situation she is in. These imprints from our time in the womb and our birth can influence and impact our lives greatly. Very often finding these imprints from before we are born are the key to moving us forward so we can change our lives now.

☉ EXPAND YOUR ENERGY WITH EAM

Check your timeline during your time in the womb and ask how many of these RESISTANCES or REVERSALS you experienced during those first 10 months of your life. Use the 5 Steps of EAM to release these imprints in your energy and allow yourself to come into alignment.

Inherited Anger from the Womb

LISA HAMMOND, AGE 41

Cat, a client of mine, was living a life in darkness, focusing on others to stay away from her own pain. As she grew up she was estranged from her mother and family and had to live with sexually abusive family members. The anger and hatred she felt inside had become so destructive that the world was an unstable place for her and she needed an escape. Having to deal with her anger, the only way she could release this pain and frustration was to self-harm.

I worked with Cat in an EAM session. The sway helped to identify that this anger and hatred had been picked up when she was in the womb. We discovered that she had been conceived in an abusive situation. This had impacted her thoughts that had been created at that time and she held the anger and judgement because of what her mother had experienced. We worked on releasing the energy, thoughts, emotions, and patterns her mum had carried which had become imprinted in Cat's energy.

The mind-blowing moment was when we discovered that these thoughts did not even belong to Cat. Her mother felt worthless and as Cat looked so much like her dad, she had found it hard to cope, even though she loved her. We let go of this anger and judgement with EAM in one release. She was able to find a new perspective and see how things had been for her mother over the years. We allowed in with a Step 5, more love, acceptance, and honour into her body.

After the session Cat cried for the first time about her mum. She is no longer self-harming and she's been able to connect with her family in a whole new way. After holding onto this pattern for more than 45 years, EAM enabled her to have a conversation and to understand other family member's stories. She is still blown away from how EAM has helped her release this pain and find a sense of love and happiness inside.

GENERATIONAL PATTERNS

We can also carry the energy of things that never even happened in our lives. Studies have shown that we can carry the beliefs of families before us. On an evolutionary level, this is designed to 'protect' us so that we learn to remain aware or afraid of things that may harm us. Have you ever noticed that similar things seem to happen to the members of one family? Examples might include a family history of debt or a thread of illness in the family line. We can and do pass these onto our children too.

◊⫶◊ EXPAND YOUR ENERGY WITH EAM

Look at your family. Can you see any themes which have been passed through the generations? Use the 5 Steps of EAM to work on releasing these patterns. By working on this you change this energetically for everyone in previous generations and those to come in the future.

SLOWING DOWN TIME

What would your life be like if you could actually slow down time. How much more would you get done? How much more of your life would you enjoy? What moments would you savour? I know for sure you've experienced time running away from you. The truth is we control our experience of time. We control how fast or slow it goes by our presence in the moment. Have you ever noticed that on holiday while you're dozing on the lounger you shut your eyes and it feels like hours have gone by? When you check the time it's only been 15 minutes. But when you have a deadline to meet the clock seems to speed up the closer it gets. Well thankfully we have EAM to slow it down. By changing the momentum of energy, shifting our perception of time and slowing our train of thought, we become more present.

◊⫶◊ EXPAND YOUR ENERGY WITH EAM

Use the 5 Steps of EAM to work on how you feel about the things you have to get done. Ask the sway whether you can slow down or speed up time. Follow the 5 Steps to change your experience

LET GO OF THE PUSH, OPEN UP & ALLOW

Throughout this book and this journey, we'll explore all the areas where you can use EAM to align the key aspects of your life. That said, alignment isn't a thing to be done once and ticked off your list. It is something you must do in each moment, each day. I want you to become so tuned into how you feel so nothing takes you away from that. So, whenever you feel like you're pushing or creating RESISTANCE or you're unsure or not clear or you feel low vibration I want you to stop, and do some EAM.

Am I Pushing?

ELEMENT 1 EXERCISE

Here are a few examples of questions you can ask to get started. (Then follow the 5 Steps):

- Am I feeling RESISTANCE about_____?

- Is there RESISTANCE in my energy when I think about_____?

- Am I pushing to make_____happen?

- Am I working against the FLOW about to make it happen?

- Is now the right time for me to be doing_____?

- Do I have resistant thoughts / feelings / beliefs about_____which prevent me from getting on with it?

These are a few exploratory questions you can ask to get you started using the 5 Steps. Get used to asking these questions all day, every day. Again, this is part of noticing how you feel and how in or out of FLOW you are in each moment. NOT PUSHING does not mean not taking action! In fact, far from it — I want you to take action, and ALIGNED action always. Aligned action trumps PUSHING action because it is following your HEART and is guided by your HEAD. If you are in RESISTANCE and try to take action you will never create the life you desire or are aligned to; you will just create more of the same chaos and confusion. Alignment allows the right inspired ideas, thoughts, and actions to come to you want to take action.

Create an Abundant Mindset

ELEMENT 2

In this element, we're working on transforming the mental level of our AURA and energy. We're working our way in from the outer levels of our energy. As we release the RESISTANCE we expand, making it easier for us to heal and grow.

We used to believe that to master our life it was just our MINDSET and our BRAIN that we needed to 'control', that once we could tame that beast then everything would be fine. Yet many of the more traditional cognitive processes only address part of the story. We now know that to change our beliefs we must also address the energy. In fact, our beliefs are just an expression of energy. Let's see how we can get the mental level of our energy to support us.

This is about aligning all of those 'hidden' pieces which make us... well, US! You will recognise this as our cognitive thoughts and experience of reality. We want to bring to light and life those unknown parts of our conscious and unconscious energy, integrating them in a way which serves us now. Many of the beliefs, thoughts and patterns we have, come about from a place of protection or fear. Our work through this journey is to transform the fear, the RESISTANCE, and anything which is constrictive or low vibrational in our energy.

The good news is that our life is probably very different to how we think it is. The flip side of that is that we are living the life that our 'mind' has constructed. We know from Chapter 1 and 2 that this mental level is made up of our thoughts, beliefs, memories, fears, hopes, and experiences. They cloud our ability to be objective. Everything we see is subjective. We want to change our interpretation of experiences to ones which are supportive.

YOUR POWERFUL THOUGHTS

From a spiritual or energetic perspective, our thoughts are forms of fast moving, higher vibrational energy, which cannot be seen with the naked eye, yet we experience them in every moment. In fact, they ARE our experience!

Remember, I said our aura is a recording device? Well our thoughts are often replayed over the soundtrack from those records. Whilst you may be having a new experience there is always this background noise and filtering from our past. Every thought has it's own vibration, every vibration is energy.

Remember energy is always omnipresent meaning it can be in multiple places at once.

Thoughts reside in the mental layer of the aura. Each thought has its own vibration; every vibration is energy and energy is omnipresent (meaning it can be in more than one place at a time). Which means, a thought can BE anywhere at any one time — in our aura, in our brain, in our physical body, and our energy. Some thoughts are higher vibrational, therefore lighter and quicker and some thoughts are slower, heavier and denser. We have thoughts which are supportive (higher vibe) and thoughts which aren't (lower vibe).

WHAT ARE THOUGHTS?

The dictionary defines a thought as an idea or opinion produced by thinking or that occurs suddenly in the mind. We are led to believe that a thought is like a piece of 'data' stored inside our brain like a filing cabinet While it's a helpful analogy, however, it isn't the truth.

Neuroscientist are still not clear what our thoughts are or where they originate from, yet they do know we must have brain function in order to have them. With instruments like EEG's they can see what is happening with the electromagnetic energy in the brain yet they don't fully understand its source. Energetically, we know our thoughts originate from the mental level of our aura.

Each thought has its

own vibration.

Every vibration is energy

& energy is always

omnipresent.

UNDERSTANDING OUR THOUGHTS

On our journey of development, we want to transform our thoughts to be ones which support us, so that we can allow ourselves to be more in FLOW. More coherent in each moment!

We've already spent lots of time exploring how our thoughts impact us on an energetic, psychological and physiological level, but let's have a quick recap. If we are holding a lifetime of resistant beliefs, they are literally weighing down our energy, preventing other information coming in, and sending out the incorrect information through our aura. This is part of the reason we mis-manifest because those beliefs are still in our energy. In addition, we have our trusty friend momentum. If you have many thoughts of a similar lower vibration, they begin to attract one another. It becomes a waterfall of RESISTANT thoughts, which creates resistant feelings, which send out resistant messages, which create resistant situations in our reality! I am sure you can see WHY we begin with raising the vibration of our thoughts first and foremost!

PSYCHOLOGY

From a psychology perspective, by releasing resistant thoughts that keep us stuck in circles and prevent us from being focused in the moment, we allow ourselves to get ore in flow. If your thoughts are doing their own thing, they can easily divert your energy, focus and attention. Become the creator of your thoughts rather than let yourself be at their mercy. This comes over time, the work we do here is designed to support you and let go of the previous patterns which held you back.

PHYSIOLOGY

We are literally rewiring the brain when we change our set pattern of thinking. Our thoughts also influence our behaviour — if we THINK a certain way — we DO a certain thing. In order to start changing the ACTION that you take, you have to have the right energy, thoughts, and emotions first.

CHANGE THE MOMENTUM OF YOUR THOUGHTS

Maybe the reason you're on this journey is because you already know that some of the thoughts you have don't serve you. You probably have some thoughts running on key subjects already (which are just thoughts that have a momentum). For example, you're currently worrying about MONEY, because you think you don't have enough money coming in to cover your bills. You wake up in the morning, thinking you need to make some more money. You are constantly thinking, "I need more money, I need more money, I need more money, I need more money. I don't have enough, I don't have enough, I don't have enough. Where is my money, where is my money, where is my money? Why isn't it coming, why isn't it coming, why isn't it coming? It's not fair. It's not fair, it's not fair."

And you wonder WHY the universe is bringing you MORE of the same things.

More NEED for more MONEY.

More NOT having ENOUGH money.

More NOT knowing where your money is.

More NOT coming of money.

More NOT being in fair situations.

What if you could find a way to change this momentum of energy and start to consciously think about what you're doing. You could change your thinking to be – "I have more money, I have more money, I have more money. I always have money, I always have money, I always have money, I always have money. My money is here. My money is here. My money is here. Money comes to those in alignment with it. Money comes to those in alignment with it. I'm in alignment." Consider how this new perspective would change your life. You have more inspired ideas on how to make money, and feel EASIER about allowing money in. You shift your whole perception and your whole reality, when you make the choice of consciously changing the words you use.

◊:◊ EXPAND YOUR ENERGY WITH EAM

You can now recognise when your train of thought is running away with you. What is the repeated pattern that keeps drawing you in? Use the 5 Steps of EAM to explore these resistant beliefs which have momentum. Use momentum to speed up the manifesting of beliefs you want to keep.

Creating an Abundant Mindset

LORRAINE SINYARD, AGE 44

I definitely knew there was more to life than what I had. Employed as Head of department in a secondary school I was feeling overwhelmed and demoralised by the system so I decided to leave teaching. I set out as self-employed and was keen to expand, grow in knowledge, and to change.

A Facebook advert about EAM kept popping up. I opened it up and there it was — a chance for change. I joined the Energy Evolution 10-month programme and things in my life started to change for the better. I expanded my training business, moved house, built my massage business, changed my view on life and, more importantly, changed myself. With my mind and energy now focused completely on all the things I wanted, I was ready to take on the world.

My mindset has completely shifted to what is important in my life and I have constant signs and gifts from the universe. Without a clear mindset and focus, I would not be where I am now.

MANAGING YOUR MEMORIES

Our memories are a type of thought. Scientifically, they are shown as a series of neurons in the brain firing in specific patterns. Our memories are our interpretations of past situations. They are our understanding and recording of what happened, which is distilled and distorted through our filters. The big question is always, 'Are our memories REAL?' Have you ever noticed over time a memory can seem to change? Maybe the next time you relive or tell someone the story it's changed ever so slightly; maybe there's a little bend of the truth or an elaboration of a certain fact. Now if you continue to tell that story for long enough it becomes a 'TRUTH'. Did it really happen that way? Or is it now just another story you tell?

WHY DO WE NEED TO CHANGE OUR MEMORIES?

It ALL comes back to whether those memories serve us. We naturally refer to the past in order to assess our present (and our future). We must change our memories if they hold RESISTANCE or REVERSALS, as they take us out of FLOW.

Energetically our memories are also recorded in the mental layer of our aura and these 'stories' are what we refer back to in order to make sense of current situations. They form the 'filters' we put on our life. If you have memories (stories) which serve you, they create a picture of a time when you felt good. You were happy, alive, and all was well. However, if you have memories or stories which are painful to relive, they hurt you, or you have made judgements about things and people based on them, these we need to transform.

WHAT IF YOU HAVE TRAUMATIC STORIES?

When I was about four or five I was playing at a friend's house and fell into the swimming pool, underneath the pool cover. I wasn't a very good swimmer. I remember having to fight my way up to the surface under the cover, gasping for air, swallowing water and trying to breathe. As I grew up what do you think my experience of water was? Did I jump in and love swimming — definitely NOT! I can swim but I was never a fan because I always felt like I was drowning.

I have since worked on those memories so that I am now MUCH more confident in the water. Am I an Olympic swimmer? Again, definitely NOT! But I LOVE being in the water now, especially taking my son swimming. Making the time to do this work on myself means I am able to be in the water and teach him a very important skill – learning how to swim. Had I NOT done this work on myself, I would have stayed away from water all together. It would have been easier to not let him swim and allowed that fear to affect me and what I did, but what would that have created? Another child who is afraid of and isn't safe near water.

Changing your memories can have an amazing ripple effect. When you change them and no longer have RESISTANCE, you make new choices, take new steps, and find new ways of behaving. This begins to change your life AND the life of others around you.

⚉ EXPAND YOUR ENERGY WITH EAM

If you have experienced incidents in your life or you hold stories or memories that are unsupportive, then use the 5 Steps of EAM to let them go. You could also try using the bubble method to help you explore it. By doing this you will change your internal reference points for things in your present and help you create a better future.

YOUR CORE BELIEFS

Your beliefs about yourself are just repetitive thoughts you will keep on thinking. These are some more standard set points that you have (remember those neural pathways)! Beliefs are like the lenses through which we view our world. They are your window on life and determine your outlook and approach. Beliefs are based on personal life experiences. They are opinions and views and generally come from others, be it family, religion, media, education or social circle.

Some of the beliefs we hold serve us; they can enlighten and support us. They provide us with a sense of love, guidance and well-being. Some beliefs limit our perception of ourselves and the world around us. They act like that 'voice' inside our head that makes us question / doubt / hold back / give up on our life and our dreams. Without awareness, we are likely to think and act as if our beliefs are *actual truths*.

Have you ever heard or read a statement which felt as if it challenges the core of you? Have you ever struggled to transform these core beliefs which do not serve you? When you can transform your core beliefs, you will to see your life getting better and better. This is because what you believe internally will be reflected back into your external world and reality, through the Law of Correspondence.

You express core beliefs as, 'I AM' statements. There is immense power in 'I AM'. Be aware of, and note, what you attach to it because, 'I AM' is literally you. Nobody else can say, 'I AM on your behalf.' Tell yourself, 'I am fat and need to lose weight' and you simply reinforce the opposite of what you want. 'I AM' acts as a command to your higher source. When you believe 'I AM one with life', you are co-creating and honouring your inner light and brilliance. With EAM we can create our own destinies, using the 'I AM' power.

Our core beliefs run every aspect of our life. From the age of 0 – 7, our entire focus is to learn and absorb. We are literally like giant sponges soaking up everything in our experience. We do this by learning about the things we SEE around us, things we FEEL from others and the WORDS others say. Then we create our OWN perception of a situation and from that we make a decision about the way the world works. We call them beliefs.

These core beliefs aren't always TRUE and yet they may be TRUE for us. Very often we are running our adult lives based on the core beliefs we created as a child.

۞ EXPAND YOUR ENERGY WITH EAM

I want you to pay attention to the statements you give to yourself, the 'I AM' statements you believe. We want to engage with the beliefs that serve us and transform the beliefs that do not. Use the 5 Steps of EAM to shift any beliefs which stand in your way. By aligning to more supportive 'I AM' statements you will feel more empowered.

CHANGING OUR PATTERNS

A pattern is still a thought; it just has a LOT of momentum which creates a habitual way of thinking or behaving and becomes the easiest way to THINK about something.

Energetically – Patterns can be learnt, inherited or passed down. Patterns can also come over from our past lives.

Physiologically — Again it's those neural pathways. On a structural level, every time we think a thought our brain gets wired together in a certain way. After a while of repeating that SAME type of thinking, those neural pathways embed and repeat the same thing on auto pilot.

Psychologically — Our brain just deals with similar information or situations in the same way. These patterns are created via a process of generalisation. We create patterns in many ways. We are born with some beliefs as you sense everything your mother experiences whilst you develop in the womb.

Other experts believe our patterns are learnt by observing people when growing up. They also come from our experiences, through which we created beliefs, and, then respond to similar situations in the same way. I believe all of the above are true.

WHY DO WE NEED TO TRANSFORM PATTERNS?

It is important to understand our patterns because we are often not even aware they are there. Why is that? It can be difficult to see something in yourself which is just normal for you? We create patterns because they make us feel SAFE. We like routine and predictability. That way there are no scary surprises. There can be no danger if we have a learnt strategy for coping with every type of situation. Then we know what to do time and time again. Voila — a pattern!

This process of creating patterns has kept us safe. It is inherent in our fight and flight response. Think for a moment about the basis of that. Most reasons for creating patterns are out of fear, danger, or a need for protection. Do any of those feel open or expansive to you? If most of our patterns are based on fear and a need to protect, my question is - are they all serving you? Probably not. Our role here is to find a way to step outside of those patterns and see them for what they are - forms of protection.

HOW PATTERNS AFFECT US?

The biggest patterns we see in self or personal development is self-sabotage, I see it all the time (and spent MANY years doing it myself!). Self-sabotage is again a pattern of coping, a way of keeping us safe, many people are familiar with FAILURE and FEAR from a young age. They are used to being around dysfunctional people or situations, or they are used to situations not working out for them.

Self-sabotage is a way of destroying something that could be so promising. It is a way of us keeping ourselves in line, so everything in our life is safe and predictable and it stays within the status quo! You've seen self-sabotage. We all do it, and you see it most in those people who ALWAYS have some kind of drama going on in their life. Some people ACTUALLY thrive off the excitement of the drama. No matter what the subject is, they are driven to create this drama, even though it is deconstructive! Does it mean that everyone with drama is a self-saboteur who is enjoying it? No, but there will surely be some momentum of energy around that subject. If left long enough drama can become a way of life, passed down through the family like an heirloom!

In the simplest terms, self-sabotage is an unconscious need to be in control, even if what you're controlling isn't good for you or your journey. To me, that is a sure-fire way to keep manifesting exactly the same thing.

How many times have you heard someone say "I haven't had time for that. I've been too busy" or "I can't do that. I've been working so hard"? Then you find them on the sofa watching TV. The issue for them is twofold, a) they say those words (which means the Law of Attraction will keep on bringing it to them) and b) they are spending most of their time feeling overwhelmed and therefore unable to take action or get clarity on everything they have to get done. So, they waste time sitting in front of the TV. This creates a pattern and eventually a self-fulfilling prophecy, which will continue to until they do something to step outside of it. Which in your case means it is time to EAM.

Letting Go of Patterns

ELEMENT 2 EXERCISE

I could create an endless list of self-sabotage patterns. Let's start with some of the most common ones, which stand in our way. Ask the sway which of these are true for you. Say the statement out loud. For example, "I have a pattern of achieving happiness or success then ruining it". If you sway YES on any, work through them using the 5 Steps. Here are a few to get you started. Feel free to add your own or work on anything you know gets in your way.

PATTERN	DESCRIPTION
Achieving happiness or success then ruin it	Once happy, or when something good is happening, do you behave in a way to make it not an enjoyable situation?
Believing you are your feelings	e.g. something feels hard and overwhelming so you believe YOU are incapable of achieving it
Compromising your health	Do you have a habit of over-eating/health drinking/doing things that affect your health and wellbeing?
Everything is bad	You just believe everything and everyone are out to get you, or that things or people in general can't be trusted
Focusing on your biggest problems	Always focusing on what is wrong in your life rather than what is right
Giving up, or hiding away from the truth	A habit of stopping doing something when it feels a challenge or never even trying
Inability to commit to or hold on to long-term relationships	Do you have a pattern of ended relationships?
Believing you do not deserve	For example, saving money or getting it in and then blowing it all on a spending spree
Procrastination	Putting off completing things you don't like to deal with
Seeing everyone else as wrong	You believe that you are always right, your way is best and others are incapable
Staying in negative thoughts	Your consistent pattern of thought is a train of general negativity

Transform Your Emotions & Vibration

ELEMENT 3

Now we're still working inwards from the outer layers of our aura as we move from mental to emotional. This is about aligning ourselves to maintain high vibrational emotions. This element is all about EMOTIONS. Here we investigate your emotions and how they impact your everyday life. You will get to know the Emotional Scale, and let go of addictive emotions, patterns, and resistant energies which create habitual ways of feeling. Together we will raise your Emotional Set point, so that you are more consistently in a positive place.

We used to believe that our emotions were just an outcome of our thinking. Many of us were brought up to ignore our emotions and only trust our logical thinking mind. Now we know our emotions are powerful. The new paradigm of understanding is that they are something WE control. It is a wonderful mix of energetic, physiological, and psychological influences, which is an output from our brain and ALSO our heart. By learning how to consistently raise your emotional set point you'll begin to see your life change and expand for the better.

WE ARE BORN TO FEEL GOOD

Your emotional health is all about how you feel on a day to day – moment by moment basis. We want to get you connected to what is happening in your body and what your emotions are doing. Our emotions are one of the MAIN ways we experience life. Everything we do in life is because we want to feel good or at least better than we do right now. We would never consciously do anything to ourselves that makes us feel worse. Yet you can see how we are unconsciously doing things which make us feel worse all the time, through a lack of knowledge.

I hope by now you know you CAN and DO control your emotional experience. In fact, it is OUR job to FEEL GOOD and we CAN choose to feel good in each and every moment. No matter what is happening outside. We are meant to FEEL good! It's our innate nature to be this way. Remember everything in the universe is designed to grow and expand and be in FLOW. That includes us.

Either way, you experience it as a place of calm and patience, because you feel so secure in yourself. You no longer criticise yourself or others, you know and own your emotions! How amazing will it be to feel like that each day?

In EAM we call that ALIGNMENT. The more emotional health you have, the more self-esteem you have. This means you no longer react with knee jerk responses, anxiety or panic to the events that occur in your life. Instead, you are usually calm and patient with yourself and others. You are an emotionally safe person to be around because you feel secure. Emotionally safe people do not judge or criticise themselves or others. Instead of trying to avoid them, emotionally healthy people feel safe with their feelings and emotions and can express themselves in healthy, assertive ways.

NEGATIVE EMOTIONAL PATTERNS

Our negative emotional patterns are one way that neural set points are expressed. They are physically created in the same way. Remember neurons that fire together wire together, so it is our habitual way of feeling. Having a habitual way of feeling negative thoughts or feelings does not mean there is some kind of dysfunction. It is perfectly normal AND a part of our natural process. It only becomes an issue when it is repressed or becomes a HABIT. Experiencing negative thoughts and emotions is natural because we're human and it is part of the human experience. Energetically, these habitual patterns are recreated through the momentum of energy.

۞ EXPAND YOUR ENERGY WITH EAM

We want to UNWIRE the parts of us energetically, which are just running these patterns of emotions on autopilot. Pay attention to the way you feel. Get connected and tuned in to what you feel on a moment by moment basis. Is it in flow or in RESISTANCE? Use the emotional scale from Chapter 3 to help you. By doing this you will create a new habitual cycle of emotions that serve you.

Forgive, Love & Be Happy

LOUISE PRICE, AGE 60

When I first came to EAM I was disillusioned and unhappy with my life. At 52, my husband had chosen to leave our marriage and set up home with another woman. I was inconsolable and angry. For a long time though I didn't tell anyone - not even my closest friends, or my family. I felt ashamed, a failure.

I had lost not just a husband, partner, best friend, but also his family, who I loved, and joint friends who I couldn't face. Somebody else was taking my place and I couldn't bear it. Somehow, deep down, and for a reason unknown to me at the time, I wanted to approach the break-up from a place of love and not of bitterness or hatred. I had seen so much of how this could destroy people. I couldn't bear to not love him; doing so would destroy a part of *me*.

I searched for a better way. Returning to my psychology roots, I retrained in psychotherapy, neuroscience, life coaching, NLP ... but it was EAM that finally showed the way. With EAM I began to realise that I could live my life my way and change the way I thought about HIM, HER, LIFE and ME. With EAM I began to rebuild my life, attracted new friends, reconnected fully with my family, developed wider interests, started a holistic business, and began my spiritual journey.

By working through this process, I came to understand why the way to peace is through love and in the process, I discovered a new relationship — yes, I could love again!

UNDERSTAND OUR CONFUSING EMOTIONS

Emotions can be confusing. The first seven years of life are crucially important to how our life unfolds. Think about it for a second: what is the main method of communication of tiny baby? You land in this world with your parent(s) there to care for you. You're unable to speak, or move, and you can barely lift your head. So, what can you do? You use your senses.

Children are giant sponges. They have an inbuilt sense of what is happening in the world because their ONLY method of communication is through the senses. They have to use touch, sound, feeling emotions, and the energy they feel to read people's body language. These skills develop way before verbal communication. This is where we develop our emotional intelligence, meaning you are able solve emotion related problems. We need to learn this skill from a young age because it keeps us safe. Being able to read and understand others keeps us protected. We learn to trust these methods of communication because they are unmistakable. This is why children are so sensitive to energy or emotions and they can easily pick up on someone's vibration or vibe.

Imagine we had an emotion like LOVE demonstrated by our parents through stress, anger or irritability. How confusing for a small child to have someone saying, "I LOVE YOU" through gritted teeth or whilst shouting or trying to control them. Their inner senses would be telling them one thing (because they are picking up on the vibration and facial expressions). At the same and they are believing in the words of someone they TRUST – for example, their parent, teacher, or another person they are learning from. In this situation, we are always taught to defer to the judgement of parents. They think, well my feelings MUST be wrong because Mum (or Dad or teacher or brother or sister _____ you fill in the blanks) SAYS that it is something else. For this reason, we can also become confused about which emotions are which and learn NOT to trust ourselves as we grow older.

It's through a lifetime of these experiences, that we disconnect from our own guidance and let other people explain our feelings! This is how we become disconnected from our own emotions (positive and negative). For example, you were jumping around and having fun in the kitchen, someone shouted "stop doing THAT" because you were playing near a hot oven. In that moment, your perception is that you shouldn't be playing and feeling excited. Meanwhile, they just wanted to keep you safe.

We've also been taught that thinking about how we feel is selfish. We believe that we should put other people first because it's the NICE thing to do! So, we learn to swallow what we think or feel and bury it so we never express ourselves. As a society, we are conditioned to disconnect from positive emotions by things we see in our family, news, politics, soap operas, magazines. We perceive what is OUTSIDE to be more important than what is within.

CONNECTING TO POSITIVE EMOTIONS

Sometimes people find it hard to engage or connect to any emotions at all. They either feel numb, or everything feels like one giant lump with different levels of heaviness. If you experience numbness instead of emotions, there is nothing wrong with you; it can mean a number of things. It could be a long period of time suppressing your emotions. It could be an energy REVERSAL created at a time when you expressed emotion and had it shut down. It can be medication or other energy toxins. Just understand that these are all just energy, which means it can be changed. During this element drink plenty of water, get lots of sleep and rest. Remember that everything we unleash and transform has the equal and opposite amount of energy at the other end of the scale. As you release this numbness, you are in for one hell of a ride into love and joy.

In general, we are not raised to be joyful and happy and to do what we FEEL is right. We are constrained by so many rules and other people's ideas of what we SHOULD and SHOULD NOT conform to, when there is really only ONE universal rule: to always do what makes you happy or experience love! Imagine what the world would be like if we all lived that way. The irony is that positive emotions are what we NEED to create the life we want. Remember the things we WANT are only because we want to feel better – SO just choose to feel better.

Emotions are

powerful manifestors.

If you want your life

to change you have to

feel good first.

The more areas you feel positive about the better it will get. You will naturally attract more positive things to you. If you catch yourself saying "I just need to do ... before I can be happy or fall in love.... "then you have work to do. Everything is ALWAYS about how you feel FIRST.

◐ EXPAND YOUR ENERGY WITH EAM

Get in the habit of noticing what you're feeling when you do things. Are you emotionally engaged or detached? What is your predominant emotion throughout the day? Are you stopping yourself experiencing the positive emotions? Are you holding yourself back from feeling good? Use the 5 Steps of EAM to explore and use the emotional scale to help you see which emotional frequency you are vibrating at. By deliberately raising your emotional set point you'll change your ability to attract.

WHAT IS HAPPENING ON A PHYSICAL LEVEL?

In our bodies, there is believed to be a specific area known as the limbic system. This is a set of brain structures, which are found at the top of the brainstem and underneath the brain cortex. These structures of the limbic system are involved in many of our body's emotional responses especially those parts which relate to our safety or survival. In evolutionary terms, this part of the brain was the part which enabled us to extend our awareness and perceive things with more than our eyes and ears.

This system influences both the peripheral nervous system and the endocrine system, which means it is able to pick up on information from outside of our body (for example, from our aura or other people's energy) and triggers the endocrine system (which is connected to our hormones and our chakras), which in turn creates the physical sensations we experience as emotions — which literally means energy in motion.

HOW DO EMOTIONS WORK?

On a PHYSIOLOGICAL level, our emotions are created via hormones in the body. These hormones are protein molecules known as peptides. It has been shown that we have the same receptors for these peptides throughout our body as we do in the brain. For example, a peptide could have receptors in the kidney for reducing blood pressure and the SAME receptors are found in the lung and brain. This led scientists on a search for neuropeptides (brain peptides), which they discovered were found in almost every area of the brain.

The neurons in our brain, which are thought to trigger emotions and act a little like wiring, are actually operating more like hormones floating in the blood. These chemical substances travel far outside the brain and into the whole body. Studies have shown that repressed traumas caused by long standing or overwhelming levels of emotion can be literally stored in the physical body, actually affecting your ability to feel or move our physical self. Think about this for a moment; if these receptors are everywhere, then there are an almost infinite number of ways that our mind-body is connected. This is how emotions create our physical dis-ease (which we will explore more in later chapters).

On a physiological level our emotions are usually an outcome of our brain and mental level of energy. Remember we have mental, emotional and energetic set points. With emotions, we may consciously, or unconsciously, remember particular times that we may have felt like this before. Because our psychology works primarily through matching patterns, our brain is automatically looking for a time when our physiology felt like this before, when it had this same mix of hormones and signals coming from the heart rhythm.

We are also experiencing the 'set wiring of the brain' which is where the neurons in our physical brain have a set pattern of things which are wired together – again from our previous experiences. This wiring creates its own hormonal experience and often triggers us to start thinking habitual thoughts associated with this way of feeling, too (for example, negative thoughts and beliefs) which we are so used to experiencing. It just feels normal. This is because these hormonal and mental experiences are tied in our brain. With EAM, we are able to break old habitual patterns by changing this "wiring" of the brain and creating new emotional experiences. Step 5 of the EAM process empowers you to connect new emotional experiences and associations with these thoughts, beliefs, and patterns so you create a new set point that serves you.

With EAM, our goal is to change our internal set points to retrain our energy on a mental and emotional level so that the messages being sent around the body and sent out in our energy are something we would choose.

TRANSFORM OUR EMOTIONS & OUR REALITY

To change our reality, we must get into the practice of FEELING good. This can be hard if you're still in the OLD paradigm way of thinking, observing what is happening now instead of creating what you want by directing your energy, especially if you keep noticing that you are yet to manifest what you want. If you continue to talk, think, or take actions based on what is happening now – you will only get more of what you have now.

If you feel RESISTANCE about something you perceive, you cannot change what you see whilst you feel that way. Your work is to note what you feel or think and begin to transform your life. Denial is not a river in Egypt! To create change we must first accept that it's down to us to change how we feel. Remember emotions are just energy, which means they can transform in an instant. As you use EAM on this you're rewiring your energy, too. So, you're transforming your OWN perceptions of reality in an instant, as well.

Remember our energy has a carrier wave, a message transmitter which means we must get clear on our energy and understand what our emotions are. If we are disconnected from our emotions, and unable to feel what is happening in our energy, we could be misfiring emotional messages all over the place, which explains our misfired manifestations, too!

⊙∷⊙ EXPAND YOUR ENERGY WITH EAM

In the same way, we have momentum of energy with our thoughts, we can have them with our emotions. Pay attention to your predominate emotions throughout the day. Stop resistant emotions before they gather speed. Use the 5 Steps of EAM to explore the emotions that come up and align to higher vibration. By doing this we prevent situations emotionally escalating and create a greater momentum of positive emotions.

We'll talk more about some of this when we look at the physical body in the next element. For now, understand that your emotions play a KEY and powerful part in your physical and mental health as well as your ability to send energy and attract.

Rise Up the Emotional Scale

ELEMENT 3 EXERCISE

Pay attention to your emotions, what you are you feeling. Are you finding yourself stuck in a habitual way of feeling? Are you seeking experiences which validate your current emotions and feed more them? Use this emotional scale and check in with yourself throughout the day. See how many of each of these emotions you are carrying using the numbers method. You can then work to transform them all and release habitual patterns.

Align to more of the positive emotions about the neutral line. Really feel what they are like in your body. What size, shape colour are they? Allow them to expand and fill your energy. Connect back to them often.

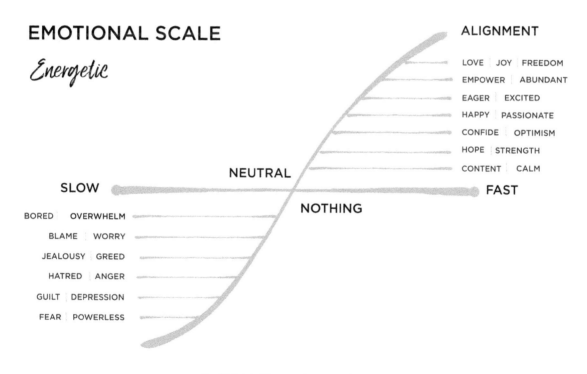

EMOTIONAL SCALE

Energetic

ALIGNMENT

LOVE | JOY | FREEDOM
EMPOWER | ABUNDANT
EAGER | EXCITED
HAPPY | PASSIONATE
CONFIDE | OPTIMISM
HOPE | STRENGTH
CONTENT | CALM

NEUTRAL

SLOW   **FAST**

NOTHING

BORED | OVERWHELM
BLAME | WORRY
JEALOUSY | GREED
HATRED | ANGER
GUILT | DEPRESSION
FEAR | POWERLESS

Improve Your Physical Health

ELEMENT 4

We're ready to start changing our physical health. We are still working our way inwards and looking at the etheric and physical layer of our aura to bring them into alignment. Changing our physical health will be so much easier now. As we have worked in from the outside of our aura we have reduced the spiritual, mental, and emotional RESISTANCES and REVERSALS which will have been impacting our physical health. By doing the work in the last 3 Elements we're able to allow the body to go into healing. We're about to explore some of the key ways you can transform your physical health with EAM.

HEALTH CARE IN THE NEW PARADIGM

Traditionally in the west we've been brought up to believe that our physical body is mechanical. It is a machine that operates different systems functionally independent to one another, and you can affect one area of our physiology or cut something out and it will not affect something elsewhere in the body.

Yet now modern medicine is starting to recognise the mind-body connection. That in fact what we eat, drink, and think are affecting our physical health and our capacity to heal. Whilst they are yet to be as open just yet to the Eastern medicinal practices, I have hope (and a strong belief) that one day EAM and other energy tools will be the norm. I believe that we have the power to shape and change our physical health, and by working with the energy first we can prevent many physical health conditions from even arising! That is my biggest wish: to empower each and every one of us to take care of our health on every level.

WHAT IS YOUR PHYSICAL HEALTH?

Your physical body is the beautiful vessel that we use to define who we are. This body is what we identify as US. It is the most manifested form of our aura. Your physical body reflects your thoughts, feelings, and emotions. The size, the shape, the tone of your skin, the colour of your tongue. The thin bits, the fat bits, the toned bits, and the wobbly bits are ALL a manifestation of your energy. Our physical health is created by the practiced thoughts and feelings we have. Your health reflects your alignment. The ill health and disease you experience is a reflection of your misalignment.

The development of our physical body began at conception and throughout our time in the womb. Many of our energetic patterns and potential are set in place from our parents. The blueprint of our physical body is created at conception, but we can still influence it. What an extraordinary journey our energy and physical bodies go on before we take our first breath. Much of our lives are shaped by the thoughts, feelings and emotions of our parents during conception and pregnancy.

Disease (DIS-EASE) in the body is simply a clear manifestation of some area of our lives which is not in FLOW. If you have manifested a disease, it means there has been a LONG practiced resistant vibration of energy. There are many different models, which explain the mind-body connection. The ones which we correlate most with EAM is known as Meta Health and Lifestyle Prescriptions. Whichever mind body connection model you follow they are all different interpretations of the same thing, a LACK OF FLOW or being out of alignment! If you choose to, you can just use these correlations to guide you into exploring possible areas of RESISTANCE to transform with EAM.

Our physical bodies are the most manifested form of our energy, and we must take care of this 'container'. Whether you feel sick, tired, exhausted, eat too much sugar/fat, or you are dehydrated, suffer from a lack of sleep, or forget to exercise or find time to relax, you will feel more out of FLOW. By nature, you will also be keeping the things you WANT to manifest away from you. If our PHYSICAL body is a lower vibrational match, how can it manifest something of a higher vibration? We live in a physically manifested world. There are many additional elements which can (and do) influence our health. We are affected by diet, wifi, chemicals, our physical environment, diseases and our genetics. All of these are just different types of energy. So, if everything is energy, we have the power to influence it with EAM even if they are 'manifested' illnesses or conditions!

To change things on a physical level in our body or our lives, we must MAINTAIN a habit of positive vibration on a physical level. If your physical body is under stress, it is CONTRACTED. By definition, you are unable to expand and ALLOW in things you want to manifest! If we are feeling tired, have headaches, body pain, or experiencing really ANY uncomfortable physical sensation we experience, it is an indication that we're out of FLOW in some area of our life. Every single time.

Our energy has been trying to communicate to us energetically for a while. The reason that we experience many physical health conditions is that we ignore the messages when they affect us on mental, emotional, or etheric level of our aura. By the point something has turned into an acute or chronic physical health condition, we have ignored the earlier energetic signs. It can also be that we've had an energetic shock significant enough to create changes in our energy and on a physical level.

Remember how the aura and chakras are communicating with the body through the nervous systems. Our nervous system is always reading what's happening in our aura and if an energy imprint, thought, belief, or emotion has continued for long enough, it will create a physiological health response.

Within EAM, we believe that everything is possible and that anything can be healed energetically. It's just a question of how to do it and the time, energy, and changes which are needed to turn it around. When paying attention to the metaphysical meanings of pain or illness in the body, you can see the connection between your consciousness and your physical body. It is a map of your energy, thoughts, beliefs, and emotions. Our MIND is everywhere. In the body, it is the influence of our brain and the consciousness of our individual cells. The tissues and organs in our body are little energetic storage places for emotions and memories.

Our physical bodies can be changed by emotions we experience. Our bodies store and have memories at a molecular level. So, neither mind nor body can be treated without the other being affected. This is exactly what we're doing with EAM. We're releasing the energy, emotions, memories, and thoughts from the aura and our physical body. They are all connected anyway! By releasing this RESISTANCE, we are allowing our bodies to heal on a physical level. In turn, this transforms our ability to manifest things on a physical level.

◊:◊ EXPAND YOUR ENERGY WITH EAM

Take a look at your physical body, where are you feeling tension, tightness, pain or RESISTANCE. Using the 'what happens to your energy' principle of EAM, describe the size, shape colour and location of the RESISTANCE and release it with the 5 STEPS of EAM. By doing this you align to a greater free flow of energy in your physical body. It resolves the stress phase and will enable that part of your physical body to go into the healing phase.

LOVE AND FEAR

Now when we take this back to our emotions remember we cannot be in a state of LOVE and FEAR at the same time. Bruce Lipton, who studied the impact of the environment on the cells in our body, was able to show that LOVE is the emotion which enables us to grow. LOVE opens our cells and allows them to interact, to transform toxins, to heal, to grow. FEAR is the emotion which keeps our cells contracted, shut down, unable to transform toxins, and vulnerable to disease. In EAM we call LOVE FLOW and FEAR RESISTANCE or REVERSAL. It is all the same stuff, just working on different levels of our experience. This is one of many reasons we are aiming to move ourselves to a place of love, it the highest vibration which will enable you to attract and heal your physical body. The more we are in love the healthier we will naturally be! Love is the maximum nourishment our body can receive for growth; love provides the whole system with everything it needs. When you are in the state of love, FLOW, or whatever you call it, your body can fix anything.

Releasing the Resistance in Physical Health

HELEN JONES, AGE 46

I wanted to deal with the pain in my body. I've had a bad neck for as long as I can remember and put it down to car accidents and fibromyalgia all in the last 20 years. When I tried to ease the pain through questioning it became very deep.... My sway was really strong saying I had REVERSALS linked to my neck pain. After trying different questions, I found out in a previous life I had broken my neck and needed to forgive someone for causing it. I went through the 5 Steps of EAM and for the first time ever my neck feels light and loose.

Since releasing the trigger to my fibromyalgia my life has changed — not just releasing the pain buttbeing able to love. My confidence, all my barriers I'd put up to not being hurt have gone — not just the pain and fatigue. It truly is amazing!

RELEASE THE STRESS

What do we need to do to stay healthy? We can start by regulating our stress levels. We've already explored that stress is RESISTANCE — RESISTANCE is stress. We have all experienced stress in our lives. This is our everyday term for being under the influence of our fight or flight response and being out of FLOW. Stress is dictionary defines stress as "the body's natural reaction to any change that requires an adjustment or response; these changes can be physical, mental and/or emotional responses". Sadly, for many people stress is a normal part of everyday life.

When we are stressed our body is somewhere in the cycle of the fight or flight, freeze and appease response. We've all heard about this! This is the physiological response to an outside stimulus, and it has served us for a long time during our evolution. This response is designed to empower our bodies to run away from a big scary dinosaur, or lion, or something which would threaten our lives! Although there are fewer scary animals prowling the streets, this stress response is still useful because it gives you a SHORT burst of energy, for the physiological increased speed or strength in anticipation of the attack. It sends an increase of blood to muscles in the extremities, raises the heart rate, creates more tension in muscles and increases the blood clotting functions in the body. Remember, earlier when we stepped in front of the bus?

FIGHT and FLIGHT engages and affects our entire body, including the nervous system, respiratory system, circulatory system, immune system, digestive systems and reproductive systems. These changes are designed to give the body the best chance of survival. Essentially it shuts or slows down internal functions in the viscera, our trunk, because it needs to divert that energy and those resources to the muscles and bones on the arms and legs, so that they can do their best to protect us when under attack!

When we are in FLOW, feeling love or in the growth phase, the blood and circulation is sent to the central organs, heart, lungs, liver, digestive and reproductive systems. These are the essential organs in our body, which we need to be functioning effectively to maintain our health. When in FLOW, these organs work to maintain homeostasis. When in protection, the blood and energy is all sent to the extremities ready to fight, which means that normal bodily functions are naturally impaired, including our brain functions!

Stress itself ACTUALLY makes us lose intelligence so we are unable to think clearly. Whilst our blood and nutrients are being circulated to the extremities, our arms and legs ready to run, there is a reduced amount of blood in our internal organs, which means our body is more prone to attack from illness through bugs, bacteria, and viruses. This is one of the leading reasons so many people get sick under stress. Our body is unable to deal with an externally perceived threat and an internal one at the same time. Because the immune system has shut down, the viruses which naturally live inside us can have their way with you, so you get ill more easily and take longer to recover.

◐ EXPAND YOUR ENERGY WITH EAM

You know when you are feeling stressed out (everything in this book has been about resolving stress — stress is RESISTANCE). I invite you to pay attention to your stress levels. Use them as an indicator that you may need to do some EAM. When you notice that you feel stressed use the 5 Steps of EAM to release the energy, thoughts, and emotions you are feeling. Change your focus and align yourself to the most positive possible outcome for that situation. By doing this, you will change your neural pathways to create new associated patterns in the brain, which will influence your whole physical body and energy, too.

NUMBING OUR BODIES WITH DRINK, DRUGS & FOOD

One of the most common ways that we now deal with stress in our modern world is to turn to external substances like alcohol, tobacco, or drugs to try to relieve stress. How often have you said it yourself or heard others say something like, "I just want a glass of wine to wind down" or "I need a cigarette as I am feeling so stressed out?" We numb ourselves in so many ways, to prevent us from *really* connecting with ourselves, whether it is with things such as food, drink, drugs, TV, Facebook, and shopping. They create a disconnect in our lives. These things create additional RESISTANCE in our physical bodies and in some cases, create REVERSALS in our energy. So, we can be in a constant reversed energy state because of the substances we put into our body.

❂ EXPAND YOUR ENERGY WITH EAM

What foods do you notice you're addicted to? What substances could you choose to eliminate from your diet in order to improve your energy flow? Use the sway to help you find them and then release with the 5 steps of EAM. By doing this you will allow your body to be more energised, feel aligned and vibrate at a higher frequency.

WATER, WATER EVERYWHERE

Water is vital to a healthy body. It loosens waste, cleanses our internal systems and allows our bodies to eliminate toxins. Humans are made up of 60% is water; in some tiny organisms, up to 90% of their body weight is from water. Our brain and heart are composed of 73% water, lungs 83%, skin 64%, muscles and kidneys are 79%, and our bones are 31% water. That is a LOT of essential body systems being made up of, and needing, water. Each day we must consume a certain amount of water to survive. Of course, this varies hugely across age, sex, location, lifestyle, and gender. An average rule of thumb is approximately 3 litres per day for men, and 2.2 litres for women. Water is important for our health and well-being. It is one of the key building blocks for every single cell created in our body.

Many health conditions and ailments which we medicate with additional chemicals can be resolved, or even healed, by drinking the correct amount of water every day. The sad thing is we are often adding more toxins for our already dehydrated body! How many times have you been to the doctors and they said, just drink 2 litres of water a day? NONE. How many times have they handed over a prescription for medication instead? Please know this is just an observation, not a bash on medicine I just believe that medication should be a last resort, once diet and lifestyle have been addressed! Our medical health care could be vastly improved by working WHOLE-istically with people to change their lives. Yes, that is another book in itself!

If more people were educated about the signs and symptoms of dehydration, we would barely need to go to the doctors at all; it is the root of so many common conditions, for example, digestive pain, arthritis, back pain, neck pain, knee pain, headaches, stress, depression, hormone imbalance, high blood pressure, excess body weight, asthma, diabetes, sleep conditions, urinary conditions and so much more! Imagine how quiet the waiting room would be if everyone was just drinking the water they are meant to on a daily basis!

Energetically, water can change vibration faster. Some exciting experiments carried out by Dr. Usi Emoto showed that by freezing water which had been infused with the intention of words the crystallisation of the water, changed. Water infused with hate, fear or pain would create small or unformed crystals. Water infused with the intention of love or sent healing prayers would create beautiful patterns and crystallised forms. What they were able to show is that water can change based on the thoughts or words projected at it. Remember we are made of water; by purifying your body as frequently as possible with high vibrational water, you will send positive intentions to everything you consume.

☯ EXPAND YOUR ENERGY WITH EAM

Using the sway, ask how much water you need to drink a day for your body. Start following the steps and notice your energy shift! Use the 5 Steps of EAM to release any RESISTANCE to consuming more water. By aligning and allowing yourself to drink more water, you speed up the clearing process. Your sway will improve, and you will get in flow much more quickly as your body is clean and hydrated.

"I NEED MORE SLEEP"

We all need ample sleep, yet we rarely get enough. Remember the YIN and YANG of life? We need to sleep and allow our physical and energy bodies the time to relax. When you sleep, your energy bodies draw in towards you and allow the day's experiences to process. In medical terms or whilst thinking about the physical body, sleep problems come from disruptions in the brain and nervous, cardiovascular and immune systems, as well as functions of our metabolism. It can also come from other sources like drugs, alcohol, medication, the list is endless, and LACK of sleep clearly indicates an imbalance in our energy. Energetically, it is usually caused by a lack of YIN energy in the body, which has been burnt out through too much activity and created excess YANG so your body is comparatively energised.

Everyone's individual sleep needs vary; most healthy adults need around 8 hours per night with around 16 hours of awake time, while some people can survive on 6 and others may need 10. Whatever is right for you, listen to your body? If you have issues with your sleep like trouble falling to sleep or waking up, this indicates an energetic issue elsewhere which you can address.

ALTERNATIVE THERAPIES

People often ask which other therapies work well with EAM; I would say anything which works on energy. My favourite and go-to is acupuncture. Having completed my degree in this area, I am a huge fan. In fact, much of my understanding of energy comes from there. If I ever stop teaching EAM, acupuncture is the only other treatment I would do because it is so powerful, quick, and effective. It is also heavily researched and used in the mainstream healthcare systems in many eastern countries. That said, many other complementary therapies get you in FLOW; they improve your mental, physical and of course energetic wellbeing.

PHYSICAL EXERCISE

We are 'meant' to exercise but sometimes we feel pretty uninspired to do so. Maybe because we've joined those classes that make you feel like jelly afterwards or perhaps you've tried yoga but the thought of staring at someone else's bottom in yoga pants doesn't fill you with excitement. There are lots of way that we can get some regular exercise that can be fun instead of regimented. There are many reasons to exercise. Purely from an energy standpoint, it increases the free flow of energy through the body. For these reasons and all of the others we've already addressed, it helps us sleep, it helps mood, it helps metabolism and digestion. It also helps our vibrancy and controls weight, and it reduces the risk of diseases and can lower blood pressure.

There are different types of exercise which may help you. Aerobic exercise helps the heart, strength training helps the muscles, and flexibility training helps joints remain bendy! Since you want to reduce any RESISTANCE, you may have to begin exercising and also find the right exercises that your body wants you to do AND that you'll enjoy doing.

HOW DO WE TRANSFORM ILL HEALTH?

You don't have to wait until you've manifested a physical condition. Is there more you could do to nurture your physical body? I spent many years working in complementary health, and I can only share things I know which have worked for me and my clients. Please seek your own advice when making changes to your physical body; the advice given here is not in place of a medical expert, your doctor, GP, consultant or mental health professional. I advise you to seek your own advice and make the best most informed choice for you.

DEALING WITH PHYSICAL HEALTH CONDITIONS

We are yet to find the one magic thing you can do to transform your physical health, in the same way that no one thing enabled it to become so manifested. There was something of a repeated or repetitive nature about it which enabled more thoughts, feelings, or patterns to accumulate which created the RESISTANCE and lack of FLOW! Within EAM we do have a step-by-step approach to begin dealing with your physical health conditions. Yet again another book in itself. You already have much of it here to help you.

CHANGE YOUR STORY

We all have a story about every aspect of our life. Do you have a health story, a 'reason' why you can or can't? Why you don't weigh the weight you want? Why you don't sleep? Why you can't exercise? Why you don't_____ (you fill in the blank). In its simplest terms, it is the reason (excuse) we are using for not transforming our energy around our health and well-being.

◊:◊ EXPAND YOUR ENERGY WITH EAM

Whilst you hold that story it will continue to be true for you. We want to explore this with EAM. There are a few things you can do to get started. First of all, let's lose the story. Like anything we keep giving energy to it will continue to grow. I invite you use the balloon method to work through your health story too. By doing this you allow your energy, thoughts and emotions connected to it to change and stop impacting the physical body.

META-MEDICINE & LIFESTYLE PRESCRIPTIONS

One of the best ways to begin to understand the impact and influence of our mind-body connections is a body of understanding known as META-Health ®. In META Health and Lifestyle Prescriptions, they have a precise bio-psycho-social understanding of stress and the mind-organ-brain connection. It enables us to determine exactly which types of stress cause which physical symptoms. It is not a therapy; it is a system to help us pinpoint the reasons why we may become ill, which is why I believe it is such a fantastic fit with EAM. This method has the potential to heal what is uncovered through the exploration with this work.

Meta Health is founded in scientific studies and research using CT scans of the brain to correlate the different effects of thoughts and emotions in the physical body. To understand more, you could read the book *The 6 Root-Cause(s) Of All Symptoms: Fear No More. Know WHY You Have Symptoms* by Johannes R. Fisslinger. There you'll discover many connections and correlations between specific diseases, emotions and organs in the body. You will discover how the conscious actions of self-healing and understanding disease progression can be helped by resetting your beliefs and ways to heal yourself using techniques like EAM.

META-Health® and Lifestyle Prescriptions provides a scientific framework to explain everything, which has been talked about by these thought leaders, and it is also backed up via CT scans.

10 KEY PRINCIPLES OF META HEALTH

1. The body, mind & spirit and social connection

2. Awareness, prerequisite for health, and personal growth

3. Traumatic life experiences – the starting point of physical and psychological changes

4. Brain – The Central Control system of our organism

5. Disease as a process – major points and phases of all health issues

6. The biological and psychological meaning of symptoms

7. The evolutionary development of organs

8. Microbes – Viruses, bacteria and fungi as biological helpers

9. Self-healing and integrative therapies

10. Patients as responsible and knowledgeable decision makers

HEALING RESPONSE

A key part of this understanding is the Stress and healing responses they talk about an energy and physical healing process. We already explored this in the previous chapters. Health conditions can either be a stress phase or healing phase condition! This is a whole field of study which I would suggest you explore as it fits so beautifully with EAM.

CHAPTER 5 — WHAT TO REMEMBER

That was a real journey to transforming YOUR SOUL, all the elements that make you who you are. We've explored some ways to bring your universal connection into alignment. You've looked at how to create an Abundant Mindset; we've transformed your emotions and seen some ways to change your physical health, too. We've worked together to raise your overall vibrational energy of the part which you recognise as you. Now it's time to begin expanding your energy and influencing those parts of your life that are outside of you.

Transform Your Physical Health

EXERCISE - ELEMENT 4

It has taken more than one thing to manifest this physical condition, so there may be more than one area of RESISTANCE which has contributed to it. These questions are just a starting point. I suggest getting a BIG sheet of paper and mind mapping the answers to these questions:

- Look at when it began. What was happening? Who was there? How old were you?

- Look at emotions you experienced back then and how you feel about it now?

- Who do you blame for your current health condition and why?

- Look at your thoughts about your health condition. Do you believe it will heal? Do you believe it was inherited? Do you believe there is nothing that can be done?

- What are your regular symptoms of this condition? List them all even if you don't experience them all the time.

- What does this prevent you from doing?

- What does it allow you to do?

You could explore finding the 'meaning' or the beginning of the condition using something like Meta Health, Lifestyle Prescriptions, Debbie Shaprio, or Louise Hay. This will help you unravel the emotional and mental connection. Using EAM, work on each of the answers you find to the questions. This process may take a while but is so worth it to allow your body to heal. The BIG secret is to rest after you do this work, too!

And ALIGN, ALIGN, ALIGN to a powerful transformative healing too!

CHAPTER 6

Your Life

"Find ecstasy in life; the mere sense of living is joy enough."
~Emily Dickinson

We've explored our inner world with YOUR SOUL, it's time to explore the outside world and begin to influence our environment and everything in it. Our energy and physical health are stronger and more in flow, which means we now have more energy and strength to influence other areas in our lives. As we look at your life in this chapter we'll discover how to change your environment, your relationships, and create the dream lifestyle you've been waiting for. It's much simpler than you think. I promise.

Your Life Phase Of The Energy Evolution

Creating the Right Physical Environment

ELEMENT 5

This element — Physical Environment, is about looking at the space around you. Energetically, we're working still on the physical and etheric level of your Aura and energy as we start to move back out and expand our energy into the world. Is your physical space supporting you and your energy, or is it depleting, hindering or draining you? Our energy is massively influenced by the space we are in (and the people who are in it), and if your space is unsupportive to you it is MUCH more difficult to influence other energy or outside influences.

Other than working on our physical bodies, this is the first time we've worked with REAL manifested stuff — solid objects! This is about more than manifesting new things. This is about being in alignment with our physical environment, spending our time in a space that we adore because it raises our vibration. As human beings, we are designed to observe what is in front of us. It's so easy to look at what we have right now and judge it. What we observe around us also influences our thoughts – if we're spending our time somewhere which we would rather not be, we are putting out resistant energy. If you live in a home that makes you feel ashamed, with tatty walls or décor that makes you cringe, then you're taken out of FLOW. The easiest thing to do is to clear up the vibration of what you have and take some practical action to change it. This will make it EASY to spend time in your space and to love it and make sure it is supporting you.

WHY DO WE NEED TO CHANGE OUR PHYSICAL ENVIRONMENT?

Our physical bodies are the most manifested form of our energy; everything which comes into our physical space is impacting us through our aura. Depending on our energy levels for the day, our aura can expand between 2 and 20 metres away. Therefore, even if you're not touching it, the things (and people) you spend time with are impacting you on an energetic level. In the same way, we are clearing each layer of our aura to allow more 'good' to FLOW in, we have to do the same within our workplace and our home. If we want to start MANIFESTING things on a physical level, the space must be a vibrational match to it. And there has to be SPACE.

Remember the Law of Correspondence – what is within is outside, what is outside is within? Our home is such a clear representation of that. If you live in a shoe box with no space around you – then you have no space to grow and expand; you're literally restricted by the space you have and what is influencing your energy. Consider the type of newspapers, magazines, and books you read. Do they inspire you or bring you down? Do you listen to the news on the TV or radio? Do you need it? Are you in environments that support you? Do you have enough daylight? Fresh air?

We begin of course with aligning ourselves to what we have right now – by transforming any RESISTANCE to what we have around us! This does NOT mean settling – it DOES mean getting your energy to at least a place of neutral feeling (or more) about what you have.

LOVING THE HOME YOU HAVE

In order to create what you want; you have to learn to love what you already have. Whilst you may not be living in your dream home just yet, it's important to feel GREAT about where you live. How many times per day do you gripe to yourself or others about your current home?

◊፧◊ EXPAND YOUR ENERGY WITH EAM

Go around you house and stand in each room; notice if you feel a change in your energy and what emotions come up for you. Notice all the thoughts which run through your head when you are in there. Use the 5 Steps of EAM to release any RESISTANCE. By doing this, you'll allow yourself to be in a more in-flow state when in your environment and raise your alignment level.

YOUR DREAM HOME

It's time to get creative. If you've listened to the visualisation meditation, perhaps you've 'seen' your dream home. What does your dream home LOOK like? What do each of the rooms look like? What colours are on the walls? Is it an old home or is it a new build? What is outside or near to your home? Do you want to be in the countryside? Do you want to live in the city? Maybe you live in your perfect house already and you know it needs a revamp! Start planning the changes to your space. If you know how to do an EAM vision board then get it pinned up on your wall or on your computer for the type of house you want to create.

◊:◊ EXPAND YOUR ENERGY WITH EAM

Transform any RESISTANCE thoughts, beliefs, or emotions that you hold about allowing your dream home to manifest. Use the 5 Steps of EAM to get into alignment with what you want to have in your new future environment at home, and at work, so that they are able to be attracted to you.

ENERGY IN YOUR SPACE

Electromagnetic energy is all around us in many different forms, some of which support our physical and energy bodies and others which are harmful. We can be influenced by energies in our home; they can come from many places.

To manifest on a physical level, your space must be a vibrational match too.

GEOPATHIC STRESS DETECTION

This is the method of assessing the impact of underground waterways, energy courses and grave site locations is part of geopathic stress detection and there are only a handful of truly skilled practitioners in the world. The natural frequency of our earth (7.5 – 8 Hz) anything which affects that frequency can cause a vibration of energy in the building or geographical place which then affects the people living in it. Over time, this change in energy vibration can cause many issues such as insomnia, irritability, fatigue, and chronic fatigue and in some cases, severe illnesses such as cancer and leukaemia. In certain situations, Feng Shui remedies are far more effective once the geopathic stress has been dealt with. Interestingly, people with nomadic lifestyles rarely suffer from cancer, as they are never exposed for long enough to any harmful concentrations of earth-born radiation.

FENG SHUI

The art of Feng Shui is the Chinese practice of harmonising ourselves with the surrounding environment, by creating energy FLOW of qi the physical space to influence the FLOW of qi in different areas of our lives. We can alter our environment to support us in every area of our lives, our work and in our home; this support allows us to become more in FLOW with what you are allowing or able to receive. Imagine if something in your home is affecting your qi flow, every time you are there you are in RESISTANCE or REVERSAL.

When it comes to understanding the flow of Qi in our physical space I would only trust my good friend Sarah Mcallister, creator of the Feng Shui agency, London. She is a genius in her own right who has been working in this field for more than 20 years. Sarah knows all there is to know and uses Feng Shui to design towns, cities, houses, and interiors. When we moved, Sarah used Feng Shui for our new house layout, gave us the ideas for colours and placements of furniture plants and lighting. It made such a huge difference in the way we felt, how we slept and also the changes in our key life areas too.

So, I asked Sarah to explain. Here is what she said. "When aligning with our highest aspirations, our passions, and desires, what many of us don't consider is that we are already being profoundly influenced, and in some cases sabotaged by, the design of our homes and buildings. Just as every person has a unique DNA, character and body type, each home and building has a unique energy imprint which is caused by many factors: the type of land and environment the building sits on, the orientation of the building, the placement of doors and windows, the garden design, the colours used internally and the layout of furniture and symbolic artwork. The land itself can emit healthful vibrations (think of a mellow meadow) or 'geopathic stress' (think Oxford Street or most downtown shopping streets!) which weakens the immune system, making the body more susceptible to illness over time.

"While some psychic debris can be cleared by using methods like EAM and the power of prayer and intention, really understanding how to design or make changes to a building is a completely unique set of skills. Classical Feng Shui is the world's oldest and most comprehensive 'environmental design' method that is increasingly crucial in our modern world to create supportive wellness homes instead of draining environments. As with nature, there is no such thing as perfect Feng Shui, but if you can have an expert help you create really good Feng Shui around you, then you can much more easily find and maintain your flow state."

Clear the Space to Change Your Life

RUTH BRADSHAW, AGE 41

I was working for myself and was in a very slow-moving transition in my life. I felt I needed to move away from multiple groups of people, old friends, customers, and connections as I'd buried my head in study learning more about energy work, animal communication and holistic animal care, and all the while my was energy changing. My wrists and hands had issues, and nearly everything I used to enjoy, like horse riding and cycling, were out of bounds.

I used EAM the moment I learnt about it to weed out anything that didn't feel good. As I began to feel less harassed and enjoy life more, I was able to work on aligning to my soul mission and creating the life I saw in my vision board. I love using EAM for everything, from swaying on food, to swaying on meetings, to swaying on what decision to make. It has guided me to and created the path I am currently on. I knew I wanted to be a kick arse animal communicator, deepening the animal and human connection. I just couldn't find a way out of the rut I was in.

I thought that I still needed my massage couch to offer reiki and facials, both lovely treatments to give, but not animal communication. When clearing my space the sway said to sell it and the universe was listening! Literally the next day received an email from a journalist wanting me to give her exclusivity for her media channel. Additionally, I landed a feature in a national magazine and a feature in a European magazine, and I was featured in a national newspaper e-mail supplement to over 24 million readers. I made it onto This Morning with Phil and Holly, a UK morning breakfast show with millions of viewers. I have to say this stuff is nothing short of magic.

ENERGY IN YOUR HOME

Just like everything else in life your home, work, or any physical space holds its own energy too. There can be parts of your home which are in flow, some in RESISTANCE, and some in REVERSAL, too. You can have ley lines and vortexes of energy, which influence your physical health and well-being. These are often created when people 'release' resistant emotions. Imagine someone has had a big argument or some drama has happened in a room. It leaves an energy imprint there. Have you ever walked into a house where someone lived alone for many years, or a room where a fight had broken out? The energy of the room still remains.

ELEMENT 5 — WHAT TO REMEMBER

If you have clutter in the rooms of your house or where you sleep you will have a cluttered mind that doesn't allow inspired thoughts and ideas to be given to you. If it is in your bedroom, it will also affect your sleep and your ability to heal. Clutter also affects your ability to allow things in. If you have no space in your home because it is full of OLD stuff you have hanging around (from your past) then you literally and metaphorically have no space to allow it in.

Think about an object which you 'keep' because it holds memories or energy for you. Is it a memory of love or does it take you out of FLOW every time you look at it? Are you holding onto it for fear of loss, or is it holding onto the past? Who does it serve you hanging on to things? Who else would benefit from it? How can you transform your clutter into money?

Sway on the things you need to let go of You would be amazed how much spare 'cash' you have sitting around you. I would highly recommend eBay or Gumtree for furniture, toys, good quality clothes, shoes and expensive items.

Is Everything Supporting You?

ELEMENT 5 EXERCISE

Now we have cleared some space, we want to make sure that everything you have left is supporting your energy. We want to ensure that you can at least enjoy the space you HAVE, because that is the BEST way to manifest something new or make the meaningful changes to your home anyway.

YOUR COMPUTER, PHONE, OR TABLET

Technology is a huge energetic distraction. It is essential to carry out housekeeping on your technology and here are some suggestions:

- Check your computer is working properly. Does it load when you open it and connect well to the internet?

- Are all your computer files in order so that you can find everything easily? Organise them and delete the ones you don't need.

- Go through your inbox, and delete old emails and unsubscribe from things you no longer want to receive (you can also sway on who to unsubscribe from).

- Social media contacts: delete people you don't want to connect with or connect to those you do.

CLEAR THE CLUTTER

- Do you need to empty drawers, cupboards or wardrobes?

- Get rid of old paperwork which is no longer needed

- Let go of memorabilia which brings up resistant emotions

- Does your space feel welcoming or overcrowded?

Use the sway to help you to decide what to let go and what to keep. Release any resistance using the 5 Steps of EAM and align to living in a harmonious space.

Revolutionising Your Relationships

ELEMENT 6

In this element, we're taking another step back out to expand our energy and working again in the emotional level of our Aura to be able to connect to a place of love in all of our key relationships with ourselves and others.

WHAT ARE YOUR RELATIONSHIPS ABOUT?

Our relationships are one of THE most powerful pulls on our emotions. From a young age, we use relationships to establish meaning in our lives. Our parents are often the first people with whom we create dependency because they are all we know, and they literally keep us alive. We learn everything about relationships, communication, interaction, love, hatred, anger all from our parents or caregivers at a young age! Depending on who they are and how they behaved, a LOT of this will have shaped how you are as an adult!

Many families are unconscious of their behaviours, their verbal and non-verbal communication, or the impact of their actions; they are simply operating on patterns learnt and observed, many of which they picked up from their parents. This means they are often making unconscious decisions about how they see life and how they connect and how they interact. They may often behave as if they are powerless. They take the knocks from life and let it take them down with it, as if they are unable to control what happens. Often people in this frame of mind point the finger, place blame, and believe it is something outside of them that has made their life this way. Why? Because they are yet to wake up to how powerful they are. They don't yet know that they are the creators of their reality and they can shape what they see around them just by transforming their thoughts, emotions, and actions.

This way of creating and running relationships is the OLD paradigm way of thinking. What we're looking to do in this element is to stop perpetuating that story and to let go of the beliefs, thoughts, emotions, and patterns that are disempowering us. That way we become RESPONSIBLE for our own lives, what is happening to us and changing it. This empowers us to create something new.

WHY DO RELATIONSHIPS PLAY WITH OUR ENERGY SO MUCH?

We learnt how to behave in relationships before the age of three. Our mental and emotional development is guided by key milestones being met at certain times in our lives. However, if we witnessed negative dynamics or were an unwilling part of the game when things were being played out at such a young age, we will have internalised thoughts / words / feelings / actions and behaviours at an unconscious level, because we absorbed and soaked up the environment like sponges in our early years. On an energetic level, our energetic foundation (the base chakra which is formed from age 0-7) represents the core of our energy. It is literally based on the actions and behaviours of others. So, the growth of our entire lives is based on this foundation. In a sense, we ARE victims of our circumstances, because at that point in time we had no conscious awareness of what IS right or wrong. We just assumed that is HOW life is!

As we get older the relationships we developed from watching our parents extend to brothers and sisters, friends and family, teachers, colleagues, boyfriends, girlfriends, husbands and wives until we repeat the cycle again perhaps with our own children. These important and powerful relationships have great significance in our lives and they are often the reason behind WHY we do so many of the things we do, which means these unhealthy interactions impact our lives and theirs on a daily basis.

Before we can begin to heal these relationships, we should look at the energetic power plays we have happening first.

ABUNDANT THINKING

Many of the 'issues' we have in relationships come from a feeling or belief of lack; we think that we are short or scarce of something – that somehow, we are not enough, or someone is not doing, being or having enough! These beliefs come from a place of scarcity. When WE talk about abundant thinking, we are talking about more than money in the bank. We mean time, money, food, love, kindness, freedom, support, attention and connection. So we look for other people to fill those gaps which are missing in us. Imagine being able to let the other people in your life off the hook. Become your own source of everything because it is all just energy. When you KNOW that this is true about everything in life, you no longer want or need to rely on others to be that source of anything for you, because you trust the infinite abundance of all of them coming from the universe!

◊:◊ EXPAND YOUR ENERGY WITH EAM

Look at the important relationships in your life. Where are you expecting others to meet your needs, fill your gaps or give something to you to make you feel happy. Use the 5 Steps of EAM to sway on what you have, who with and how you are draining your relationship. By aligning yourself to being able to receive these abundant resources with step 5 you can free yourself and others.

BE FREE OF THE ENERGY DRAMA

Many relationships interact operate within an unconscious dynamic known as the Karpman drama triangle. It explains the interactions where no one is at fault, everyone else is blame, and no one is accepting responsibility for their words, thoughts, or actions (and we would add, their alignment!). We've all fallen into this at some point and might default back to it when under stress. We are often completely unconscious that this is even going on. You'll find that most people believe that LIFE JUST HAPPENS to them; if something good happens they believe it's JUST luck. If something bad happens, it is someone else's fault! The basis of this type of understanding is a Puller energy or victim consciousness – meaning "It's NOT MY FAULT". Everything outside of me has the power to influence my life, and therefore I am unable to accept responsibility for what happens".

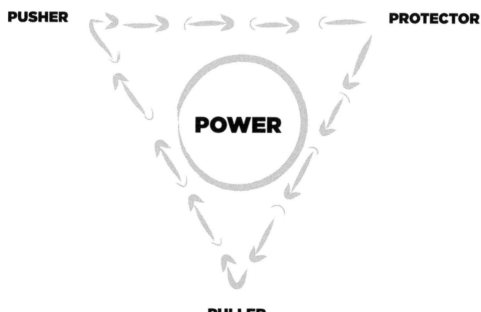

The EAM Energy Game

This theory is based on Transactional Analysis. Within EAM we call it the Energy Drama because it is more about the PUSH, PULL, and PROTECTOR energy, which keeps this drama cycling. The communication always looks 'honest' yet there is often a hidden and unconscious motive to the communication, so the interactions are energetically communicating the hidden meaning. It is these hidden 'unsaid' messages, which cause the drama. Remember we spoke about the energy of truth. We KNOW when someone is telling a lie; the more in tune you become the more easily you spot this, too. So, the drama unfolds as people miscommunicate verbally and energetically with pushing energy, drawing from others and placing blame. This is all coming from a place of LACK, a belief that to win someone else has to lose.

This drama triangle is one that we play out unconsciously in so many situations, we often have a default position in one of the three areas and we can flit between the three roles of the PULLER, PUSHER and PROTECTOR depending on who we are talking to, which is what makes the drama continue. Most of our relationships and interactions in life are based on this dynamic, as are the plot of most soap operas/films/books/newspaper stories. This is why we believe it is so normal and natural to communicate and interact in this way: we see it around us all the time. In truth, it is unhealthy because energetically it takes us out of alignment. This dynamic is all old paradigm, based on control and taking away other peoples' power. You need to be conscious to this kind of work and actively take full responsibility for your life the way it is. You do this by focusing on being in alignment. We call this your place of POWER.

THE BLAME SHAME GUILT GAME

Where does this energetic power play come from? Usually from our families or community growing up. In unconscious families if we ASK directly for what we want we are often shamed or called names by people in our family: for example, "you're spoilt", "you're selfish", "you're self-centred", "it's not all about you" or "you're greedy".

This is based on a common human belief that there is LACK or not enough of something to go around or that there is a limited supply whether it is time, money, love, freedom, attention, food, or kindness. Asking directly for things you want or need is often a big NO NO in many families, which means you learn to go without (creating beliefs of lack or low self-worth) or you find ways of manipulating people to give you what you want without asking for it (which disempowers you to get/receive or achieve things yourself (hence the powerless victim mentality is born!).

Learned helplessness is a mindset whereby we have learnt to get our needs met by being the helpless victim (the PULLER). These people see no possibility for good things to happen. They feel powerless to change things, which means they become unable to respond to opportunities and situations in their lives which contain something good. It's like an aversion to good things happening in our lives. Learned helplessness is a belief and you can use EAM to work on it.

If you find yourself making excuses or giving reasons for the way your life is, believing that you are powerless to make changes, there is some of this dynamic going on. Whether that is because of something someone else has said or done, or maybe you believe you HAVE to be there to support someone who is helpless and unable to do it themselves. It's okay. It is just a state of energy, which means you have the power to change it. I spent many, many years as the PULLER. Then I moved to being the PROTECTOR and when I wanted to lash out I would step into the PUSHER. We all do this in our lives bouncing from one energy to the next, and it is energetically DRAINING, causes RESISTANCE and is unbelievably OUT of alignment!

STEPPING INTO THE TRIANGLE

These interactions are always a two-way thing. Remember two energies moving in opposite directions create tension and RESISTANCE. The PUSHER is not only directing their PUSH energy at the PULLER; they are also receiving BLAME back from the PULLER, too. The PULLER at the same time is pushing their energy BACK against the PROTECTOR in defending their position. The PULLER is now being PUSHED on by the PUSHER; they are also PULLING energy from the PROTECTOR and pushing back the responsibility onto the PUSHER. The PROTECTOR is now PUSHING onto the PUSHER; they are drawing energy from the PULLER by taking their power away and instead of encouraging them to support themselves. Confusing, right? That is exactly what it is like when you are in the drama. A constant push, pull power play where everyone gets lost. Let's meet them.

THE PUSHER

The PUSHER likes to be 'RIGHT'. They want to feel in control and they often avoid looking inside. The PUSHER is often the person who is considered the bully, using their power and energy to PUSH their will, intention, thoughts, beliefs, or feelings onto someone else. When on the receiving end of this, you automatically feel like you want to push back to prevent your energy from being overcome. This is usually perceived as some kind of attack (energetically it is) on the PULLER and the PUSHER will gain their power by feeling superior to the PULLER.

The PUSHER's thoughts and pattern will be to blame ("It's your fault, look at what you made me do.") and they set ridiculous unnecessarily restrictive rules and limits. The PUSHER will provoke conflict, believes they are justified and likes to be in authority.

THE PULLER

A PULLER is the one will has been attacked by the PUSHER. When you meet a veteran PULLER, you can feel them pulling you into their energy like you are circling down a plug hole. These people tend to get what they want by any means and are often trying to get supported by other people without directly asking. Most importantly, they get to stay where they are. The PULLER draws energy from a PROTECTOR (and everyone else around them too); they are often giving their power away by blaming everyone else for their situation. The PULLER wants to and is often seen and often behaves as innocent and helpless.

They want people to feel sorry for them, that it isn't their fault. They often feel helpless and oppressed and act in a powerless way. They refuse to resolve problems or take responsibility and use conflict situations to create drama. The emotional pay-off is a confusing game because everyone is often switching 'roles' depending on HOW the game is going and who they are talking to! Secretly, everyone wants to be in the position of the PULLER, because they are free of responsibility and looked after, and everyone else takes the blame.

THE PROTECTOR

The PROTECTOR is the one who gets to be a hero or the 'good' one of the three. They feel strong and get to do the RIGHT thing. You will find them riding in to save the day for a PULLER. This is the soul aim of the PROTECTOR. They get their high and 'good feelings' by being the saviour and it is a must for them to be relied upon by the PULLER for emotional, or moral, support. They will often intervene with the PUSHER to protect the PULLER and fight for what is 'just'.

The PROTECTOR feels obligated to rescue the PULLER even if they loath doing it. They want to help and they feel guilty if they don't. Most of the help is given begrudgingly with an underlying expectation that at some point in the future the PULLER owes them. Then if that energetic debt is not repaid they talk about others behind their back. The PROTECTOR keeps the PULLER dependent on them and while they think they are avoiding drama, they end up creating it. This is often a co-dependent energy dynamic where neither person is happy. Their energy demands credit for the help that they give.

Can you see how any and all of these energy positions are disempowering? We could write a whole book on this one subject alone. It is one of the the biggest energy drains in our lives as we are PUSHED and PULLED from one energy state to another. All the time our energy attention and focus is taken away from the important topic of changing our life.

STEP INTO YOUR POWER

So how you do you step OUT of the energy drama. It is simple. Now that you have this knowledge, you will see it happening everywhere. You have a choice. You can choose to step into the drama or you can choose to step out. By using EAM you can work your way through ALL of these interactions by recognising that any energy, thoughts, beliefs or emotions which come up about what other people have said or done, *is about you*. When you can own that and commit to doing the work on yourself first THAT is where you can step into your POWER. This is about recognising your energy before you communicate and coming from the new paradigm. It is an art learning to do this. You may slip back to the 'old' ways occasionally. I promise the energy you regain in your life by living this way is worth it. You'll see your life change in front of your eyes. I'll share an exercise with you to work on this at the end of this element.

Releasing Anger Set Me Free

JULIETTE, AGE 45

I left my husband after experiencing patches of physical and verbal abuse, at times I feared for my life. As a single Mum, I felt deeply unhappy and unsure of what to do next and not finding it easy to talk to friends about either I internalised all the pain and hurt. I made the bold decision to move my life and my clan to Somerset and when I arrived I was exhausted, drained, and empty. The weeks got worse with insomnia, more stress, and my heart was ready to burst.

I was a co-dependent and I knew this was going to be a challenge to shift. A relationship with an old friend from college raised the patterns of being controlling and needy and despite the fact that I believed we were so good for each other in many ways, I couldn't stop trying to control everything and him. It was after we took some time out the relationship that I found EAM. I knew I'd found something special and a deeper part of me knew this could help change my life around.

My first goal was to build a stronger more trusting and loving relationship with my eldest son. Our relationship was on very rocky grounds as he felt unheard, unloved and disconnected from me and more recently from school and the outside world. Using EAM daily, things started to shift and turn around. I loosened the control I had and feelings of suffocation, being trapped and not able to do 'my own things'. I felt lighter, happier and a lot more open to receiving and giving love more freely. My son saw this and started to open up himself. He started hugging me and telling me he loved me. I was completely wow-ed by how quickly EAM can work. I realised I was putting so much stress and negativity on him. It was my stresses, frustrations, negative beliefs and mindset and this was keeping me stuck. I am so much more comfortable in my own skin now and with my emotions. I think my children realise that I am coming from a place of love now...so when I say I love you, they say it back not because they feel they have to but because they really feel it! Now Family life just feels amazing.

FINDING NEW LOVE

If you're on the search for a new relationship, whether that be a friend or partner, you need to know that before you can do so you must transform any thoughts, beliefs and emotions you've held about your relationships from the past. If you hold a belief that all men are assholes or that all women are just after your money, what do you think you'll attract in to the next relationship? If you want to change what you attract in your relationships, you must first change yourself. By changing your past stories and changing your energy, you allow in the possibility for the new things you want.

⦂⦂ EXPAND YOUR ENERGY WITH EAM

Get clear with yourself what beliefs, patterns or emotions you hold. Align yourself to allowing in only the best possible experiences for yourself in a new relationship. Follow the 5 steps of EAM and use the sway to help you define the important traits you want to attract

UNCONDITIONAL LOVE

As you can see above, our relationships are often pretty complicated with SO many well-meaning intentions and emotions flying all over the place and unrealistic expectations on how other people should behave. From birth, we are conditioned to think that LOVE is given when we DO as we are told or behave a certain way, in order to make someone ELSE feel good!

So many relationships are built on CONDITIONAL LOVE (meaning "if you behave a certain way, I will love you! If you DON'T, then I won't!") Now we never say that out loud, but we certainly act that way! How often have you withheld your hugs or kisses from someone because they upset you? Or used your emotions and affection as a way to get your own way? I know I have! When we do this, energetically we are shutting ourselves down from the state of FLOW and disconnecting from love. Yet for many this is how we are often raised to behave by our parents. We do it to our partners. We do it to our friends, and we do it to our children! This CONDITIONAL LOVE teaches us many things from a young age which create many of the patterns, issues, and RESISTANCES which we experience as adults.

◐ EXPAND YOUR ENERGY WITH EAM

Look at the way you connect and communicate with others. Where are you being conditional with your love? Where are you closing yourself off from love and FLOW? Use the 5 steps of EAM to work on any RESISTANCE you feel about them; use the bubble method if you need to. By aligning yourself to more unconditional love, you will receive more of it from life and those people around you.

REAL SELF LOVE

What we want and need is to create an amazing relationship with ourselves FIRST and foremost, by taking responsibility for ourselves. By that I mean BEING in alignment, which is when you FEEL in LOVE anyway. Why live a life which is dependent on someone ELSE being in a good mood and loving you in order to feel good? We want to be able to feel LOVE in ANY and ALL circumstances because without that we have NOTHING to give or share with anyone else anyway!

For me, learning to love yourself is what EAM is all about. Whether you call it FLOW, LOVE, or ALIGNMENT it is all one and the same thing to me. I am so proud to be a leader and part of the Real Self Love Movement, a collection of like-minded individuals who are on a mission to empower more people to reconnect to themselves and find that place of true love for who they are. I recommend the awesome book *I Love You, Me! My Journey to Overcoming Depression and Finding Real Self-Love Within* by Dr. Andrea Pennington for your self-love work. In it you'll discover a simple 5 step framework to help you explore more about who you really are at your core and learn to love and forgive yourself. You'll then authentically express the real person you are right now.

Our connection to love IS being in alignment; when we have our own connection to our source, we are connected to the infinite, abundant source of love. Why would you wait to receive it from people or other outside forces as our source of connection? We have it within us always!

◊:◊ EXPAND YOUR ENERGY WITH EAM

Ask the sway if you love who you are. Use the bubble method to explore any RESISTANCE to really loving yourself completely. Follow the 5 Steps of EAM to release any RESISTANCE to loving yourself. Align to allowing true self-love into your energy and your life.

WHAT TO REMEMBER ABOUT RELATIONSHIPS

So now you know how to connect to your own source of love. You can see some of the power plays and drama that can play out in our lives with others. You now know the power you have to stay in your own energy. It is time to connect to unconditional love for yourself and every area your life. Remember you have the power to change your life and all your relationships.

Time to Release the Drama

ELEMENT 6 EXERCISE

Using the sway, I want you to explore which of the 3 energy archetypes you are.

- Am I a PUSHER?

- Am I a PULLER?

- Am I a PROTECTOR?

It is common to be all three. You will have a tendency to be one of them more than the others. You can also ask the sway which one of these you are in relation to key people in your life.

You can use the 5 Steps of EAM to release this archetypal role you play and align to being in your POWER.

You can also use the lists of patterns outlined above for each role and ask if you have that habit. If so, how many times have you repeated it? Pay attention to your interactions with others. Learn to recognise when you are slipping into these energy dynamics. Use the 5 Steps of EAM to release these habits and ways of behaving so you can change the dynamic of your relationships and reclaim the power in your life.

Living Your Dream Lifestyle

ELEMENT 7

Now we're back at the mental level of our aura, it is time to expand our knowledge, skills and expertise. It is about enriching ourselves and our life experience with those 'things' you previously only dreamt of.

CONNECTING TO THE FUN

Life is meant to be fun. And yet we probably all allow ourselves to put practical responsibilities, things that don't necessarily fulfil us or that we don't necessarily enjoy before enjoying ourselves. Very often, enjoyment is one of those things that gets put to the bottom of the list. When was the last time you truly, truly let your hair down and had some FUN? Not a nice time but a time when you just went out and acted like a child again. When was the last time you played bat and ball or rolled down a hill like a small child? This element is about that childlike nature. Believe it or not, life isn't just about work or being a parent or a wife or husband, life is about how you're spending your time. Are you enjoying what you do?

Everything we do in life is because we want to experience the emotions of love, happiness, joy, and freedom, yet most of our time is focused on things that do not bring us joy or happiness. They don't bring us that feeling of excitement. From an energetic perspective, what we experience as fun is actually the feeling of alignment. We are in alignment because at that moment, when we're experiencing that side-splitting laughter, we're enjoying ourselves. When we're rolling down that hill, we have let go of resistant thoughts, beliefs, feelings, emotions about the subject and probably everything else. We are truly connected to our inner selves, and we are enjoying that moment in time without RESISTANCE. That is what the feeling of alignment is. That is what it feels like all the time.

Having fun and laughter also enables you to easily change your perspective. When things are stressful or feel like a disaster, starting to shift your way to feeling the humour around it or even just going out and having fun. Being in this energy state enables you to release the resistant thoughts and beliefs.

Obviously, you now have EAM too, but in those moments of fun and laughter you are no longer in a resistant state and which means the solution to the problem can come to you.

Fun and recreation and living your life is an essential part of human life. Anything can be fun because it is all about your vibration. It's all about your energy.

)⦂(EXPAND YOUR ENERGY WITH EAM

How can you bring the energy of more fun to your everyday life? Use the sway to help you identify 2 or 3 things which will help you connect to that inner joy, that childlike sense of fun and adventure. Then follow the 5 steps to release RESISTANCE. Align to doing it then take ACTION to make the magic happen.

Fun & laughter

light you up inside,

so you can shine

like a beacon.

RECONNECT TO YOUR CHILD ENERGY

Do you remember how when you were young everything was about giggling, laughing and having fun and playing jokes, hiding behind the sofa and feeling like nothing in the world was important other than being in the moment? That childlike nature has been drummed out of too many of us. We've also curbed it by our own perceptions from other people, from ourselves, from what we've seen with others, and from other people's comments. Maybe your parents yelled at you to "Stop doing that," "Don't climb on the sofa!" What this created was a sense of doubt. You disconnected and stopped allowing yourself to have fun, enjoy life, and be spontaneous. It makes us these grey, boring 'adults" before our time.

If you have children, please pay attention to the times that you find yourself saying "No", or "Stop" and ask yourself if you really need them to stop. Could you let your 'adult' go and jump in and join them instead? Allow them to experience that sense of joy, excitement, spontaneity, wonder, and fun in their connection to life. Help them to stay children and create happier memories.

☼ EXPAND YOUR ENERGY WITH EAM

Take a look at the silent beliefs which pop up whenever you're about to have fun. What are the voices you hear? What do they say? What did you hear growing up? Follow the 5 Steps of EAM to work through them and align to having fun, feeling excited, playing, and laughter.

LIVING YOUR IDEAL LIFESTYLE

This part of the journey is also about enjoying the lifestyle you want. I know life is about more than the materialistic elements of your life. There is also no shame in enjoying the good stuff either. If you were allowing yourself to live the life of your dreams right now, what would you be doing with your time? Would you be doing what you're doing today? Would you be on holiday? At the spa? Or travelling? It can be so tempting to hold off starting to live the life we want because of practicalities or by thinking about how our current life is. The whole idea with manifesting is to align your thoughts, words, beliefs, behaviours, and actions. All of this must come before it will begin to manifest.

EAM Has Opened Up the World to Me

HAZEL ADDLEY, AGE 38

I was scared of flying. I was anxious of just about everything to do with the process of flying... getting there on time... getting from the parking to the hanger... going through security... being stuck on the plane for hours... fear of being bored or uncomfortable or not liking the people around me... and the biggie for me - a fear of being shut in, trapped on the aircraft. I would find myself lying in bed involuntarily playing videos in my head of getting on the plane and I'd feel as if I had fallen head first down a well. I'd feel breathless. My heart would be thumping with panic and dread.

So I chose not to fly. That is until a dream opportunity came to visit New York. It was on my bucket list and this time would be different because I had EAM! I used EAM on everything negative that came up for me around flying. I did this in advance every time I though$t about the trip, as well as on the drive to the airport, whilst going through security, waiting in the airport lounge, queuing to get on the plane, finding my seat, sitting waiting for the plane to fill and take off, and whilst taking off. It was an amazing feeling when it hit me that I was flying and I felt okay. I felt good, in fact (a side effect of all the EAMing I had been doing) and I hadn't taken any medication!

EAM has massively changed my relationship with flying. This year I have five flights booked which I arranged without it even occurring to me to be scared. EAM has opened up the world to me!

RELAXATION FOR MANIFESTING

Our ideal lifestyle probably has us resting a little bit more than we do right now. As much as I talk about taking action, there's also magic in the relaxation. And in sitting still and doing nothing. In fact, the sitting still and doing nothing can be your activity. This is just as important, if not more so, than doing the work. As with everything, there is a balance of both.

We are conditioned to think that the only way to create is to do. The truth is, the benefits of laughter and enjoying yourself and getting in the FLOW of being in the moment, far outweigh the action taking. However, you can't do any one of them in isolation. You can't just go out and take action all the time and not relax. Likewise, you can't sit there and relax and expect things to happen. You need to flow between the two.

Have you ever noticed that when you go on holiday things miraculously seem to happen? The reason I want you to really connect to this relaxation is because as you stop and relax, you aren't putting out any contradictory energy. You aren't creating new thoughts or feelings, or moving the goalposts on what you've been asking the universe for again. When you take time out to relax and stop still for a while, physically and energetically, the universe can find you and deliver the things that you've been asking for.

In a similar way to how the energy of fun and laughter expands your energy, the energy of relaxation does the same. It almost lights you up like a giant beacon and the universe can clearly see you. If you spend time running around doing, going from place to place, it's like a lighting jock in a theatre trying to follow an actor on stage who is running around from side to side. The universe cannot find you. One minute you are in focus and then you are off again doing something else. So, spend time sitting still and relaxing and enjoy being in a place where you can discover your next inspired action, and then follow your next impulses from there. Even if they don't make logical sense.

ENGAGING YOUR LEFT BRAIN

You are an expanding being and expanding your knowledge is another way that you continue to grow. It may be this journey we are on is filling this gap for you. When did you last embark on learning something totally new for you? The process of learning and education engages our left brain. Our left brain is our sensible, practical, logical part. We need it to be on top form, as much as we need to engage our right brain. It is not enough to sail through life. To keep ourselves expanding, we need to challenge ourselves: to take on something new and learn new things, like acquire a new skill which stretches us. This keeps the excitement in our lives and keeps us engaged. This is about engaging your brain, expanding your knowledge, and engrossing yourself so that your brain can re-engage itself and stay active.

YOUR CREATIVE ENERGY

How can you find ways to get connected to your creative energy, while manifesting all those things in your lifestyle?

The right side of the brain is the creative side. It is about allowing yourself the time and space to be in FLOW. Creativity, art, or craftiness puts you in the space of being in your right brain, which naturally connects to a higher source. It takes us out of our left brain thinking. Finding a way to switch off your normal mental activity and be in that open, creative space allows the inspired thoughts and ideas to drop in.

The state of creative energy is a powerful place. Creative energy is the energy we use to manifest. When you can allow yourself to be creative, you generate the energy that enables things to manifest. The more you connect to your creativity, the more quickly things are going to manifest for you. Creativity doesn't just mean painting or knitting; it can also be your work. How can you, or do you, use your creative energy in your everyday life? It's more about the energy of what you are doing than the task itself. This is a wonderful way to connect to doing it. This is about you being in that new FLOW, that new source of creativity, the new manifestation.

CHAPTER 6 — WHAT TO REMEMBER

This has been all about YOUR LIFE. So now we've explored how to align your environment, the places you live and work so that they support you. We've explored the power dynamics in our relationships, too, and aligned to more love. We've understood the power of connecting to fun, laughter, and happiness in our lives and starting to live that ideal lifestyle right now. Now it is time to look at our work in the world as an expression of who we are.

Do Something for You

ELEMENT 7 EXERCISE

Use the 5 Steps of EAM to release the RESISTANCE to doing the activities that are part of your dream life. Pick 3 things you would love to do but that you always say you are too busy for. Pay attention to all the energy, the thoughts, the beliefs, the patterns and the emotions that surface when you think about what stands in your way. Use the bubble method to work through it and align to allowing the energy of them into your life. Then go out and take action. Book them in. Tell the universe you're serious about changing your life. Then watch the magic unfold.

PART THREE

Making Your Difference in the World

CHAPTER 7

Your Work

*"There is no passion to be found in playing small –
in settling for a life that is less than the one you are capable of living."*
~ Nelson Mandela

This is where we begin to create the real magic. The key elements of YOUR SOUL and YOUR LIFE are in flow. Now it is time for us explore and expand our newly aligned selves into our expression of work in the world. That means finding a way to be in flow with the money and wealth you receive so that you can use it to make a meaningful impact. We'll define your passion and purpose and enable you to get clarity on how you can make an impact with your work.

Your Work Phase of The Energy Evolution

Expanding Your Money, Wealth & Abundance

ELEMENT 8

It's time to connect to the abundance of wealth. Now we're working in the outer levels of our energy bodies; we have connected to the sources of wealth inside, so now we can tap into those around us. Money is like everything else, it's JUST energy. Usually by now the 'need' we previously had for money has disappeared. You've already done most of the work to shift your money story. You see money is never about the money; it is what we think the money will bring us.

CREATING MONEY AND WEALTH IN THE NEW PARADIGM

The meaning of money and abundant resources is ingrained in us from birth. We are brought up in an old paradigm system which believes that MONEY = POWER. So, to HAVE POWER (and therefore happiness and therefore love) is to have money. Subsequently, we inherently believe that MONEY is the source of our power. We also believe that WEALTHY people have more TIME and therefore scarcity of TIME is a lack of abundance resource. We believe that more MONEY = More TIME = More Freedom. We see happy, smiling pictures of wealthy people having free time with friends. So, we connect MONEY to FRIENDS, FUN and HAPPINESS. We also have a connection with TIME, MONEY and CLIENTS. With all of these important and implicit meanings connected to money, no wonder MONEY means so much.

In the new paradigm, you know that MONEY, TIME, HAPPINESS and POWER are limitless resources. They are all sources of energy. They are not limited. No one owns them. They are freely available to you. You just need to tap into the energy of them. When you discover and truly live your life knowing that money and abundance are all just energy, you will be able to tap into the flow of wealth around you.

WHAT IS ABUNDANCE ALL ABOUT?

We have been taught to BELIEVE that being happy is dependent on having money. It's true that having money DOES make things FEEL easier; it makes choices easier and gives you freedom to do more in your life. However, if you ask anyone what they want money for, whether it is a car, a house, a holiday, to pay the bills, whatever it is, if you ask the same person the question "and WHY do you want the_____?" it usually boils down to the same answer. What they actually want is the FEELING they believe their desire will bring them — freedom, peace of mind, love, happiness. You can have those without needing the money first just by being in alignment. To get the money you must FEEL those emotions first anyway.

For many people the issue around money is that they have quite a tidal wave of energy Flowing in the opposite direction when it comes to abundance. This is because we have so many mixed up and conflicting beliefs, thoughts, feelings, patterns, and emotions around money, wealth, and abundance. These are often created at a young age and through significant events in our lives. Very often money has been a subject which caused conflict in relationships. We learnt inherent patterns in our families and deep emotions about what we can or can't create. Abundance is a mindset, which means money is a mindset, which means wealth is a mindset. Like all things we are manifesting, it takes some gathering of momentum by giving our focused energy, thought, feelings, and actions to see it manifest in our reality.

WHY IS MONEY & ABUNDANCE SO IMPORTANT TO US?

We are brought up to believe in a system of society where MONEY = POWER. We are taught in so many ways that the way to have power (and therefore happiness) is to have money. When you look at this concept on an emotional level, all everyone wants is to be happy, and therefore they believe that money is the route to make that happen. Many people believe that the money comes before the happiness and that only when the money is here can we be happy (I know for sure I used to have some of that going on myself). The irony is it's that belief which motivates us to 'work hard' to 'push through' to 'make it happen', and we all know what those patterns create, more RESISTANCE, which makes it harder for us to actually reach the thing we want, so it becomes a self-fulfilling prophecy.

Will having money really make you happy? (Come on, you know the answer by now!). Being happy and in alignment makes you happy and *then* the money will come. As you know, you must THINK and FEEL abundantly before you can manifest money, and it must be habitual thinking. It should be a way of life for you. Just one or two days of thinking abundantly will not make you a millionaire!

I have a secret to tell you: we are BORN to be abundant! It is a way of being, not a thing to have. The universe has an infinite FLOW of everything ... and I mean *everything*. When you transform yourself, and come into alignment with your life, you will see there is enough of everything for everyone. When you trust that the universe is always supporting you and will bring you everything you ask for (if you stay in alignment with it!), the FLOW of abundance manifest in your life very quickly.

On a more practical level if we want to change the world, having wealth and abundance in our lives makes our mission so much easier. I will never be one of those people who says, 'You don't need money to make an impact'. That's true in many cases, but it sure helps. Mother Theresa was one of the greatest people at raising capital to invest in her projects. She understood the importance of this resource in enabling her and others to make a real difference. Having money enables you to mobilise resources, people, and ideas more quickly, and have a bigger impact. It also allows you to share the wealth with others, and focus your time, energy, and attention on projects that empower ourselves and the wider community. I hope that for you, gathering wealth means more than buying Christian Louboutin shoes or a snazzy red sports car! When you're clear what the wealth is for, it will manifest so quickly and so abundantly that you might surprise yourself.

HOW DO WE TRANSFORM THIS MONEY STORY?

You're already halfway there. Everything we have been doing so far has led you to this point, to be ready to work on money, wealth and abundance. There are a few principles to understand. These apply to anything you want to manifest.

- **YOU MUST LET GO OF TIME**. We are so used to controlling everything around us, we get frustrated or think that it is doomed if things happen outside of OUR schedule. There are so many factors that influence when things manifest. Firstly, your energy; if your energy is swinging around all over the place then every time you take yourself OUT of FLOW you hold off the manifestation of things you have coming to you, which is why we have worked on bringing these areas into alignment for you. You must let go of timing and trust the universe to deliver what you want when you're READY.

- **TRUST THE UNIVERSE.** I know we like to believe we control every aspect of our lives, and to some extent we do. We have the power to create anything we want, with the support of the universe; therefore, we must TRUST the universe to bring us the things we want. Also, know that the universe has a bigger plan for us, so if it happens in a different way to what you want, know that there is a reason for that.

- **SIT STILL AND ALLOW.** As we discussed in the lifestyle element having fun, sitting still and connecting to the FLOW of abundance is one of the best things you can do at least once a day. The more you sit still and relax, the more open your energy becomes to allowing, which is essential. You must be able to ALLOW and be open to receiving. Then go and take inspired action.

TRANSFORM RESISTANCE TO WEALTH

- **SHIFT YOUR ATTENTION AWAY FROM LACK.** Forget about money and wealth. You have to see the abundance in everything. Whatever the resource, whether it's time, love, people, clients_____ (You fill in the blank), it is what you focus on which sends a message to the universe that "I don't have enough_____" This is the opposite flow to abundant thinking.

- **BE GENEROUS WITH EVERYTHING.** This is about FEELING generous in everything you do. We give from a place of alignment because whatever you're giving you KNOW there is much more of it to come.

- **TRANSFORM HOW YOU FEEL ABOUT MONEY.** What happens to your energy when you think about money? Do you clam up, get scared or paralysed? Does that feel like the right vibration to be sending out to the universe? We need to transform our FEELINGS about money so that we feel these expanded emotions about it consistently.

- **'NEEDING' MONEY DOES NOT BRING IT.** If you need anything it keeps the very thing you want away. NEEDING is like affirming to the universe that you can ONLY be happy when you have that thing; the energy of NEED is resistant and prevents FLOW. To manifest money, wealth and abundance, you have to TRUST that it is coming and release the NEED!

- **CLEAN THE CASH**. Think about the RESISTANT or REVERSED energy which is being passed around as people spend money. Do most people hand over money with love? Or are they sending it with loathing, lack or fear mentality? As you come into contact with cash or when making payments, check in with your sway. Is this money holding resistance? Align the money using Step 5 and send it on with love.

◊:◊ EXPAND YOUR ENERGY WITH EAM

Pay attention to your energy. What happens to your energy when you think about money, wealth or abundance? How do you feel when you spend it? Then follow the 5 Steps of EAM to release the RESISTANCE in your energy. With Step 5 allow yourself to align to receiving more abundance on all levels.

YOUR MONEY MINDSET

One of the easiest ways to begin raising your abundance set point is to work on your money mindset. I wish there was space in this book for me to share the 88 most common money mindset beliefs and patterns which stand in your way. Things like 'I find it hard to save money', 'I spend money as soon as I get it', and 'I believe I don't have enough money'.

You can download them here as part of the downloads for the book. www.energyalignmentmethod.com/tush-freebies

You can create your own as well by just paying attention to yourself. What do you find yourself thinking, saying or mulling over in your head time and time again?

◊:◊ EXPAND YOUR ENERGY WITH EAM

Write a list of all of the things you have found yourself saying, thinking or doing over the last seven days. Then follow the 5 Steps of EAM to transform any resistant energy. Make sure you align to the positive mindset messages you want to maintain around money.

The MEANING OF MONEY

We know we have all this integrated neurological and energetic connections to money and what it means. Like Money + Power = Love, Happiness, Friendship and Fun. The reason we may have RESISTANCE to wealth is because of all these complex meanings around money and what it REALLY means to us. It is never really about the money. Rather, it is about what we believe the money will bring. Rarely are these meanings we ascribe to money that we hold, even our own! We've picked it up from friends, family, and society.

For example, we may have love demonstrated through the giving, receiving or removal of money. So, money is often tied to love. When you look at this concept on an emotional level, what everyone wants is to be happy. Therefore, they believe that money is the route to create it. So many people believe that the MONEY comes before the HAPPINESS, and that we can only be happy when the money is here. The irony is that belief motivates us to 'work hard' to 'push through' to 'make it happen!' All of these patterns create more RESISTANCE, so it is harder to reach the thing we want = the money. In the end, it becomes a self-fulfilling prophecy.

০:৹ EXPAND YOUR ENERGY WITH EAM

Take a look at what money really means to you. What do you believe having money will bring you? What emotion do you believe you will feel when you have it? Use the sway to ask questions around what money means and use the 5 Steps of EAM to let go of the beliefs and meanings you have attached to it. Use the bubble method to help you work through this. By doing this you can align to the positive meanings and connect to allowing a flow of money into your life.

YOUR MONEY STORY

Maybe you've had experiences in your past where you lost money, were in debt, or made money but had to sacrifice something — free time, time with family or friends, or even relationships — to get it. You will have a story about money, good or bad. The question is does your money story support or hinder you? If you know you have a story going on, then it's time for you to do the work. By changing your money story, you also change your reality around wealth and abundance.

⊙⊙ EXPAND YOUR ENERGY WITH EAM

Using EAM, explore your current money story. Use the bubble method and the 5 Steps of EAM to investigate and release any energy you have around your current money story. Align yourself to creating a new story, one that serves you and the journey that lies ahead.

EARNING MONEY AND FINDING WORK

There is, of course, a practical element to creating your own wealth. We have focused so much on energy; this is where the ACTION taking part really needs to kick in. Whilst we can always manifest income from other sources, most people look at their wealth capacity through their work. Your VISION, ENERGY, THOUGHTS, EMOTIONS, and ACTION; what you think feel and believe about your work affects your ability to manifest wealth. You must take aligned and inspired action, too. For most that means working. We will cover some in this element and more in the next two chapters.

If you hold resistant or reversed beliefs about capacity to earn money from your work, these will be reflected in your life. For example, if you think *my job only pays me £7 per hour and that's all I can earn.* That is what you will manifest. Conversely, if you change your belief to *I am ready to receive abundant sources of wealth from anywhere in my life, and I am ready to allow more money through my work*, you will see money flow begin to come.

ALIGNING YOURSELF TO THE JOURNEY

Now money doesn't just come through what you earn; it can come into your life from anywhere. Manifesting and receiving money is a vibrational energetic journey. You can't go from £0 - £1,000,000. You must experience your way there. It begins with earning a small sum, like £2000. Then you can enjoy that feeling of money and align yourself to the next chunk of money. You can then enjoy that, know what it feels like and align yourself to the next chunk of money. Each time this happens, the chunk of money grows!

ELEMENT 8 — WHAT TO REMEMBER

This is just a drop in the ocean about how to get yourself in flow with more money and wealth. It's part of a much bigger picture. I know that by doing this work outlined here you will begin to create a real shift in your life. Change your story about the past and create a new story for your future. Act like you have it. Think and feel like you have it. Start doing the things you will do when it is in your bank.

Remember, it's all just energy. When you can transform the meaning of money, your energy, beliefs, and emotions you can see your life (and bank account transform.) If you really want to talk shift your ability to attract, money, wealth, and abundance then you can download the 88 Money Mindset Messages which will help you transform your abundance.

Life Evolves When You Are in Flow

JACQUI TILLYARD, AGE 54

Last year, I felt full of turmoil especially with my work. My whole workload ground to a halt and I felt very stuck. I had no income and was isolated and not sure what to do or where to go. At the same time, I was also totally distracted with relationship issues and felt very uncertain about where I was heading. I was looking to shift how I felt and get out of my stuck state fast.

Having already discovered the benefits of EAM a couple of years ago, I decide to attend a live event. I used the 5-step process to release RESISTANCE around work, abundance, health and relationships. I felt much better and lighter for doing this work. As a result, I made the bold decision to become an EAM mentor.

What a year it's been, with so much transformation. My journey has been a voyage of self-discovery in every area of my life. I am now feeling totally in my power. My soul is now complete and I feel on purpose. Having done the release work on myself I now feel connected, calm, confident and happy in all areas of my life. It's a wonderful feeling when you live in alignment with your energy.

I have a superb technique that works for me on a daily basis and I am now sharing this with clients in EAM sessions and in personalised wedding and funeral ceremonies as a celebrant.

I'm so happy I said yes to my myself and my future and it's all paying off for me. I highly recommend it to others open to being in charge of and aligned to their own energy.

Be an Energetic Millionaire

ELEMENT 8 EXERCISE

When working with the universe, no one pops out of the sky and leaves a map on your desk to tell you how to get there. Your guidance comes as little signals, messages, thoughts, words, and actions. Find a way of making a list so that when inspired ideas come to you, you can write it down. THEN take the action! Don't put off taking the action because the ideas have not come to you in this moment. Take at least one step towards making it happen.

It really IS time to change. If you want a new money story to come true YOU must start doing, thinking and saying things differently. Just for a minute close your eyes, relax your body and get the FEELING of abundance in your body. Affirm "I am a millionaire" until you get a big sway forward (if you sway backward then release RESISTANCE first until you sway forward). If you knew next year, or in the next six months that you would be a millionaire no matter what you did, write down the answers to the following:

What is the NEW story that we want to create? What is the new powerful story that you want to tell yourself AND everyone else? Think about things like what you do for a living. How much money you earn? How long it has taken you to create it? How much free time you have? How easy is it to work? How much support do you have? How much freedom you have now?

Use the sway to help you construct this story to get clear on the details and to help make sure you're aligned Use Step 5 to align to the answers you have to these 3 questions.

- What would you THINK differently?

- What would you DO differently?

- What would you SAY differently?

Finding Your Passion & Purpose

ELEMENT 9

Here you'll discover how to use your energy to follow your heart, live your purpose, and create or define your mission in life. We're still working to expand those outer layers of our energy and connect to our purpose in the wider world, whether you're here to do bookkeeping or save animals, to collect recycling or feed starving children, to be a plumber or bring up our next generation of children. Each and every single job we have is important. This is about you connecting to your passion and living your life on purpose. It is about your expression of what is aligned to you.

Most people believe that their passion is about what they DO in the world, that their passion is external. They often spend more time at work than they do at home in a job they hate, so they can make ends meet. Dreaming of a day when they can truly live their passion. Or they go on an endless search for a job title or promotion, they push and sacrifice themselves to get there only to realise they are still unhappy. Your passion is something INSIDE of you, that once expressed you get to DO in the outside world.

NOW it is time to start thinking discovering your passion and purpose and finding a way to work with the right people so that you can make a difference. Whether you work for someone else or you work for yourself, it is about what is inside of you and how you express it. Living your purpose is about who you are every day. The way you do it is JUST an expression of that.

◑ EXPAND YOUR ENERGY WITH EAM

Let's first explore what energy, thoughts and beliefs you hold about being able to find or live your passion and purpose in life. What do you find yourself saying all the time? What do you believe is in the way of you living your passion? Do you believe you have a purpose? Use the bubble method and the 5 steps of EAM to help you explore and align to being able to find and live your passion and purpose.

In elements 9 and 10, your mission is to bring it all to life. Your work is an extension of you. Living your purpose is about bringing your skills, knowledge, and expertise to life, in a way that only you can. You want to create a life, job or business that excites the pants off you AND at the same time is of service to others. You do that by being SUPER clear who you are, what you want to do or be known for and who you want to work with. By now you know the power of working with the universal laws and living in alignment. When you are clear and make these decisions then life can send you the people and opportunities to support you. Which in turn means you make the difference and attract the income you want.

If you wait for outside circumstances to change you will never be 'ready'. Your journey so far has been about aligning to this. You have done so much of the energy work already. Now it is time for you to take action step outside your 'outer limit'. Allow your purpose and passion to lead you in the right direction in your life.

FIND YOUR PASSION, PURPOSE & PEOPLE

You've done so much work looking inwards at who you are and how to bring yourself into FLOW in by working on your thoughts, feelings, and beliefs. You've looked at your home, lifestyle, friendships, relationships, and money. We have laid the foundation for where you want to go. If you had looked at what is meaningful to you in your work before now, you may have made choices based on fear instead of love and passion. You may have decided to do something that your partner, friends, brother, sister or mother thought you 'should' do instead of listening to your own guidance. You may have made choices based on money or lack of it. I've seen it happen a thousand times (and repeated it myself for the more than 15 years until I finally figured it all out!). The truth is a choice based on any of those things will never serve you in the long run. What you create in your life must always be connected to your vision and in alignment with what makes you happy.

WHY THEY ARE IMPORTANT

Being on PURPOSE is what is authentic. Anything else is false and fake, and this creates a level of RESISTANCE. Our mission is to transform that and ALIGN ourselves in every way possible. This applies to more than your work; it is every area of your life, and if you're spending over 30% of your life working in some way, surely you want to be happy and in FLOW. Imagine how the world would be if everyone was living their purpose, happily doing the thing they loved that served the people they cared about. What a different place the world would be.

PASSION is important for the same reason. Passion is something we experience as an emotion, and it is brought about through the MEANING that something has for us. Let's look at this energetically or emotionally for a second. When you do something meaningful, which makes you feel proud, is it a happy emotion or sad one? It's happy. That emotion of passion and meaning is a representation of the fact that you're in FLOW. So, living your passion, working on your passion and sharing your passion is a primary way of keeping yourself IN FLOW for 30% of your life.

We all want connection; it is one of the underlying things which everyone is searching for, connection with other PEOPLE. If you look at any survey around happiness or what motivates us to keep going, it is usually something to do with other people. That could be our children, parents, friends, family, partner, or clients. When you look at any experience which has the deepest impact on us in life, it is usually to do with our connection with others. We are made to live in communities; we are made to connect. We are meant to play our part within a group of people. Right now, the world needs more people who are connected to their purpose, who understand their passion and the people they want to support. Are you ready for that to be you?

Living authentically with passion and purpose and working with people who support and inspire you begins with getting clear on the values which are important to you. It is then that you can bring it all to life in a way that works. Whether the outcome is running a business, working for a charity or being employed, the important thing is who YOU are being.

We all need to have connection, passion & purpose in life.

DISCOVER YOUR PURPOSE

Often people believe that your purpose is your job. Your purpose is something you do all day every day. When you look back at your life, you've probably been doing it since you were young. It is usually a skill, a quality, or a way of being. Something you do wherever you are. I believe that living your purpose is often our way of contributing to the community. Whether that means people nearby you in your street, and people around the world who need to know what you do. Living your purpose is when you're most in FLOW. It just feels natural, easy and simple.

Along my journey I was lucky enough to befriend a wonderful lady, Helen Elizabeth Evans. She has an incredible method of analysing your finger prints to help you to discover your life purpose. She uses the analysis to help people design their business so you can express your passion and your purpose. It was one of the biggest turning points in my personal journey to realise that all along I had been using my gifts. My gift is to be a mentor, teacher and guide. We are all born with a message inside, that message can be decoded in your finger prints. It was mind blowing to finally see someone explain what I had been feeling inside all my life. My natural brand is to come from a place of service and empowering others. Once I had a one to one session with Helen to discover this the trajectory of my work changed. You see it no longer mattered 'what I did' so long as these key elements were included in everything I do. If it had not been for my session with Helen I am not sure EAM would even exist.

To find your purpose, ask yourself what values in life are important to you? What do you believe is needed in the world? How can you turn that into work or a business? The first and most important step is for you to discover your purpose. To be clear: your purpose is about WHAT and WHY you do something, it is NOT about what you do for a living. Your work is more like the application of your purpose. It is the HOW.

DISCOVER YOUR PASSION

There is also something (maybe more than one thing) that you're passionate about. It is something that you feel compelled to do. Usually it is something you want to change or that you can see a new way of doing. Often this comes from your own journey: it is your story. As we discussed earlier, your passion is about discovering what REALLY lights you up. It may feel like something you want to 'fight for'. If it feels like a fight we may want to transform the RESISTANCE around that, and it will show you that it is something you passionately believe in and want to do something about. Your passion can also be a way that you express yourself; for example, art, music, painting, or speaking.

YOUR CORE VALUES

Every person needs to know what values they live by. Your personal core values will then map across into your work or business and become the ethics by which you live. What makes your work unique is YOU! It doesn't matter how you channel it. Be clear on YOUR personal values. You should summarise these down to 10 core values. These will not just apply to your work, and you'll find them important in every area of your life.

Finding Good in Something Bad

JO TOCHER, AGE 58

I lost a baby boy at 24 weeks — he was a stillbirth. It rocked my world. I was not the same person going back to work. Something inside me had changed so profoundly. I retrained as an aromatherapist and in many other modalities, such as Reiki Healing, (this was what helped me come to terms with my loss), hypnotherapy, wellbeing coaching, meditation and mindfulness. It was then that I discovered EAM.

I worked on myself in a way I hadn't before; this was deeper and more significant than anything else I had worked with. As a therapist, I had never worked with anything as powerful as this. It somehow got to the core of me and I knew big changes were afoot. I worked on the module for finding my passion and purpose. I started out being sure that my purpose was to help others; however, after writing my Soulful Story about the biggest, pivotal changes in my life, I realised this was when I had my miscarriage. This became my passion and purpose in life... to help others who have similarly lost babies in pregnancy.

I was like a butterfly coming out of my cocoon that had kept me safe for many years. I was now ready to break out and raise my head above the parapet. I trained to become an EAM mentor and I've now have worked with many women helping them through this trauma. I am in the process of writing my own book about how to heal from pregnancy loss. I would never have had got this level of clarity for my passion or purpose or even had the courage or self-belief to write a book, without doing EAM.

FIND YOUR PEOPLE

Now we are clear on our PURPOSE and our PASSION, let's define WHO we are passionate about doing things with and for. People and community are what should matter most to us. We want to be around people we love to spend time with. It doesn't matter if you're building a business or thinking of where to work, if you're building a charitable movement or changing the world. You want to build a community of likeminded people around you, friends, joint venture partners, employers, contacts, family, partners. You want to be able to attract these types of qualities in people to help you with your mission, and likewise you may be able to help them with theirs.

Part of living your passion and purpose includes being part of a community of people who need you most. Who is ready to hear your message? To evolve and grow, it's important to be in a community or work with team of people on a similar mission, whether you join one that already exists or you create one of your own. What is wonderful about the universe is your team is already gathered somewhere. You just have to find them or bring them to you, energetically.

This now leads us to the community of people you want to make a difference to. You have a natural gift or talent which other people need. The BEST way for you to work with the people you are passionate about is to SEE what is possible for them. As a leader or someone who wants to make a difference, it is up to you to see the potential in them and keep that vision of what is possible in their future alive (even when they have given up). It is then that you have something to give.

BUILDING CONNECTIONS

Whilst you're thinking about people, you've given some thought to who you would like to talk to. This is about building a community of people around your passion. Who else has a similar passion or mission? Who else is already working with the people you're passionate about? Who else cares about the people you're passionate about? We are designed to work in communities, on teams, and as groups. Working collaboratively achieves goals so much quicker. We work better together. So, let's start thinking about who you can bring on board to support your mission and whose mission you can support.

◊:◊ EXPAND YOUR ENERGY WITH EAM

Use the sway to define the traits you want to see in people around you and in your work community. Align yourself to attracting the traits you need. Create a list of people to connect with. Who can enable you to achieve your vision? Who do you know that can support you in getting to where you want to be? What communities can you be part of who will understand you?

ELEMENT 9 — WHAT TO REMEMBER

So now we have some more clarity around what fulfils us inside. This is really a big piece of work. When I work with clients, it really takes us a while to deep dive on all of the questions we have to explore your passion, purpose, your values. You need to do this to understand the people you want to connect with and the problems that they have and face so that you can see how YOU are meant to support them in their lives or businesses. No matter what your passion or purpose or even industry, we all solve a problem for someone. That is what makes the world go around.

Discover Your Purpose

ELEMENT 9 EXERCISE

You may want to use this space to discover your purpose in life

Some questions to help you explore your purpose are:

- What do you find yourself doing all the time in every situation?

- When you look back, what have all of your job roles included? Is there a theme?

- When you were at school, what did you find yourself doing the most? (It doesn't have to have been in the classroom.)

- What do you get so engrossed in that you forget to eat?

- What do you spend your time fantasying about?

- From these questions does there emerge a key theme? Are there 2 or 3 words or qualities which draw them all together?

- Using the sway ask, "Is this my purpose?"

Use the sway to help you get clear on this and release any RESISTANCE to discovering your purpose. Remember the most important thing in every situation is who you are, not what you DO.

Selling Your Soul & Making an Impact

ELEMENT 10

Now we're at the edge of our energetic experience. How will you really show up in the world, take action and put your life's work into practice? Now that you have done all the work in the previous elements, you're ready to create the massive impact and financial success and recognition you want and deserve. This is now the greatest expansion of our energy; we are beyond the edge of our energy and now using our aligned and expanded self to make our difference in the world.

LIVING YOUR MISSION

Whether you're working for yourself or working for someone else, the important part is that YOU are making your difference. You can live your passion and make an impact inside an organisation just as much as you can by building your own business. You've been through this entire journey. It probably feels like a million years ago since we first began doing the work on getting you in FLOW, working on your RESISTANCEs, straightening out your timeline, and looking at the thoughts and beliefs that have been standing in your way. I hope that by now, you should be feeling like an entirely different person and your life should be looking very different too.

What is making an impact really all about? For me, I believe that making your impact is important whether you influence 10 people, 100 people or a million people. It's about the difference that only *you* can make. You've done so much in this journey to allow you to understand who you are here to work with, what lights you up inside. I hope the work life you are now designing is coming from a place of FLOW, that it's coming from vision, your heart, from understanding yourself, your mission, your story and all of the things that have brought you to this point in your life.

If you are yet to start doing work which is meaningful to you then now is the time. If you are already doing that, then hopefully this might give you some more ideas on things that you can tweak or share or new perspectives.

We spend 30% of our life at work. Let's be sure that you enjoy that time you are working, so you stay in alignment as much as possible every day.

WEALTH COMES WHEN YOU SHARE YOUR GIFTS

The best paid work comes when you're doing the work that you're here for. I've seen it time and time again. When people start doing the work they are meant to do, the money comes. Yes, you can earn money. Yes, you can build a business doing almost anything. Unless it is filled with passion it will feel like hard work, stress and being overwhelmed.

In my previous life (whilst I was hiding from my true calling), I spent many years teaching and sharing with thousands of people on how you can build a sustainable, profitable business that takes your clients on a transformational journey. I loved it in some ways and made me cry in many others. I now understand why I needed to do that so that I could take EAM out into the world in the way that it needed to be.

GET PAID WHAT YOU'RE WORTH

Why do we need to make an impact? As I just shared, we spend over 30% of our life in work. If you're not doing what you love, you're spending 30% of your life out flow. Most people in the world get up every day and go to work. They hate their job. They hate their business. They get stressed out. They feel overwhelmed and tired. They spend so much time and energy dreaming of winning the lottery, so that they can be free. What they really want is FREEDOM. They just believe it is the money which will give it to them. We know that FREEDOM is a choice. It is a state of being. What if you just took the leap and did that anyway? We have one life, so f****ing live it. If you are or have spent years of your life doing work that you hate, please stop. The world needs YOU to be doing that thing which is calling in your heart.

How do we get in FLOW with the work that we want to do? This is about looking at the practical action steps that we need to take. Now, remember your life needs to be in alignment. Everything we have done so far in this Energy Evolution Journey has been about bringing your life into alignment. Now more than ever you need to ensure that your energy, your vision, your thoughts, your words, your emotions and your actions are all in FLOW. Unless you are putting yourself out there, sharing your big vision, and doing the work that's meaningful to you, how can the universe respond to that and the other areas of your life? Why should it, when you are living out of alignment with yourself?

WHAT TRANSFORMATION CAN YOU CREATE IN THE WORLD?

This is about bringing all those elements of your life into an aligned place. The world needs you. The world needs you to be doing your thing. *You* need to be doing your thing. There is no more time for you to put it off. You are the only person in the world who has had the experiences that you've had in the way that you have, with the beliefs that you have, with the resources that you have.

Nobody else has lived their life in the same way as you. Nobody else has the same answers, the same insights, the same ideas as you do. The world has given you that; you've got that insight for a reason and there is someone somewhere that needs what you know, whether that's one person, 10 people, 100 people or 1,000. There are people out there who need what you know, and it is your love-bound, life-bound duty and journey to be living your passion. Put your vision out there. Share your vision on social media. Tell everyone you meet and see the opportunities, the connections, the joint venture companies, and the clients begin to turn up.

LISTEN TO YOUR VISUALISATION

Go back and listen to the visualisation. Hopefully, you've been listening to it on a regular basis as you've worked through the journey. We know how important your vision is. It's a key part of your journey. I want you to reconnect your vision and really focus in on your life, your ideal dream lifestyle, but also about your work and your passion.

Making Money & Difference

CATHERINE PAGE, AGE 43

When I found EAM, I had just come out of a 10-year toxic relationship that had left me heartbroken. It had shattered my faith in humanity. I was absolutely exhausted, my business was completely running me, and finances were hard. Initially it was tough stepping out of the drama triangle that we humans live in... blaming others, not taking responsibility, RESISTANCE to doing inner work, and thinking it impossible to cut years of conditioned thinking.

As therapist for the last 26 years I have worked more than 50,000 client hours using other healing modalities. I have been blown away by how simple and effective EAM is. Fear, old beliefs disappeared! I let go of the old and transformed my life into one that I truly wanted to live! I became an EAM mentor so I could enable others to rebuild their lives and unlock their own potential.

I went from skint and broken at the end of every month to bringing home 4 figures monthly. This made such a huge difference to me and my life. The support with all of the internal chatter and the practical steps to building a business on my terms has been amazing. I've used EAM to help me shape my work and business around me and discover what I wanted to do and be able to make a difference in the world.

PERCEIVED HURDLES

Look at the perceived hurdles and obstacles that you think may get in your way. Maybe that's technology, family, not having the money, or not having the skills or knowledge or expertise around business. Perhaps it's that you know your passion, but you feel like you haven't trained enough yet in what you want to do, or you don't feel like you're fully qualified to really go out there and help people. Whatever those things are, we need to identify them now. Once you let go of the belief, that's when the magic can truly start to happen.

What are your perceived hurdles? Sometimes it might be a very practical answer; it might not just be an energetic answer. For example, if you don't know how to build Facebook fan page, you need to find out how to do that. Other people might be able to connect you with somebody or might be able to recommend something. Sometimes the solution is just outside of us and all you need is someone to point you in the right direction.

◊:◊ EXPAND YOUR ENERGY WITH EAM

Look at beliefs and energy of emotions which are standing in the way of you taking your leap into the world through your work. I would get the bubble method for this one and write down everything you think is stopping you from making your impact. Then use the 5 Steps of EAM to release the RESISTANCES and align to allowing yourself to do the work you are meant to do.

CREATING A BUSINESS IN FLOW

Now I would love to share with you the work I used to do in helping people to design their ideal life and business that works in flow with who they are. It is called the Soulful Entrepreneur System and it is based on the Chinese 5 Elements and the way in which all things grow and generate. It is based on the energetic connection and relationship with your client. It is designed to continue growing and evolving itself as you evolve, creating its own wheel of momentum. Again, this is a book in itself. You see the success in your business or work only comes from having all of the elements of your life in alignment. People would spend hours screaming at me to fix something in their business when actually it was their energy which was totally out of sync.

Their businesses inevitably ended up collapsing, never getting any traction, or getting off the starting blocks or being as free Flowing as they could have been because they ignored the other work before. They were trying to go for the end result first and ignore everything else and then working their lives backwards. Through years of doing this and sharing this with thousands of people, I saw time and time again where it was going wrong and that's exactly the journey that I've now just shared with you. That is what enabled me to create and share The Energy Evolution.

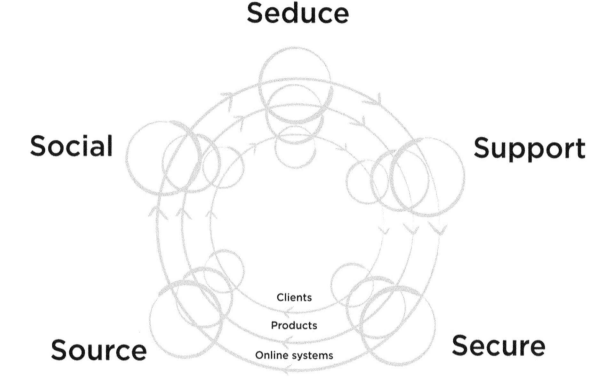

The Soulful Entrepreneur System

YOUR SOULFUL SYSTEM

It begins with YOU, YOUR LIFE, and YOUR WORK. Then you can start thinking about how to build that into a business model. If you're working for someone else, it is a system for sharing your ideas with the community of people you want to buy into your philosophy. If you've done all of that work on yourself, it should be a business model that represents you, your values, your mission, the transformation you want to make and then this business model becomes all about your client. This is all just an energy journey that your client needs to go on, so that they understand what you do for them.

There are 5 stages to this client journey, which are all about their energetic and emotional connection to you and your message. This in itself is a huge piece of work but for now I want you to know that building your business and finding clients is an energetic journey. Everything you create for it must be in alignment with you, the message you want to share and the things your potential clients or community need to hear. Even though I no longer run this business it is still the model I teach and share in more depth for those inside the Energy Evolution for those who are on the journey because it is an extension of you. We enable all of our mentors to implement it in their businesses too. The same principles still apply because it's all just energy.

As we discussed earlier, in Chinese philosophy one of the main principles is the 5 key energy FLOWs. The five element energies are Wood, Fire, Earth, Metal, and Water. The five stages of your client's journey, those five element energies, also apply to the growth of your business and your evolution too. It depends on where you are already in your passion journey and your business journey.

YOUR BIG MESSAGE

Whether you're running a business, finding clients, aiming to work in a charitable cause, or needing to convince the boss that you should be the one to run a project, you will have to find a way to educate people and deliver an idea that is fun, engaging and educational. You'll need to get people to buy into the idea of what it is that you want to share at the end. You want them to understand your story. You want them to love what you do and know your message, which means that they can go out and spread that on your behalf. It's a win when people know what you do because you never know when all those people are going to start sharing your message with somebody else.

It's your key philosophy and your key teachables that enable you to take this presentation and be able to rock up anywhere and start sharing your message.

◊:◊ EXPAND YOUR ENERGY WITH EAM

Use the sway to help you identify 3 key messages that you wish everyone would know. If you could stand on your soap box and shout at everyone, what would you say? Use the 5 Steps of EAM and align yourself to sharing this message and embodying it so it emanates from you.

BE IN FLOW WITH YOUR WORDS

Practise this. If you have an important presentation to do, please do yourself the honour of practising what you're about to share. Make sure you are in flow with your words. Use EAM to work through any RESISTANCE in your words, so that what you share comes from a place of alignment. You want to make sure your message is congruent, that it feels right for you, and that it is what you believe. Work on releasing any RESISTANCE about anything you're sharing with others. Particularly if you are inviting people to buy from you or take some action. Make sure you've released RESISTANCE, because RESISTANCE travels. Even through the internet, RESISTANCE travels. People will be able to pick up on what you're feeling, what you're thinking, what you're saying, and what you're doing. Even if you think that it's not, they absolutely will.

Our voice, our energy, and our passion is all communicated just as much through the internet as when you're meeting somebody face to face. If you are out of FLOW, in the wrong energy when you record something, feeling resistant, or feeling scared or overwhelmed about any of this stuff, that all transfers as well. You want to make sure that you are as in FLOW and as prepared as possible.

☼ EXPAND YOUR ENERGY WITH EAM

If you have a big presentation, event or talk where you need to speak, make sure you are aligned to your words. Use the 5 Steps of EAM to release any RESISTANCE and align to them hearing the true meaning of your message, so that they take the action you need them to.

CHAPTER 7 — WHAT TO REMEMBER

This last element was really looking at the OUTSIDE world, at what makes you sing. How are you creating your wealth and making an impact in the world? Everything is energy and it all begins with the emotions, thoughts, and beliefs we hold about every area of our lives. Now you've expanded yourself and your energy out to be in alignment on every level of your aura. Your life should be feeling FAR more in flow.

What Are You Here For?

EXERCISE - ELEMENT 10

It is time to be truthful with yourself and to align to what you are here to do. If you need to you can go back and listen to your visualization to connect to your impact in the world. Use the sway to ask questions and get ideas you are meant to do for you work. Do you know what it is yet? Has it been shown to you? Do you need to wait or take some action to find it? Unless you are doing it already, align yourself to knowing what you are here for and start taking action towards it.

_____

_____

_____

_____

_____

_____

_____

_____

_____

_____

_____

_____

CHAPTER 8

The World

"The power of mass intention may ultimately be the force that shifts the tide toward repair and renewal of the planet."

~Lynne McTaggart

CHANGING THE WORLD WITH EAM

What a journey we've been on together. Whilst I hope that it has been an epic adventure for you too, this is REALLY just the beginning. In this last chapter, let's explore what is possible when we come together. What could we do if the world was aligned and in flow? What could you do better with the community of support and people who understand you?

YOU ARE LIMITLESS

Our basic human nature is growth and expansion; the universe was created that way. We are born to be successful; we are born to want more so we are always searching for something else. We find ourselves looking at the future and where we are going, sometimes with hope or hopelessness, sometimes with fear or joy. We all have a dream. We all have a vision, something we're working towards, whether that dream is having one more day off a week or living on a beach in Barbados. It is a projection of ourselves and our lives in the future.

My ethos is that this is a journey of EXPANSION. If we are expanding, there must be a limit to where we are right now. Imagine it is like an edge or an outer or upper limit. Energetically, we're talking about the *edge* of our aura and what is contained within it. To allow more into our lives, we must move past the limits of our current experience.

We have created our own limitations; these show up as self-sabotage and are designed to keep us safe. They kick in when we reach the outer edge of our current self-imposed bubble and you're about to break through. For me, limitations are connected to our growth and more related to our future and where we want to go. There is also something many people refer to as the GLASS ceiling! Gay Hendricks talks about it in his amazing book *The Big Leap*, which offers incredible insight into 'the upper limit' and what these limitations are.

PUSHING THROUGH

We will ALWAYS have an upper limit. No matter how 'successful' you are or what you're aiming for, there will always be a limit on your current potential because it is the boundary line of our current capacity. The limit is created by your current mind-set, thoughts, beliefs and experiences. The journey we are on is about continuously expanding our limits. So, every time you break through your 'glass ceiling' and onto the next level, there will be another one there to greet you. I say that to inspire you because your glass ceiling could be way beyond your current experience.

This is why I bang on so much about releasing any and all RESISTANCE, so you continually expand by being in FLOW and living your life aligned in the best way possible. The more you do, the more you expand. The better your life gets, the more your capacity to receive improves.

HOW DO THEY AFFECT US?

We can limit ourselves in so many ways, mainly by doing things which are out of FLOW. In *The Big Leap*, Gay talks about four hidden barriers that trigger your upper limiting behaviour. All of them are beliefs or ways of thinking about ourselves.

'Hidden Barriers' that hold the Upper Limits in place

1. Feeling fundamentally flawed

2. Disloyalty & abandonment

3. Believing that more success brings a bigger burden

4. The crime of outshining

When we have these hidden barriers in place, we will find a way to ruin situations around us even when things are going great. We will focus on everything that is wrong rather than everything which is right. These are all just RESISTANCE or REVERSALS created by unresolved issues in our energy.

These could be in the form of beliefs, stuck emotions, memories we hold, or stories we keep on telling. There is no end to what form the limitation may take. Your work is to recognise when they are showing up because they will continue to ruin your efforts to change your life and be successful.

First, let go of the pattern of allowing these self-imposed limits to kick in, so that you can prevent yourself from creating more of these situations. Then you can start to recognise all these upper limits. They are not in fact 'real'; they are just the limit of our current experience. You can use EAM to break the 'hidden barrier" and let it go with ease so you can step into your next level of alignment. So, when they pop up celebrate you are about to become the next level version of yourself.

SELF-IMPOSED LIMITS

A great example of an upper limit kicking in is something like this. You meet someone you love, you are really happy with them after a string of previously unhappy relationships where you've been hurt before, and this finally feels like the one. You've been together a few months and you know inside it is something special. Your partner organises a surprise trip to Venice. You're having a wonderful time, you know you're in love, and you've had a great evening. You've had flowers and champagne and have been serenaded. Your partner pays the bill and doesn't leave a tip. After all of this, you just cannot shake it from your mind that they didn't leave a tip. So, you go quiet, you sit on it for an hour or so, not really looking at them and secretly FUMING because you think they are unkind and they should have left a tip. Then you burst out with "WHY were you so tight and not leave a tip for the waiter? I can't believe you wouldn't spend your money on that ..." This starts an argument and ruins the whole trip (and possibly the relationship).

The TRUTH was that the waiter had been quite rude when you had popped off to the loo, and your partner had chosen to let it go because they wanted you to enjoy the special evening with you. The reason this is an upper limit is because in amidst all of this wonderful experience can you see how you choose to focus on the one small thing rather than receive the good. You have finally receiving everything you wanted, when something inside feels "oh, stop a minute this is unsafe. This is unknown territory" (edge of our current experience). So, you do something to bring yourself back to a situation where things feel normal, within your range. Even though it is not enjoyable to argue, you know how to experience that. Your work here is to make sure you recognise this phenomenon, so that when it arrives you can recognize it and react accordingly! Understand that the issue is very rarely about the what is in front of you. It is always about something else. That 'something else' is something that YOU have going on in your energy. So, own it fully, take responsibility for what you think and how you feel.

ARE YOU LIVING IN REALITY?

Reality is very subjective. We can think that we are all living in the same world having the same experience. Yet as we have seen throughout this journey, we can interpret situations differently. We all think that only our reality is the right one. Yet how do we know whose is real? The answer is no one's. We are co-creating our experience of life. We affect what we see and what happens all the time. We are all one.

Your identity, the part you think makes you, is not real either. It is made from changeable elements of our life like character traits, experiences of the past, and the stories you have told or been told which make up your life. So, if they can change, how can it define who you are? They only make you YOU whilst you hold them. The journey we've been on together will have allowed you to change them.

If the reality of our lives is perception and the identity of who we are is changeable, how can we know what is real? The easiest way is to just let go. To recognise it is all a story. None of it is real and everything is real all at once. By knowing that you can change your reality with EAM, you can change your life.

Usually these (and many other things) are excuses that many people allow themselves to believe because they are looking at life through the 'reality' they are living. Ultimately these stories they create are all based on fear. Fear of not enough, fear of failure, fear of success, fear of the future and of what will or won't happen. Or self-doubt, lack of self- belief or self-worth, and feeling unworthy. The list goes on. All the time and money in the world won't change those things in their life they until you change your energy. Now of course you know this now. If you've reached this point of the book, I hope you've implemented what you've learnt and moved past it. I want you to bear this in mind when interacting with others in your life and in the world.

ALIGN TO THE RIGHT RESOURCES

To really be able to go on the next phase of this journey, you may need to find more resources. Now if your current 'reality" has been that you need more support, time or money as well as doing the energy work, there are some practical things you can do.

Think about ways you can 'buy back' your own most precious resources, your time and your energy, and the right support. We all have access to the same resources; you have a choice about what you do with what you have. So, if you want to go on a bigger journey to change your life. You need to make it a priority. This means allocating time and energy.

Have you ever heard someone say, "If I had the money to do XYZ then I would be able to ...." or "If I had the time for XYZ then I would be able to...." You see that kind of thinking can be the very thing standing in our way. Whilst we believe it is our reality, we will create more of the same. To create more allow support and find time and money, we have to do the energy work first.

ALLOW MORE SUPPORT

Most of us have other responsibilities. It may be work, children, caring for parents, social activities, and clubs; the list is endless. The biggest question you can ask yourself is does it have to be me who does it? Could someone else step in? Find ways of getting support. Or maybe finding supportive communities who understand where you are and can give you guidance along the way. No one can change their life alone. If you feel resistant to finding the right support or allowing people in, use the 5 Steps of EAM to release that and allow in "I am ready to allow myself to be fully supported. I allow this into my energy in all forms on all levels at all points in time".

MAKE MORE TIME

How many times do we tell ourselves that we're too busy or don't have the time? Even if not out loud, how many times have we thought those things? Ask your sway.

Let's find some time in your life. Look at what you spend time doing and ask yourself, is it important to me? Do I love it? Is it taking me towards my vision? If the answer to any of those things is no, then let it go. It starts from the moment you wake up. Do you lie in bed in the morning scrolling through

Facebook on your phone, or do you write in your journal and make a plan for your day? Do you watch TV, play video games, read magazines and newspapers, or listen to the news or radio? What could you listen to? What could you choose to read instead? If you commute, what do you do on your journey? Do you listen to inspiring books or training or do you watch people on the train and play on your phone?

What do you do when cooking the dinner? Do you do the cleaning, putt on the washing, finish the ironing or do a bit of gardening? What if you got up an hour earlier in your day? What if you went to bed an hour later? What if once a week you asked your friend to look after the kids for an extra morning or afternoon? What if you asked your partner, friends, or family to chip in a bit more around the house? What if you got a cleaner to do 2 hours work a week, which brought you a bit more time? What could you achieve in that time?

We all have the same 24 hours in the day. It is what you choose to do with them that counts.

CREATE MORE MONEY

I hear this all the time. I get it, I really do. I know that sometimes there is more going out than there is coming in. I spent years in debt and fighting people off whilst busily trying to build businesses or recouping money I had lost. It all feels so real.

Of course, we can work on your beliefs around money and notice whatever happens to your energy when you think about it, like we did in Chapter 7. You also need to take action.

What would you do if you knew that someone would give you £1 million pounds in 10 days if you could raise £10,000. You'd get a plan into action and make sh** happen, wouldn't you?

You'd probably go through your house and put everything that you no longer want or need on eBay or in for sale groups. Maybe you'd throw yourself a garage sale in the garden. You'd cut down your spending on your bills and cancel subscriptions you didn't want. Maybe you'd get a loan from a bank or ask a friend who is cash rich. Perhaps you'd start charging more per hour for your work. You'd put some services up on sale on Facebook and use your talents to raise some extra cash. You'd basically get REALLY creative about it and you would FIND the money. So how can you apply that same energy to what you're doing right now?

Now that you understand some of the key elements of applying EAM, it is time to put them into practice.

CONNECT TO YOUR SUPPORT GROUP

To create the success, you want, it is vital to find the right resources and support. I am yet to meet someone who has created epic success in their life and done it alone. Even the greatest people in history have had support and the right resources to create their achievements. We all have a wealth of responsibilities in our lives. Whether it is looking after ourselves, our children, friends or family. It could be our health, our work, home, charitable cause; whatever it is you are choosing to focus on, you can ONLY be in one place at a time.

If have children and you're at work, do you just leave them on their own? No, of course not. Rather, you get support through organising childcare or making sure they're at school. If you are at work and there is a task which is outside your skill set, do you try and push through or do you delegate it to someone who loves that task and can complete it far more quickly and with more passion than you? Think about a child at school. Do you expect them to just suddenly know how to do everything the first day, or do you provide them with support and assistance, people to guide them and enable them to put in place simple and practical methods to learn?

The same goes for resources. Do you think that Mother Theresa achieved all she did on her own with no budget, no time, and no team? Did you know she was an incredibly prolific fundraiser, gathering support and resources for her cause which enabled her to do the work she was here for.

The same goes for changing your life. You will need support along the way. It is up to you to put the right support strategies and find the resources to put them in place. How will you prioritise yourself enough to get the support you need, and to find the energy, time, and money to implement these changes in your life. I would love to be there with you through it all.

SHARE THE RESPONSIBILITIES

If we believe we have no one to step in and support us that is exactly what we will create. Have you heard people say things like "I am a lone parent. I've got no one to help with my kids". Now we know in some cases this is true. Yet in others this can be an example of our resistances allowing us to generalise one element of our life and we project it onto everything. So, we end up creating our own reality.

People are usually more than willing to support us. It is usually we who struggle to ask for help. If you REALLY wanted to buy yourself a little time to get yourself in FLOW, how would that ultimately benefit you and your family? What support could you ask for in the home? Who else could take on some of the responsibilities you hold (even if it is was just for a short while)? What roles are you playing in the home or family, which are sucking up more of your time and energy?

Maybe you need external support and guidance. What skills, knowledge or expertise do you need around you? What mental and emotional support do you need? I know sometimes we may not have the people around us who get it. They would think that this stuff is crazy! To go on the journey to changing your life, how can you get the right kind of support from the right people? Ask yourself, WHAT resources do I need and HOW am I going to change my life, once and for all?

BE WITH THE RIGHT PEOPLE

It's vital to your success to make sure you have the right people around you. People who get it! If you have a person in your life who'd laugh at everything in this book, maybe share it with someone else first. If you're easily knocked, swayed, or influenced by others, hang out with people who think and feel the same way as you do.

If it's right for you and people around you will get it, then share this with them. Share it with your children and your friends. The more people around you who are doing it, that you can talk to or bounce ideas off, the better it will be for you.

Whilst EAM IS a self-help tool which you can absolutely use on your own, sometimes it's nice to be part of a community of people who understand it and can support you in changing your life. If you hang out with people who don't get it, you may want to give up. You do not have to do it alone, and the greatest successes come from allowing other people to support you. If you need more support around you come and join our online group. www.energyalignmentmethod.com/join-the-community

THE POWER OF GROUPS

It has been said that 'We are the average of 5 people we most associate with'. We know that energetically this IS true. Studies have shown that our energy will synchronise to the highest frequency in the room. So, if you are spending a lot of time with people who drag you down, moan, bitch, whine, and complain, it probably doesn't take long for you to jump on the bandwagon with them. We love familiarity; the brain is less vigilant for potential threats because it is familiar with the place and the people around us. So even when we KNOW we are surrounded by people who bring us down, we tend to stay there because it's 'safe' and what we know.

On the flip side, what happens when you spend time with people who inspire you, lift you up, and show you that it is possible to change your life, so that you can progress to the steps and leaps you need and deserve to take. To change your life, you need to surround yourself with people who have the same or a higher vibrational energy and view point of life.

A COLLECTIVE INFLUENCE

These energetic influences apply to all of our social situations and relationships. Collectively, we influence others' energy and they do ours. In a group dynamic, energy will synchronise; the larger number of people in that state, the harder it is to resist it. This is the energy of momentum in action. Think of it like the domino effect. As one person does it, so do 2, 3 10, 30 ... the energy ripples, expands, and impacts more and more people.

Think about a group of normal, everyday people who suddenly find themselves in the middle of a riot, smashing things up, becoming violent and hitting other people. Is it because everyone went mad at once? No, it is just because everyone tapped into the group energy. The same thing happens at a concert when everyone feels loved and connected, singing their favourite songs at the top of their lungs in a stadium of hundreds of other people. I have seen this happen at our live events too. The energy in the room is electrifying as we work together to use EAM and release the RESISTANCES and REVERSALS and align to something new. You see everyone raise up to match that synchronised high vibration.

SHARED ENERGY AND VISION

How can you be part of a group or community of people who have the same or higher vibration than you? If you want to support yourself in maintaining this level of energy, focus and attention, then be part of the right communities. This can be just in an online space or at events or meeting up with people in person. This is one of the reasons why people say that our live events are just so transformational. Not only are you in a room with other high vibe people, as one or two people start to shift there is a domino ripple effect across the whole room as everyone else is able to transform things which were previously stuck.

So, get yourself in a room with others who are the same, and be in the energy of all these other people who are in FLOW. The thing is, this carries on after the events, too. As you are more in FLOW, you've expanded your own energy so when you go home this is your new normal. You can never go back because your energy will want to maintain this new high vibrational state!

Whether you join a local meet-up group, support network, or healing circle, find a community of like-minded high vibe people to be with. People who understand this and are doing the work on themselves. Perhaps you want to join our EAM meet-ups, courses, and live events. Make sure you find time in your life to be in the energy of other high vibe people. The impact on you and your transformational journey will be huge just by being in the room.

Even if you are waiting to get to the live event, you can join the wealth of energy inside our online group visit us here www.energyalignmentmethod.com/join-the-community

Be your own coach.

Create connection.

Feel into your emotions.

Reflect back what

you see, feel & hear.

TAKE RESPONSIBILITY FOR YOURSELF

When you are self-responsible and aware of your energy you can change your life rapidly. Become your own coach, listen to yourself, create a connection with yourself and skillfully learn to reflect back what you see and hear. You can use your sway to help you ask the right questions and the 5 Steps of EAM to transform anything that comes up for you. You can become your own transformational coach. In Chapter 3, we created a list of how to know when you need to use EAM. Use that as your guide.

BE YOUR OWN COACH

We all have a story about our life. Why things are this way or how it came to be. You can use your story to identify the places where you have RESISTANCE or REVERSAL. Once we have that information and work through it with EAM, it has no use to you anymore. Share your story only with the purpose of releasing the energy in it. Then follow the 5 Steps of EAM to work through what you discover. A really powerful way to work through this with EAM is first see what happens to your energy when you think about your journey. You can follow the balloon process or you can write it out.

By writing the story down, you give it less energy than speaking it out loud. It also means we can burn the piece of paper afterwards, which can be a helpful symbolic act of letting it go. By writing it down unedited in a journal or on a piece of paper, you can go back and identify beliefs, emotions and stuck energies around it. Then work through the 5 Steps with them.

With this I would say be aware and try to avoid 'digging' to get to the core root" of the issue", as the energy of this can literally pull you down. Only work on what needs to be released until the sway says it has gone, then align with Step 5 to call in the things that you want instead.

This philosophy of not buying into your story can sometimes seem like tough love. It is never meant to be that, just that we can choose what we want to believe. I want to believe in the story of who you are, who you believe you can become. You must believe in the empowered version of you who is able to change your life and those of the people you love. That is the story we all want to hear. It is the one you should share the most. If you share that story with me, I will be there to listen and cheer you on. Let's create the energy of that and bring the life you want to you.

EXPECTING OTHERS TO BUY INTO YOUR STORY

Once you have done that work, we can take a further leap of faith. Again, it is back to being self-responsible (yes, I've said it again) and it really is such a key component of that journey. We can get so wrapped up in own story, the reasons why our life is the way that it is, why we can't do the things that we want to do, why we have made choices and decisions, and why we have yet to make changes.

It can end up feeling like a repetitive story. When we are communicating from the place of the story and telling everyone "I can't do this or that" or "I'm feeling like this because …", two things are happening. One is that as you know you are creating more of it, the more you will give energy to it and the more it will persist. Secondly, you sharing that story because you want someone else to say, "oh yes, I understand, yes you're right it is unfair, I understand why you are stuck where you are". You want them to buy your story. A little reminder here: when we do this, we are in the energy of the PULLER, drawing energy from everyone and everything.

Please do not be offended or upset because I use the word 'story'. I'm not disregarding your experience. I am sharing with you a new paradigm in how to approach it. What you are describing is your experience of past events; is just a description of what your energy was doing at that time. It is a story of how you interpreted energy. If you expect people to buy into your story and then they agree by jumping into the pit of RESISTANCE with you, you will both be stuck in this narrative.

GETTING YOUR NEEDS MET

I know many people want to make a difference. I believe as human beings we ultimately want to do good, live in a harmonious world and support one another. Yet many people are spending their time trying to help others or giving to others constantly without having their own needs met.

There are many different models about needs; one of the most famous is Maslow's hierarchy of needs. I quite like Tony Robbins' example, as it keeps things more simple. He says there are 6 human needs: certainty, variety, significance, love and connection, growth and contribution. He groups them into 4 needs of the personality and 2 needs of the spirit (we would call it soul).

When thinking about the needs of the personality, we are talking about the part of us who is driven by the need to feel that we have achieved

- **CERTAINTY** – this is about being able to predict, create consistency, and feel safe, stable or secure. This is the part of us which likes order.

- **VARIETY** – on the other hand, we also love to feel that there is some variety in life. We love to be surprised or challenged. We want more excitement and adventure. We love change and novelty.

This in itself presents a bit of a challenge: we want freedom, yet we crave certainty. We wish for excitement, yet we like safety and stability. This inner conflict creates a RESISTANCE as the different needs we have push and pull us in different directions. Or we allow others to push and pull us as we try to get these needs taken care of.

We also need:

- **SIGNIFICANCE** – a need to be worthy, to be special, and to feel needed or wanted. Everyone wants to feel important or have pride in what they have done.

- **CONNECTION AND LOVE** — We also want to be loved by others. We want to be attached and unified or intimate with the people around us.

Again, we're in this push pull scenario which creates RESISTANCE. For example, we can lose our connection to love and intimacy as we push to have meaning and significance in the world.

Then we have the needs of our spirit or soul. These are more about our meaning and depth in life, and what fulfills us. The provide us with a way to be happy and fulfil our lives.

- **GROWTH** – This is about our spiritual, intellectual and emotional development.

- **CONTRIBUTION** – We need to make a difference to serve and protect other people. We need to contribute to things outside of ourselves.

The challenges come when we do not recognise these or know how to get our needs met without having to get it from someone or something else.

UNCONSCIOUS NEEDS

Most of our internal battles are around fulfilling these underlying needs. Unconsciously we all want these things, yet we have strange ways of getting them. It is often around these needs that we create or destroy things in our lives. We can also put other people first without sorting ourselves out. Have you ever seen that friend who is running around trying to sort out your love life and giving you relationship advice when their own relationships are a mess? Maybe that person has even been you? How can you give someone the real advice they need to hear when you're still in RESISTANCE or REVERSAL about it yourself? Whilst the intentions are well-meaning, it can lead to two people running around being out of FLOW instead of just one.

Think about the need to put someone else down, to talk about other people, be a martyr, or rebelling for the sake of it. Are these supportive ways to get your need for significance? Or could you do it through developing yourself, mastering your life, doing charitable work or being successful in your life? Some of these are depleting and some are source-filling. You can choose how to meet your own needs without impacting others or coming from a place of misalignment. By fulfilling yourself first you will no longer need others to be, do or say anything. Your interactions will change and you'll become a strong source of support. Once your own oxygen mask is on and you come from a place of alignment, you will have the capacity to empower others.

PUTTING YOUR FOUNDATIONS IN PLACE

If we want to go out and change the world, we must have our own foundations in place. From an EAM perspective it means being in alignment first. By bringing all elements of yourself and your life into FLOW, you get your needs met internally. You no longer need anyone or anything outside of you.

This is exactly what the Energy Evolution journey is all about. Hopefully, by now you've done the work in this book and brought yourself into alignment. As you start looking at other people around you, first of all put on your own oxygen mask. If you try giving to others when you are out of alignment, you'll have nothing to give. Once you have brought yourself into alignment, you'll have the energy and capacity to help others. Allow yourself to recognize your own needs and get them met.

THE 'OTHER' PEOPLE IN YOUR LIFE

Let's face it: not everyone in the world is the same as us. The world would be a boring place if that were the case. It is this interplay of energy between us all which creates the differences in our lives. To change our lives, we have to change the way we interact with other people, too. This can be challenging because our relationships can be complicated and messy when they are out of FLOW. You worked on much of this in Chapter 6, but there still may be some work to do.

LEARNING TO LIVE WITH OTHERS

We're going to have to learn to live with other people in the new paradigm. Instead of us expecting them to change to make us happy, we're going to do the work to make ourselves happy no matter what they say or do.

Dealing with people who are still living in the old paradigm can be very difficult. They may use blame, shame, guilt, push, pull and manipulation to get your attention. You may still find yourself getting dragged back into those ways of communicating, too. I invite you to change the energy of it, so that you can live in the new paradigm in all your relationships (with or without the people in your life right now).

When you are able to recognise your own interactions, and choose to respond in a different way, the 'stuff' that other people do will no longer influence or impact your energy. Guess what, as soon as your energy changes you'll see the shifts inside them, too. That is when the true magic with EAM begins as you see the impact of your energy shifts changing others.

As you go on the journey to changing your life, other people will have a LOT of opinions about what you should or shouldn't do. The truth is it will be down to you. Your choice is to always come from the place of alignment.

HOW TO DEAL WITH OTHER PEOPLE

Let's talk about the way we see other people. If we see something in someone else that is pushing our buttons, it is more about us than it is about them. Many of the feelings, thoughts and emotions you hold are not about what is happening right now and maybe some of the things which have happened in the past. Those situations may be to do with that person directly or just someone that they remind you of.

Either way, we have to own our stuff and do the work on it. So, before we can have clear and aligned communication, connection or relationship with them we have to clear up our energy about them first otherwise everything they say will be clouded by your thoughts and emotions! This has an awesome two-way benefit as you work on your stuff: a) you release it from your energy; b) it means it is not there to refire anything later down the line; and c) you are clearing out your own emotional and mental filters so when they communicate back to you, you will be able to receive their message. This means we need to work on how we feel about them.

MANAGING OTHER PEOPLE'S ENERGY

Have you ever been around someone who just seems to suck your energy and create a vortex of doom around them every time they speak. This is a person in PULLER energy. Even though you know this, we can be affected by their energy, especially if it's someone who is e close to you. If you suddenly start to notice that people you once loved now seem very negative, feel different or behave differently with you, then celebrate. They are still the same; it's you whose changed. You're releasing your lower resistant energies. Your energy is raising and becoming lighter. You are becoming more aware of energy. You know what it feels like to feel good and in FLOW and you'll notice more easily when something feels out of FLOW too. Use the 5 Steps of EAM to work on whatever is pulling you down about what they say or do. Then align to more love, connection, and happiness.

☼ EXPAND YOUR ENERGY WITH EAM

Very often in the spiritual world you'll hear people talk about "closing yourself down" or "protecting yourself from negative energies" as a way to cope with the 'sucking' energy. By its very nature protection is RESISTANCE. Shutting yourself down means you are energetically making yourself (and your aura) much smaller. If our energy is being easily affected by others, this is more about us than it is about them. The only time that someone else's energy can impact ours is when we are out of FLOW.

Remember in our Step 5 aligned energy, our aura expands; it is strong and complete. This means that nothing and no one can mess with you. In Step 5 you are in the state of love, which is the highest vibration and the foundation of new paradigm living.

Make a new choice today. It all begins with working on our own energy. You may notice that people are different with you. Or you'll hear things like "you've changed". It's almost as if they find it hard to understand what is different or they will want to drag you back into their story. When you stay in FLOW they will try even harder to pull you back to the metaphorical dark side! Stay strong and use the energetic force!

EXPECTING OTHER PEOPLE TO CHANGE

In all my years working with thousands of people, I know one of the biggest things that wastes your time, your energy (and sometimes your entire life) is this crazy notion that you can change someone else! If we try to push someone to change, we are creating more RESISTANCE in the relationship. Energetically, you are pushing them and their aura, which makes them feel small. We all want to be as expanded as possible, so they will automatically PUSH back. Every single time. So, what do you do?

TO CHANGE OTHERS, CHANGE YOURSELF

Imagine if we put the same energy and attention into changing ourselves as we did trying to change others. If you REALLY want to change them that is exactly what you need to do. Our lives would change more quickly than we can possibly imagine. (And we would be so happy and focused on our own alignment that we wouldn't give a **** what they're doing anyway!)

Use that energy to change the situation instead. You have the power to change the dynamic in the relationship and let that stress or push or pull or tension go. If you have people in your life who you wish would change then follow what you have learnt in this book. Show yourself just how powerful you are. You'll find so much magic in using EAM to change your relationship with others. As your energy shifts, they will change too.

THE POWER OF WORKING WITH A MENTOR

When thinking about the right support, you may also want to consider getting yourself a guide. When you go to a new city and want to find the quickest way to visit all the top spots, do you just fumble around with a map or do you get a guide to take you? The same comes to changing your life. You need to get yourself a guide, coach or mentor. Am I saying that you should come and work with me? Nope. I am not the right guide for everyone. I want to share with you how to find the right coach or guide for you. That may well be me or one of our awesome mentoring team. It may be someone else entirely. What I want to share are some REALLY important things for you to consider and it is about much more than the letters they have after their name.

CHOOSE YOUR GUIDE WISELY

Let's take this back to energy. Our physical body is one big sensory unit. It is designed to pick up, receive and understand information from various parts of our world and environment, both internal and external. Scientific studies have shown that we are also able to connect and pick up on the energy of others, and that this energy can influence us and we can influence it. Our energy and physiology influences other people. This is happening with every person and every interaction. This knowledge is crucial to understand from both sides when you are looking for a coach, guide or mentor or if you are already someone or would like to be someone in those roles. Here's why.

We often think of 'coaching' to be the ability to ask those deep questions, watch for facial movements, tonality of the voice, subtle body movements, gestures, and ticks. It's well-documented that people who are in a 'good', deep or meaningful connected conversation will start to mirror one another, with their postures, tone of voice, and rate of speaking. In fact, it's this mirroring or similarities which create rapport; we do this all the time in normal communication. Yet there is also something happening on an energetic level. We become energetically linked to the people we connect with. Research suggests that when we are able to create greater heart coherence when communicating with others, there is increased physiological linkage, and we become more sensitive to others and enable a greater connection to occur.

Also, the power of working with someone 'face to face' helps to activate the limbic system, which is responsible for down-regulating the amygdala (the emotion centre) in our body. In doing so it also helps us to reduce the effects of stress and trauma in the body from current or past experiences. This is one of the powerful effects, which happen just by being in the presence of someone, especially if they are leading you in a coaching role. Therefore, the energy of the coach, mentor, or therapist you choose to work with is of GREAT importance. Studies have now shown that their vibration has an impact on the level of changes they can make on the physiological and psychological states of their clients, just by their presence.

YOUR HEART IN SYNC

What is actually happening is a silent energetic communication between each person's heart energy; when in rapport and in each other's presence, there is a synchronisation of heart wave FLOWs. Hearts will synchronise to the highest frequency in the room.

The most in FLOW (coherent) heart energy is stronger, larger and more fluid in structure and therefore more likely to 'win' the energetic battle between the two. The less in FLOW (or resistant) energy is more unlikely to disrupt the energy of the other.

So, what does this mean for you when choosing a guide? In terms of expansion, you want your guide to have a higher frequency energy than you, meaning they have done the energy work on themselves. It doesn't mean they have to have more money or external success than you (although it can be an indicator of their own work). It is about knowing that their energy frequency is higher, to allow you to expand your energy and reach that level and beyond.

Remember the collective energy syncs to the highest vibration in the room. When you choose to work with someone who is yet to do the conscious energy work on themselves, you are the one who loses out. Your capacity for change and transformation is limited by the level of transformation that person has made in their own energy. Think about it. When you meet someone your two auras meet. If that coach, therapist or mentor is still energetically carrying all of their own crap they bring that into your session! They will see your life through their lenses, which may influence your choices. If the room is energetically full of their baggage how much capacity is there for you to expand? This is so important to know.

If you are a coach, therapist or mentor already, I invite you to ask yourself that question. Have you truly done the level of work on yourself and your own energy? Have you invested in yourself enough to shift the imprints you are carrying so that you can be an even brighter energetic presence to transform the lives of your clients? I believe it's our duty to do so. I know this may be pushing buttons for some and it is not intended to do so. If it is doing something to you, then that's an opportunity for you to explore it with EAM. If we are here to serve to our highest potential, do you believe your clients deserve the best from you?

Think about it for a second: would you go to a fitness instructor who was overweight? Would you go to a dentist with bad teeth? Would you trust a school teacher who couldn't spell? You get the idea. Choosing your coach, mentor, or guide is exactly the same. You need to know that the person you are trusting to guide you on your journey has the skill, knowledge, and experience, AND has the energetic capacity to expand you.

FINDING WHAT WORKS FOR YOU

Whether you are looking for a new Reiki therapist, acupuncturist, coach, mentor or guide, ask yourself these questions. You can ask the sway if you like (make sure you have released any judgement or RESISTANCE about that person first). Does this person have the energetic capacity to help me grow? If the answer is yes, GO FOR IT. If the answer is no, then maybe find someone else who is a vibrational match or higher frequency energy than you.

Now of course it would be rude of me not to suggest you work with myself or one of our mentoring team too. To become a mentor every single one of our mentors has to first complete their own personal transformation, inside The Energy Evolution before they are able to join the training. I want them to be able to create massive shifts for you, and to do so they must make massive shifts in themselves first. If you want guided support from someone who has been on this journey and walks their talk, who you know will understand everything you're going through, then click here to talk to us and find out more www.energyalignmentmethod.com/book-a-call

The Magic of a Mentor

HELEN JANE, AGE 58

Whilst I was working with a mentor we identified that I had RESISTANCE to feeling confident. We discovered this was related to my dad. I was tiny when born, a month premature and weighed only 4lbs. Growing up, my parents were very protective towards me. Using EAM, we discovered that my dad's energy was around me and it was his fear keeping me stuck. He had run his own business for a while that had gone bankrupt and as a result he drummed into me whilst growing up that I should get a reliable job and work at it until I retired. My dad passed away more than 20 years ago, yet the feeling of his energy around me was suffocating.

Using EAM I was able to work on my dad's energy. The energy felt heavy. The fear was a lack of my financial stability and security. I felt lots of tingling, coldness, and emotions. We released his lack of trust in me making my own decisions and his need to protect me. We then moved on to Step 5, allowing me to be safe, supported, loved, and protected, guided at all times in all decisions.

I felt as if my heart chakra had really opened up, I felt so much lighter, more confident and trusting of myself. I felt a sense of freedom and no longer felt suffocated. I feel that my dad is still around me but in a much more supportive way and I now feel more connected to him.

HEAR YOUR CALLING TO BE AN EAM MENTOR

Have you been feeling that nudge inside you? Maybe reading this book and seeing or feeling the transformations for yourself, you've felt the difference EAM can make in your life and the lives of others. Whether you're already a therapist, coach, mentor, or guide or even if you've never done anything like this before, if there is a tug inside of you to know more about how you can use it to change the lives of others, let's talk.

I know from talking to our amazing mentoring team that they have found many different benefits to being an EAM mentor. I think the biggest shift is the version of you that you become on the journey. To become an EAM mentor is no small feat; it's an 18-month journey of self-discovery, shifts, healing, training, and transformations. You can't just attend a 2-day workshop and get a certificate. It was a big decision for us to take, as I knew we could touch the lives of millions so much more quickly if we just 'qualified' more people fast. Yet what is more important to me is knowing that our mentors live, breathe, and walk their talk. Before they are able to change the lives of others, they have to have change their own lives, too.

Every single one of our mentors who are already therapists, coaches, or mentors in other modalities has said that EAM is like nothing else they've trained in for creating the shifts in their clients. It complements much of the work they were already doing and enables them to take your transformations to the next level. Even for those who have never done anything like this before, from the first level of their training they and their clients have been amazed at the shifts and transformations they have felt in just one session. Not because of us but because THEY have chosen to let go.

Going on a journey alone to change the world can feel tough at times. I spent so long on my own trying to 'make my difference'. Yet working together as a team we are MUCH more powerful together. More than anything it's the support of the team around you. Everyone is still on their own mission but with a team of others there alongside to cheer them on and lead the way.

More importantly, being an EAM mentor is also about the sense of belonging, the friendships and the lifelong support and team work. It is empowering to have people who have faith in you when you have no faith in yourself. (In fact, this happens in all our communities and programs, not just the mentoring). Everyone is working together in the new paradigm, too. It is about how we can work together and rise up as a whole. So many of our mentors feel like they finally 'get it', why they have been through what they have so that they can finally live out their purpose and passion for change.

Think about the growth of anything. The luminaries you recognise now in any industry were often the pioneers, the thought leaders, the people who were part of the journey from the beginning. Right now, EAM is pretty new; if you're feeling the calling, it's probably for a reason. If this seems to have 'fallen in your lap' or arrived at the right time, if your vision resonates with any part of the big picture, there's a reason for it. Perhaps you just KNOW it is right for you even if you are yet to know how to make it happen. It is no coincidence that you are reading this book. Release any RESISTANCE and then ask your sway. Are you meant to help take EAM out there?

If so, let's talk to find out how you can play your part in changing the world and share the EAM magic. www.energyalignmentmethod.com/book-a-call

By changing your life,

you also change

the world.

YOU CAN CHANGE THE WORLD

Whether you are working with us or just working on your own, you can change the world. Just for a second let's take it back to the science of life. Have you ever seen those awesome pictures that pull you in as you see never-ending patterns reflected as you look closer? This type of picture is called a fractal. It is a pattern which never ends. Almost everything in nature can be discussed as a fractal. It is a term used to describe things which have a self-similar construct across different scales. Fractals are created when we repeat a simple process or structure in an ongoing feedback loop. Science has shown that our natural world is built on these incredible fractal patterns.

Our universe is made up of millions of galaxies. Inside each galaxy are millions of solar systems, which contain millions of planets, which contain millions of moons, clouds, rocks, rivers and possibly life. On our own earth, this fractal pattern has been seen in rivers and tributaries, coastlines, and mountain ranges, as well as the construct of clouds, seashells, and hurricanes. Everything in nature is a fractal pattern or its primary construct. It's the same thing in our physical body. We see ourselves as one human being working independently. Yet we just need to use a microscope to see that we are in fact one organism made up of — some crazy number — like 37 trillion cells. Each of those cells is made up of a crazy number of atoms and proteins and electrons. Whichever level you look at, we are creating this fractal-based community of living energy. Health and sickness on one level of that community is reflected across all levels of the fractal community.

Let's take that fractal and expand it out from us as individuals. Remember that our aura acts in the same way as the membrane of the cell within the body. So in the same way, we as living beings are the cells of the community which make up this planet. We live in households, in communities, in towns, cities and countries; we all populate this one giant organism, planet Earth. Together, we are one community. What affects one part of our community affects it all. When we all come back to it, everything is energy, as we are all connected by this one field of electrons. In exactly the same way as the physical body, the health and well-being of the planet is in fact directly connected and affected by the health and well-being of us as individuals and vice versa. This isn't only our physical health; it is our collective energetic health and vibration, too. This is about our collective evolution as a human race.

The EAM and energy work you do for yourself is creating change on so many levels of your own physical, mental, emotional, and spiritual health. It will also ripple out to change the lives of your family and friends, which will have an impact on your community. When there are enough of us doing it, we will have an impact on the population of our planet. In other words, YOU can change the world.

My mission with EAM is to empower a global wave of people to step into their power so we can change the world from the old paradigm to the new. This is about bringing in a new way of living: one that is empowering, healthy and sustainable for every being on this planet, plants, animals, and humans alike. After everything that life has provided for us, I believe we can play our part in helping to maintain this beautiful ecosystem. I hope that this book is just the beginning of your journey to changing your life. And you can see how changing your life IS changing the world, too.

FOR THE NEXT GENERATION

Imagine a life growing up where you know about energy and how to align with it from an early age. How different would your life have been if you'd understood the power of energy, known how to manage your emotions and let go of the pain, hurt, anger, trauma and sadness you experienced from the time you were a child? Imagine what it would be like to have a world where all parents knew how to communicate with their children from love, who created safe, respectful boundaries, and who empowered their children to recognise their abilities. How different would the world be right now? How different would your life be?

We have the opportunity right now to create this world for the thousands of children who are born every day. We are on a mission to share this widely to impact as many people as possible to make a bigger impact in the world now and for future generations to come. I know in my heart that one day EAM will be in every school and we'll see people swaying everywhere!

CREATE THE NEW PARADIGM THROUGH YOUR WORK

You can also change the old paradigm to the new with your work. It doesn't matter what you DO. Because it's about who you are BEING when you DO it. Have you ever stood at the train and had a happy attendant singing away or sending you good wishes on your commute? Have you seen a wonderful smile from the cashier somewhere as you paid for your shopping? Think about the teacher who inspires a child to recognise they are capable of so much more. You don't have to 'change the world' or be on some big philanthropic mission to make a difference and make a change. Just be in alignment wherever you are. Talk about the good things. Inspire people with hope and possibility. Show people it IS possible to change their lives and shift what they think and feel.

If you are called to do something that makes a difference, PLEASE follow you heart. I ignored my inner calling for so many years. I knew I wanted to do energy work but had no idea what it was. My life felt like a PUSH and it didn't REALLY change until I stepped into the work I was meant to do. And wow, what a journey it's been. You are here to share your story and journey with those who need to hear it. You have insight like no one else on this planet because no one else has lived your life. YOU who must share that message. If you have that call inside I would love to help you share your gifts. I hope this book already has inspired you, yet there is so much more we can do.

For you to achieve your dreams and live the life you really want you must expand into that person. It is an energy and action journey. Sometimes you just need the right people to be there with you as you go along the way.

BUILDING A SOULFUL BUSINESS THAT SERVES

If you run your own business or work for a corporation, how can you create a soulful business that serves? Imagine if teams and businesses were working in flow. Imagine leadership and organisations insisting that EAM is part of their HR programs to make sure that their team members are happy and healthy. Less stress, days off sick, unhappy team members leaving work. All of those things would be gone because the team are happy and congruent with the values and the big vision. Imagine the impact those organisations would have in the world if all of their teams are in flow, aligned and working together to make a difference. It will be an unstoppable force for good.

Wherever you are or whatever you do find out about how you can make your difference in the world. Bring in new paradigm ways of operating, of creating your business. Find ways to treat your clients that come from the new paradigm. Find ways to pay your team and suppliers that comes from the new paradigm. If we want to make a difference in this world, I believe that business needs to be the way to lead that change.

Would you love to find a way to make a difference in your work? Where every single interaction makes a difference. You can do just that with B1G1. This amazing social enterprise was created by my friend Masami Sato and her husband Paul Dunn. With one mission in mind, to create a world full of giving.

Just so you know, we walk our talk too; from you purchasing this book, you've made a difference in the lives of others. Proceeds from the sale of all our products and programs go to supporting projects that positively impact in the lives of others. You can make a difference in your work so many ways. Go over and visit them at www.b1g1.com to find out how.

MAKE A DIFFERENCE IN SOCIETAL STRUCTURES

I believe that we need a positive change in government, healthcare, education, the way we produce food, how we generate power, the way we treat animals, the rainforest, the sea and water, and the livestock we grow and consumed. How we communicate. How we teach love and inspire each other. How we parent our children. How we share the news and what we watch on TV. How we love each other ... All of these are in our hands. It is up to us to create this change. It is my dream and part of my vision that one day EAM will be a lesson in schools, taught to children by parents and prescribed by our doctors in healthcare. I'm on a mission in this lifetime to make it happen. By implementing some of the things in this book and bringing ourselves into alignment with the changes we want to see I believe we can.

CHAPTER 8 — WHAT TO REMEMBER

I believe you have everything in your hands to change your life. You have limitless resources available to you. Now that you know how to tap into this wealth of abundance, you can use it to change your life. I believe that nothing in this world is broken; it is all in the process of change. Right now, we are seeing the chaos as things move to the new way of being. To change the world, we must come together and support each other. Hang out with people of the like vibration, and come together to shift the energy and change our planet. By doing the work you have done, and I hope that you will continue to do with EAM, you are contributing to mass consciousness. You are here for a reason. You are changing the world. Together we can create this global transformation.

Conclusion

My intention is to do my part to leave this world a better place for having been in it. I hope that this book is the first of many ways that EAM will create an impact. My biggest inspiration in life is my little boy, Kye. I want to leave the world a better place for him and every single person and child on this planet. If you ever read this book one day, Kye, I want you to know you were my inspiration for it all.

ENDLESS POSSIBILITIES

To everyone reading this book, I hope you feel less alone because you are never on your own. The pain and disappointment of the past hurt you, I know. But they made you exactly the person you are today, and what a wonder you are.

No matter what has happened in your life, YOU have the power to rewrite your story. Every day is a chance to start again. Your life is yours, no one else's. The only thing that ever stands in the way of what you want, is your energy, what you think and what you feel. In this book are the answers you need to change your life. All you have to do is trust, take that leap of faith and do the steps. You WILL create change.

It ALL begins with changing your energy, thoughts, and emotions. When you master that, your amazing life will unfold. No matter who you are, where you began, what happened in your past, what happened in your family. What your parents did or did not say or do.

It is all JUST energy.

You are powerful beyond belief.

You are important, you matter. You have meaning.

You deserve a life of peace, freedom, and love on levels beyond what you can imagine.

You are meant to live your life on your terms.

My heart felt love is sent to you always.

Yvette xxx

Acknowledgments

This feels a little like winning the Oscars. There are so many people I would love to thank, too many to list here.

Among these are the thousands of participants who took part in our formative research studies into the use of EAM. You helped me to understand the questions that needed to be answered. You bared your souls and changed your lives. Thank you for making EAM what it is today.

To my wonderful partner, Adrian Ellett, who has stood by me, picked me up, and held me tight on the days when I wanted to give up. Thank you for being there every step of the way. I could not have wished for a kinder man. I love you.

Lisa Hammond, my 'wife', my best friend and partner in creation. EAM would not be what it is without you. It is an honour to share this crazy journey with you. And maybe in this lifetime we'll finally change the world.

The wonderful Andrea Pennington, thank you for seeing the power of EAM and joining me on this journey to get it out to the wider world through Make Your Mark Global. You are such a support and inspiration. I feel I have an angel with you at my side.

To Carol Taylor, our patient and knowledgeable editor. Thank you for helping to shape this book and hone the message. You have brought this work to life.

To our incredible (and growing) team of clients and EAM mentors: I wish I could name you all one by one. But you have truly inspired me to keep on going. Watching the shifts and changes in you and seeing the people you have become has been such a privilege. Thank you for hearing your calling and stepping up to take EAM out into the world.

To the thousands of experts, researchers, scientists, philosophers and luminaries who have dedicated their lives to changing the way we live. To those who have trod the path and shared their wisdom so that we could speed up our own journey, I thank you for making this knowledge so freely available so that we all have the potential to change our lives.

My mum, Gean Taylor and my sister Siobhan who despite all the ups and downs of life, have shown me how to be strong. Thanks for being there for it all. And, of course, my wonderful little man, Kye. I have already thanked you. Without you being gifted into our lives, who knows where we would be. This book is for you and all the other children growing up in the new paradigm.

For those friends and family, colleagues, associates or people from my past. Even though you are not listed by name, please know that your time, love, energy and connection played a huge part in creating this book. Along the way I have learnt so much from you and whilst it may not be written on the pages, your energy is infused in this book, too.

Resources & References

Throughout the book we've explored so many people, cited studies and other places you can explore in more depth. Below is a short list from each chapter

CHAPTER 1

Beyond the Bleep, Alexandra Bruce

Nature, Nurture & The Power of Love, DVD Bruce Lipton

Stealing Fire: How Silicon Valley, the Navy SEALs, and Maverick Scientists Are Revolutionizing the Way We Live and Work, Steven Kotler, Jamie Wheal

Rollin McCraty and Maria A. Zayas "Cardiac coherence, self-regulation, autonomic stability, and psychosocial well-being"

Rollin McCraty Ph. D, "The Energetic Heart Bioelectromagnetic Interactions Within and Between People"

Armour, J.A. and Ardell,J.L.(eds).(1994). Neurocardiology. New York: Oxford University Press.

Rein G, McCraty R. "Structural changes in water and DNA associated with new physiologically measurable states"

Rein G, McCraty R. "Modulation of DNA by coherent heart frequencies"

Randoll U "The role of complex biophysical-chemical therapies for cancer"

Cameron, O.G. "Visceral Sensory Neuroscience: Interception"

Damasio, A. "Looking for Spinoza: Joy, Sorrow, and the Feeling Brain"

Bower GH. "Mood-congruity of social judgements"

Childre, D. and Rozman, D. "Transforming Anger: The Heart Math Solution for Letting Go of Rage, Frustration, and Irritation."

Childre, D. and Rozman,D. "Transforming Stress: The Heart Math Solution to Relieving Worry, Fatigue, and Tension."

Pribram KH, McGuinness D. "Arousal, activation, and effort in the control of attention."

LeDoux JE. "Cognitive-emotional interactions in the brain"

LeDoux J. "The Emotional Brain: The Mysterious Under- pinnings of Emotional Life."

CHAPTER 2

Wings off Light, The Art of Angelic Healing, Marie Lisa Labonre & Ninon Prevost

Wood Becomes Water, Chinese Medicine in Every Day Life, Gail Reichstien

Aura Awareness, CE Lindgren, DLitt & Jennifer Baltz

The Orgasm Prescription for Women, Andrea Pennington MD

The Astonishing Power of Emotions, Esther & Jerry HIcks

Cosmic Ordering Made Easier, Ellen Watts

Gaetan Chevalier et Al. "Earthing: Health Implications of Reconnecting the Human Body to the Earth's Surface Electrons"

Scaer, R. "8 Keys to Brain - Body Balance"

Damasio AR. "Descartes' Error: Emotion, Reason and the Human Brain."

Miroslav Stefanov et.al "The Primo Vascular System as a New Anatomical Systems"

CHAPTER 3

Power Vs Force, Dr R Hawkins M.D. Ph. D

McCraty R. "Heart-brain neurodynamics: The making of emotions"

McCraty R, et al "The impact of a new emotional self-management program on stress, emotions, heart rate variability, DHEA and cortisol. Integrative Physiological and Behavioral Science"

Stanley, R. "Types of prayer, heart rate variability and innate healing."

CHAPTER 4

Nelly Alia-Klein, Rita Z. Goldstein et al. "What is in a Word? No versus Yes Differentially Engage the Lateral Orbitofrontal Cortex"

The Act of Attraction in Business Tamsen Garrie

CHAPTER 5

Molecules of Emotion: Why You Feel the Way You Feel Candece Pert

The 6 Root-Cause(s) Of All Symptoms: Fear No More. Know WHY you have symptoms (Lifestyle Prescriptions | Self-Healing Made Easy Book 1) Johannes R. Fisslinger

The Hidden Messages in Water, Masaru Emoto

The Body Mind workbook Debbie Shaperio

You Can Heal Your Life, Louise Hay

CHAPTER 6

Sarah McAllister Feng Shui Consultant, Architect and Agency www.fengshuiagency.com

Games People Play: The Psychology of Human Relationship, Eric Berne

I Love You, Me! My Journey to Overcoming Depression and Finding Real Self-Love Within Andrea Pennington

CHAPTER 7

Helen Elizabeth Evans – Discover your purpose fingerprint analyst www.hands-on-business.com

CHAPTER 8

Spontaneous Evolution, Bruce. Lipton & Steve Bhaerman

The Big Leap, Gay Hendricks

McCraty R, Atkinson M, Tomasino D, Tiller. "The electricity of touch: Detection and measurement of cardiac energy exchange between people."

About the Author

Yvette Taylor is a speaker, author and creator of the revolutionary self-help technique known as **EAM — The Energy Alignment Method** — which has been dubbed "the fastest transformational energy tool for getting in flow" by Hay House author, Jo Westwood.

Over the last 3 years she has shared EAM with thousands around the world and has certified an ever growing team of mentors in the use of this life enhancing method.

Yvette has been voted the Top 10 Holistic Therapist in The UK by Holistic Therapy Magazine and is the recipient of the Janey Lee Grace Platinum Award for best therapist and practice 2017.

She also holds multiple industry awards for "UK's Best Coaching and Mentoring Business", "Shining Online" and for making an impact and being an inspiration to women in the UK.

Yvette is also the Co-Author of *Time to Rise* and the international best selling book *Pay It Forward Book Series: Notes to my Younger Self*. She has been featured in Om Yoga, Soul & Spirit Magazine, and Spirit & Destiny Magazine. She was a co-host on America outloud talk radio show.

Yvette has spent more than 18 years studying, using and teaching eastern principles, spiritual practices and self-development throughout the UK. In her years working as a business and marketing coach she has worked with thousands of spiritual leaders and entrepreneurs.

She is on a mission to touch the lives of millions to help them feel more empowered, in flow and to help them change their lives.

Take Your Next Steps with EAM

Now you know how to use the 5 Steps of EAM and how to make them work. It is time to take aligned action. Believe me there is so much more to EAM than I can share with you in this book. If you're really ready to change your life and start putting all of this into practice, visit our website or book a call to discover more about our transformational one to one sessions, workshops, retreats and online programs. We are here waiting for you to join the next phase and ready to change your life.

WORKSHOPS AND LIVE EVENTS

- The Energy Emergence – Introductory live EAM workshop

- How to Change Your Life & Get in Flow

- Reclaim Your Power, Transform Relationships

- Create More Money, Wealth & Abundance

- Sex, Love & Power of Your Hara

- Manifest Your Best Year Ever

- Create Your Attractive Vision

- Local Meetup Groups

COACHING AND PROGRAMS

- The Energy Experience – The online guide to The Ultimate Self Help Book

- 121 Empowerment Sessions with an EAM Mentor

- The Energy Evolution - Transformational 10-Month Life Changing Program

- Become an accredited EAM Mentor - Teach and share EAM with others

You can be part of a method which is changing the world one sway at a time! Follow the link below to have a chat with one of the team and discover more about the method which is changing the lives of thousands of people.

www.energyalignmentmethod.com/book-a-call

I hope this book has lived up to its promise as the ultimate self-help book. If you've loved it, remember to just keep giving. Pass this on or gift a copy to someone you love or even a stranger. Know that you hold the answer to changing your life in your hands. It is all JUST energy. Now with EAM you have the power to change it

Thank you so much for being a part of this journey. In a million years, I never imagined I would be sharing this. It fills me up inside to see the impact that EAM is having on the lives of so many and now I hope on your life, too.

Much love as always,

Yvette xxx

PS. If you would like to get in touch to discuss corporate training, schools, talks, collaborative projects and partnerships please contact hello@energyalignmentmethod.com.

Lightning Source UK Ltd.
Milton Keynes UK
UKHW050334161019
351675UK00001B/10/P